They
Called Me
Job

A Story of Grief and Faith Resurrected

Brenda Fitzpatrick

Proverbs 4:18

BRENDA FITZPATRICK

Trilogy Christian Publishers
A Wholly Owned Subsidary of Trinity Broadcasting Network
2442 Michelle Drive
Tustin, CA 92780

For information, address Trilogy Christian Publishing
Rights Department, 2442 Michelle Drive, Tustin, Ca 92780.
Trilogy Christian Publishing/ TBN and colophon are trademarks of Trinity Broadcasting Network.

For information about special discounts for bulk purchases, please contact Trilogy Christian Publishing.

Manufactured in the United States of America

10 9 8 7 6 5 4 3 2 1

Library of Congress Cataloging-in-Publication Data is available.

ISBN 978-1-64773-598-2 (Print Book)
ISBN 978-1-64773-599-9 (ebook)

To the memory of my four children, Erin,
David, Scott, and Heather.
It is because they lived that I was blessed
with the joy, sorrow, and victory
that inspired this book. Even though their lives
were short, my life was so much richer and
fuller because of our days on earth together, loving one another
with an undying affection that transcends even death.

This book is also written for the glory of God,
my Father, who enabled me to survive
unspeakable grief to write my story. Because of
His great love and the joy that He has set
before me, I can face the future with
anticipation of better things to come.

CONTENTS

• • • • • • • • ● • ● • • • • • • •

FOREWORD

I am convinced that the best way to grow up is to have older siblings to care, guide, and lead one into adulthood. I was blessed with that experience. My sister Brenda took me under her wing at my birth and gave me first experiences as if I were her own. Through these experiences, I was prepared for a lifetime as an adult. We are now the best of friends. My oldest surviving sibling and sister. I am still learning and seeking her wisdom even as we grow closer with age. This is what makes her special to me.

As I have watched Brenda traverse the paths of life, I have sought her advice on the most significant occasions. She encouraged and led me to receive advance degrees in the field of education, just as she did. Her credentials of education and experience are not the most important things that you will experience in this book. Her most important roles of wife, mother, and daughter of the Most High have been the hallmark of her life. Everything begins and ends with those places she sees as honor. What I have witnessed over a lifetime, you will catch a glimpse of in her writing. You will see a snapshot of a time in her life where her faith, endurance, and perseverance became the bedrock of how someone can not only survive but also thrive in the darkest of circumstances. This is what will make her story special to you.

Often compared to Job, Brenda has remained faithful. Her story, portrayed in her honest, heartfelt writing, is the same picture that I and countless others have witnessed. As you read the message of hope that springs from this book, know that the ending is worth the travel through the dark grief and deepest sorrow. Each chapter reads as a diary of what this journey of loss has meant to her ability to resurrect a spiritual faith that can only come from a place of strength and hope for reunion and a purpose.

As I have witnessed and mourned with her during the grief periods of her life, I have asked along with others how one family can endure loss and recurring pain over time. How a parent survives the tragedy of losing a child is something we often ask. What we cannot conceive of is it happening multiple times until the parents become like the orphans. The roles are abnormally reversed.

Although grief is uniquely handled by different people, I believe that you will see how a life lived in faith and unconditional grace can not only survive but also thrive. I know that Brenda's story is what we all long to hear. A story of triumph as we all face uncertainty and loss in many ways. I know it will bring a confidence of survival and encouragement of faith to the reader, as it has to me.

—Judy Campbell James, MEd
corporate trainer and education consultant

CHAPTER 1

• • • • • • • • • ● • • • • • • • • •

Facing Uncertainty

It is almost midnight. Tomorrow we will sit in the doctor's exam room and get the results of the biopsy of the mass in our son David's back. How will he react? How will I or his father react? Will I faint as I almost did at the orthopedic doctor's office last week when he asked if David's oncologist suspected the cancer may be back? Where is the faith I hold so dear? Where is God in all this? Has He heard all the prayers I cried over the last two years? Does He see the anguish in my heart when David spikes a fever or wakes me in the middle of the night in pain? Did He respond when I asked him to please heal my son? So many questions! So many emotions! Can this emotional roller-coaster ride be over and give all three of us time to catch our breath?

The one prayer I have held before God, my Father, is Proverbs 11:21 (KJV), which says, "The seed of the righteous shall be delivered." I pray it over and over. God's Word will not return to Him void, so I know it must come to pass in my life too. Also, the Word says that my seed shall be blessed (Ps. 112:2 KJV), that I have all the promises made to Abraham, since I am Abraham's seed by being in Christ (Gal. 3:29 KJV). I hold on to hope, even when I am at the end of my rope, seeing nothing but pain and misery in my son day and night. I see the spark of hope, and faith is not dying but getting stronger day by day. Outwardly I shake, I cry, I fall on my face before the almighty God. But inwardly, deep within my spirit, there is a sword that holds power over all the power of the enemies. It is the Word of the almighty God, the Word of Jehovah Tsaba, the Lord our warrior. It is the Word of Jehovah Rapha, the Lord our healer. By His stripes David was healed, isn't being healed, isn't waiting for healing, but was already healed (Isa. 53:3 KJV). So, I let the flame of hope burn on until my faith is made sight.

A mother never stops caring, worrying, or fretting over her child. When my children were small, the fevers and sicknesses that would come and go would send me into hysterics sometimes, as I fretted over them and did everything possible to help them recover. But as they became adults, I still fretted but went to battle on my knees, still doing whatever I could to help them recover.

I understand the agony that God and Jesus must have felt in that time span when the Father, God, had to turn His back on His only Son as He bore the sins of the world on the cross. Jesus cried, "My God, why hast Thou forsaken Me?" (Matt. 27:46 KJV). But God couldn't look on sin. He is the Creator, master of all, the perfect one who knows no sin. The agony of that span of time had to be immeasurable. And yet Jesus knew He had to endure the pain of the cross to open a pathway for all mankind to come to the Father. That gives us an open door to the God of all, to His very throne room. I have accessed that pathway more in the last two years than ever before in my life. And the door was always opened to me.

CHAPTER 2

•••••••••●•••••••••

They Call Me Job

In case you haven't read this book of the Bible, Job was allowed by God to be severely tried to prove his faith. Satan appeared to God and asked to try Job to prove he would turn his back on God. He said Job only honored God because God had put a hedge around him. So, God said yes. The only stipulation was that Job's life be spared. So, a whirlwind destroyed Job's house, cattle, land, and all ten of his children. Job was a very wealthy, prosperous man. All he had left was a wife, who advised him to curse God and die, and a few friends, who sat around him as he sat in the ashes, trying to scrape the sores that covered his skin, to find relief. Those friends' words cut like knives in the soul of this man, who was so sorely afflicted. He said he wished he'd never been born.

More than once, people have called me Job. I haven't lost my health, my house, my land, or my husband, but I have buried the last of my children just two weeks ago yesterday. I am undone. Everything is nothing. I wander aimlessly from the living room to the kitchen to the bedroom, not really wanting to eat, sleep, or live. It's a dark night of the soul. I am filled with anger at times, at God, at the hospital where our youngest son, David, was treated, at people's words that don't comfort, at having no comfort! How easy it is to be surrounded by people who have platitudes and advice but have never walked this path or can even imagine walking it. But let me interject here that I have had a support group around me, my husband, and

David, in his two years of extreme suffering. Because of a group who supported me after we buried our precious, beautiful twenty-three-year-old Erin in 2006, I have been surrounded also by moms who have buried their own precious children, who know the agony that we have suffered and suffer now. But even some of them are aghast that we had to bury this, our last living child. And we have had family, my sister, brothers, nieces, nephews, aunts, uncles, and cousins, who have cared for us.

I am angry. I don't understand. I can't make peace with God because, right now, I feel that even He, who is so full of compassion and mercy, has forsaken me. I know deep within that He has not. Maybe I am hiding from Him because now I don't really understand Him. He, who healed everyone who came to Him as he walked on earth, came that day to take my son away from me and into heaven. I felt Him enter the ICU room. I know He was there, as crazy as that might seem to some. For the past two years, I have been on my knees continually. I would care for David during the day, and when I would lie to rest, I would not sleep well but wake around three each morning. Many times I would climb out of my warm bed to kneel and even sometimes lie prostrate on the floor beside my bed to cry out for God to heal and deliver my son. I knew all the ways to pray. I prayed the covenants that God had made with those who belong to Him. I had a whole list of covenant promises that I prayed continuously over my children. Recently, I watched a movie called *The War Room*. It was about a woman who believed in prayer. I created a little prayer space like she had in the movie. You can walk in my bedroom today and see the checklist of prayer requests, many of them for David and his friends. I intended to check them off as they were answered. It lies there still, untouched by me anymore.

When my children were little, as tired as I would be at night, I sat by their bed or lay beside them as they went to sleep, reading the Bible and praying with them, sharing the Word of life. Both had knelt beside my bed and accepted Jesus as their Savior at a young age. Both were never ashamed of the fact that they were Christians. Both asked me to pray over them when they were sick. I remember praying over Erin's back once when the pain was overwhelming. Often, when she was small, if she was ill, she would say, "Pray in tongues, Mama," referring to praying in the Spirit. And so often in the past two years since David was diagnosed with leukemia, I had put my hand over the part of his body that hurt and prayed, cursing the afflictions and really believing that the prayer made a difference. Sometimes he'd reach his hand out for me as he lay in the hospital bed and say, "Let's pray." I found out at the funeral that churches all over the world were praying for David. Both my brothers are pastors, and my two brothers-in-law are pastors. Their churches, and even a mission group who has churches all over the world, prayed. I have friends in England who prayed. The assistant manager of the hotel where Berry and I stayed as David was in the hospital had her mom in Germany to pray. My nieces and nephews, several of whom are pastors or ministers, had their churches praying. So David was covered so fully in prayer. He survived a lung infection that almost took his life after the bone marrow transplant in December 2014. They had given him a fifty-fifty chance of surviving. But after only five days, he pulled the breathing tube out and came off the lung bypass machine and dialysis. What a miracle! So I know those prayers were answered.

The question that haunts me and my husband is why. Is it okay to question God? I don't know. But I do know that David, in the Psalms, asked many questions of God. Moses argued with God.

All I know today is that I am numb. I am shocked that David didn't survive this. I am appalled that God didn't spare his life. I have no answers. Several friends and family members have sat with us in the last few days and said as much. No answers. No understanding. Many who have prayed and followed our journey so closely were shocked. We really thought David would beat this. We really didn't think we would have to bury this sweet, kind, caring, loving young man who was our heartbeat. Sure, we clung to him after Erin left for heaven. We eventually turned our attention to him, focusing our everyday existence on helping him succeed in life.

And now I am called Job!

CHAPTER 3

· · · · · · · ●●●● ● ●●●● · · · · · ·

Sharing Grief

I have had many opportunities to meet and share grief with others. Here are a few of the many people I have met at various times during my own grief journey.

Today I met my friend Nerissa Mohammed and her daughter for lunch. Nerissa lost her precious Ariel after we lost Erin. She grieves with us. She came to the hospital in Atlanta and sat with us, helping us with hotel bills, food, and whatever else we needed. She is such a kind and compassionate friend. As we sat there today, their eyes filled with tears as I cried and talked of my own grief over my David. We talked of Ariel, too, and tears came again. Two young people with bright futures gone way too soon. Our hearts were bound and torn at the same time as we shared our sorrows and tears.

A lady I met had just buried her thirty-five-year-old daughter two weeks before her brother had come in for a lung transplant. She spent hours there with her sister-in-law, as they waited and hoped. I was able to share with her the comfort I had received when our Erin left for heaven. We exchanged phone numbers, and she genuinely appreciated talking to me. One day, I was sitting there, and a well-dressed woman came in and sat alone at the other side of the room. A doctor followed her in in a minute and sat beside her, giving her the news of what he suspected was wrong with her husband. I noticed that she was taking it in stride, not breaking down with emotion, as I would have done. The doctor left, and I felt compelled to go and sit beside her and offer what comfort I could. When I did, she burst into tears and shared her fears. She said they only had one son and she felt so alone. We hugged when she left. She came back by in a few days and said she needed one more hug.

Yesterday, as I was buying more bricks for my memory garden for David, the clerk talked with me for a while, ending with a hug. As I shared David's story, she told me she had lost her fifteen-year-old son a few years ago. As we looked into each other's eyes, we shared the pain that only a mother can know. Her son had died in an accident. I told her about David's battle with leukemia. But I quickly said it really doesn't matter how a child dies; it is always beyond heartbreak.

Today I am seeing another mom lose her son. By *lose* I don't mean *lose*, but he left for heaven yesterday. I have never met this mom, Stephanie Savage. Her family attends the church where my brother pastors. But he kept me informed of her son's illness over the course of the last six years. Stephanie's son had a rare disease, and it slowly consumed his fragile body. She sent me a friend request on Facebook shortly after David left for heaven and told me she and Glenn (her son) were praying for us. Glenn left for heaven just a few months after our David. I sent her a message of condolence yesterday and shared the advice my dentist gave me that only God can truly comfort us after such a horrendous loss. My niece saw her last night and told me Stephanie said she had had me on her mind yesterday and prayed for me. Isn't that amazing that she would pray for me in her time of great sorrow? When I heard the news early yesterday, tears came because I knew all too well what the next few weeks, months, and years would look like for her. She is a strong woman of faith, which will help her. But I was too. It didn't take away the pain and the fact that I had to face a life without my son and my children. It's tough knowing what Stephanie and her dear husband and surviving children will endure the next few months especially and, well, the rest of her life. It never goes away, this grief. Never!

CHAPTER 4

· · · · · · ●●● ● ●●● · · · · · · ·

Children, What a Difference

When my babies were born, my life changed dramatically. I battled depression and feelings of low self-worth much of my life. But when I held my Erin for the first time and looked into that little miracle of a face, I began to know a love I had never known. Here was this little life, unshaped, unmolded, just waiting for guidance. There was much prayer and educating myself on mothering that would take place over the next twenty-three years. And the love. Oh my! How do I describe such unconditional love a child gives to a parent? We bonded fast, as a welded piece of metal that is stronger, they say, than the whole metal at first. It was a bond that could/would not be broken by arguments, distance, even death! And then two years later, I found we were having another baby. Another girl! I was delighted! I talked to her in my tummy and sang to her. Erin and her dad talked to her. We felt the little bumps when she had the hiccups or moved around. But her little life was too short, as she delivered at six months, only to go straight to heaven. But even in that short six months, I was forever bonded to my little Heather Lynn in a way few can understand. I loved her unconditionally, even through death.

Recently, studies have shown that because a mother was bound by the umbilical cord to her child, some of the child's cells remain in the mother's body forever, bonding her with the child. Maybe that is another reason a mother never stops mourning for a child who passes so soon.

Five years later, the most precious gift became ours when our baby boy was born. He brought into our lives a world of toy trucks, tae kwon do, baseball, video games, music (always music), and love that was unimaginable. He told his friends that he knew he was a mama's boy, clinging to me especially tightly when he was ill or afraid. But he grew into such a kind, respectful, compassionate son who hated injustice and loved his friends and family with a passion not seen much in this world. The love he gave me and his dad was huge! He would easily have given his life for us if that time had come. But his last great battle with leukemia proved it even more as he fought with everything in him to survive, only to have to leave us at twenty-four years, nine months, and six days. But his love still warms my grieving heart, as death cannot separate a mother and son. The love and bond continue throughout eternity.

The love and joy that children bring into couples' lives truly makes the bond of a family unit. What joy the new surge of life brings to a home.

CHAPTER 5

Circling the Hole

Grief is like a deep, dark hole. Someone once said, when you are grieving, you are as if in a deep, dark hole. Some friends and loved ones will circle the top, waiting for you to emerge as the person you were before the grief. Some will reach down and try to help you up but can never really touch the depths where you are. And there are a few who will climb down in the hole with you, sitting with you, crying with you until you are able to climb up a little, then a little more.

I feel, at times, that I won't get out of this one. We went through this with Erin, with Scott, my husband's second son and my stepson, even with our little baby who we never got to hold in our arms. How many times do we get knocked down and still can get back up? We know, as with Erin, that we will never be the people we were before. But with Erin, we were still parents of a living child. Now, with our baby boy gone, we have nothing left but memories of a happy, joy-filled life with our children. Today, I live in a lonely home with my husband. Just me and him. The echoes of children playing in the yards, the sounds of guitars, the radios blaring in the house, the laughter of children on the phone with friends, the coming and going, the parties, the big Sunday dinners, the endless loads of laundry, the endless trips to the grocery store, the Friday-night pizza-and-movie nights, even the echoes of David lying in his bed with me constantly going in to check his blood sugar, give him his meds, try to find something he could eat, cleaning up after he vomited, changing the dressings on the PICC line, cleaning the hole in his back that finally healed after his being in ICU three weeks, all of it just echoes in my mind. A quiet house filled with memories of days gone by. A house that haunts me and warms me. It is one that hurts me and reminds me of a full life that is behind me. I am in the minus life now.

And I stare at the walls and try to get some semblance of a life when neither me nor my husband feels like living. Can I emerge again? There comes a time of emerging from the cocoon that has held me bound. When will this happen? I've been in grief over Erin and Heather for many years and for Scott a few years. So I know it will come. Right now, my cup is empty and full. It is full of endless questions, full of not knowing, and empty of a future that will never be. Will I emerge? I am ten years older than when Erin left us. It seems harder this time. The things that brought such comfort then are not working as well this time. It is different. It seems more intense.

It is 3:09 a.m. I slept for about two hours and woke up. My stomach is a mess. My heart is too. My mind is working overtime to compensate for all the mixed emotions. My body is fighting back now as I have stressed it to the max for some time. I try to do the tasks I used to do so freely around the house. But I don't complete them in one fell swoop as I did before. I must break them into smaller tasks. Where is my strength?

The future is still fuzzy. I can't go there, lest I am overwhelmed. I remember Dr. G, David's oncologist, giving him sage advice when he told her he was so depressed upon learning he was not in remission after the first two treatments. She said, "David, just take one day at a time. Decide what you can do that day, even if it is a small thing like this office visit. When you have done that, congratulate yourself on completing the task. Don't look too far into the future. Just focus on today's task." I thought that was pretty good, especially since our Lord Jesus said basically the same thing. "Take no thought for tomorrow" (Matt. 6:34 KJV). I will follow that advice. Today is all I can handle anyway or getting through this night for now!

CHAPTER 6

Reflections

It's as if we are in one of those movies where the main character has flashbacks of a better time. I just heard it sleeting outside. I walked to the back door, and immediately my mind took me back to those times when it would snow unexpectedly and I'd say, "Come here and look!" Erin and David would come onto the little back porch and stick their tongues out to catch the snowflakes. They would get so excited. The next day, I couldn't keep them in the house. We'd all go out and make a sled from whatever we found and slide down the little hills and build snowmen. The memories are so many. The days were too few. My heart is living in the past, and what can I do?

I wander around this house sometimes, thinking back to when my husband and I were first married. It was just the two of us. We were finding our way to becoming a family. Then the children came, and the joy, laughter, houseful of visiting children, trips to movies, tae kwon do, piano, twirling, cheerleading, parties, softball, basketball, football, school field days, graduations, award ceremonies became a way of life. Life was full, rich, and full of joy and sorrow, of laughter, tears, and even disagreements. It was so wonderful. When the children are suddenly gone, the house is an empty tomb almost.

I look for David everywhere I go. His counselor wanted to meet with Berry and me just to see how we were coping with our grief. David respected her highly, so I really wanted to go. But walking into her office was just too much, so she agreed to meet us at Starbucks. I remembered the many times we sat together in the waiting room and I waited for David to finish his session. I felt I would be expecting him to walk out of her office, and it was overwhelming.

The last time I kissed Erin goodbye was as she was getting in her car to leave the afternoon of the day she went to heaven. The hug was a little longer than usual, and the smile and kiss on the cheek let her know how deeply her mom loved her. I still remember her looking up and giving me that beautiful smile of hers. I remember going around to David's hospital bed that last week and hugging him, telling him I didn't care about germs. I was going to hug him. I never left his room without telling him how much I loved him. He would always say, "I love you more." He had just started saying that after he got so sick the month before he was readmitted to the hospital. My little Heather had had the hiccups the day before she left for heaven. I felt the little bumps in my tummy as she slowly moved from side to side. I miss it all!

I heard on TV yesterday that it's more valuable to have memories than dreams. As I thought on that, I had to agree. I do value highly every single memory of my children growing up. What fun and laughter, joy, and yes, tears we shared! I was in the storage shed and found Erin's little red wagon. As I pulled it out, I remembered the last time I put David in and rode down the hill. When it snowed years ago, we'd make a sled out of whatever we could find. Laughter would fill the air as we slid down our snow-covered front lawn. The precious memories do flood my soul. But the hardest part is, no new memories are being made even as I witness other families going on with life.

CHAPTER 7

·········●●●●●●●●●●●●●········

Plus or Minus

During David's bone marrow transplant, the days were numbered, starting at minus days just prior to transplant. The day of transplant is day 1. The nurses told him it would be like a new birth. Grief is a little like that. Everything in your life up to the day your loved one dies is minus, in the past. The day of death is day 1. Or should it be reversed? All the pluses should be days up until the day of death. And then the minuses begin for a grieving parent. They are all the days you live without. You can't make any more memories. There are no more hugs. You are living in the past much of the time as you remember. You search for anything to help you stay alive.

As I look around the house, there are reminders everywhere, *everywhere*, of David's future. There's the high school diploma, reminding me of his future college diploma, what job he might have held, how he would have influenced the world around him with the intelligence God had given him. He was always a gifted student in school. As I sit here, I look at the little board beside my computer and see appointment cards for appointments that never will be kept. I think of the care I had been giving him and even long for flushing the PICC line, doling out his handful of meds, and keeping track of blood pressure and blood sugar for the doctors. I long for the continuance of his illness even, as opposed to this finality of death. People would be quick to criticize and say, "No, you wouldn't want him suffering." Of course, I wouldn't. But he would be here! There

28

would still be the long conversations, the gathering of whatever food he could eat, the big hugs every day, the "I love you" phrases that we shared. But what do I see? An empty room. A suitcase still packed with a PS3 and PS4 with the last games he played in one of them, an unmade bed that still holds his scent, a little side table with controllers he won't hold in his hands again, a little back scratcher that gave him ease from the uncontrollable itch and pain on his back. It's all the little reminders that he won't continue in this life. Game over! Grief looks at the whole picture, especially the future and all the little reminders that he won't continue in this life.

I feel I am in a vacuum. And all the life has been sucked out. I breathe to maintain my bodily functions. But it seems my soul is just there. For what do I wait? Do I wait for God, who I felt didn't answer my pleas for help for David's life, for my posterity, for Him to keep His covenant that says, "The seed of the righteous shall be delivered" (Prov. 11:21 KJV)? In Christ, I am the seed of Abraham and David, great men of God. The Bible says all their promises are mine too. I kept that close to my heart through David's illness. All those scary moments, especially when the nurse would call a code MET and I would sit back in the corner of the room, strangely calm, because I had a promise. David would get through the crisis and his vitals would look good again. So what? I was told once to never question God. Can I even question this event that changed my whole existence? Is God mad at me? Have I sinned? Did David, Berry, or I commit a horrendous act of sin that God would turn His back on us? After we lost Erin, it never entered my mind that God would punish me so greatly as to take my baby boy. Never! I feel so lost, so hopeless.

I used to take long walks early in the morning and talk to God. I felt Him so near. I felt He was my best friend. Even in the dark days, I knew He was close. Now I can't feel anything. My spirit, soul, body, and mind are so deeply crushed. Therefore, I breathe until I can breathe no more or until God sweeps down with a miracle and picks me up. I just exist. Will He? I am clueless. Will I live, or will I die? This is day -22. What does the future hold?

DAY-23

•••••••••●•••••••

Living with Minuses

I decided not to call them chapters from now own, just-days, minus days. I want this book to be a display of this grieving mother's life.

Years ago, in 1976, I sat alone in a little rental house and wrote a letter to my as-yet-unborn children. My career came first, and marriage hadn't been in the picture. But I believed I would have children. Eventually they came and brought such joy into my life for thirty-three years I couldn't have imagined.

A few months back, being the woman of faith, I have been, I penned another letter. When the doctors told David that he had a very slim chance of ever having children, I jumped on the faith bandwagon and determined that he would. I spoke the Word by faith. I got my pen and paper and wrote a letter to my grandchildren.

Dear grandchildren,

I know this seems strange because, even though Berry has three grandchildren, two of whom have called me Grandma, I haven't had you yet, you born of my seed and bloodline, David. The doctors said he would likely not have you, but I believe he will. I know time is short and the days are getting dark in this country, but I have asked the Lord for you. And I expect to see you before this life is over.

I wrote a letter in 1976 to my children, David, Erin, and Heather, before I was married. So, I can write one to you too. I know I will love you. I want to share the love of God with you, too, since it has been my strength in this life.

I can't wait to meet you.

Love,
Grandma

But now, with David passing into heaven, this letter will never be read by my grandchildren by blood. The future is just a brick wall, a thick fog. I am adrift on a sea in a boat with no sail. Ahead, all I see is thick fog. The nothingness of the future overwhelms me. There is a flicker of light that is God. One day He may loom large and be in charge again. But for today, I only see Him as an almighty God who frustrates my plans, as David said in the Psalms. He seems as the almighty, who does what He wills and leaves no control for us. We are at His mercy day in and day out. Over and over the Bible talks of Him being a just God who loves justice and mercy. I am not throwing away all that I have known and believed. It just seems so far from me right now, having to say an earthly goodbye to my last child, whom I loved so deeply and by whom I was loved in return with an unconditional love. I am adrift. Only God can save me from this darkness.

DAY-24

• • • • • • • • ● • • • • • • • •

Unending Questions with No Answers

A grieving person often deals with random thoughts, all the what-ifs, the whys, and if-onlys. And then there are the unending questions that, often, have no real answers in this life. Such are my thoughts today and a part of every day now. Here are some random thoughts today: Why was it my child, who was so good and kind and never hurt a flea in his life? Why me? Do people think I'm cursed? Throw me off the boat! Maybe I'm the Jonah! Why was his blood type still O+ when the transplant was supposed to be working 100 percent? Did they mistake the type-and-cross they did that last morning on the oncology floor and give him the wrong platelets? Did they kill him? What if I had just kept him here and treated him with natural cures, many of which are flooding social media day by day? Could he have been cured? Why isn't the doctor who saw him so frequently over the past two years contacting us? Don't they care? Is he just a number to them? The medical care team and hospital that we poured almost a million dollars into, do they have no affinity to the people they treat? Now I feel guilty for mentioning money. What was David's life worth? It was worth more than all the money in the world! I don't even care about money. I don't care about much of anything right now. I'm full of sorrow down to the pit of my very soul, very existence.

Where is my best friend? I remember telling God that if He takes David, He is taking me. Once, I even bargained with God. As I turned a corner to walk back to David's room in Emory, I made a promise to God. I told Him if He healed David, I would step out of my "shell" and speak to any size group about His amazing grace. But David is gone to heaven now! Is He through with me on earth? I go through the gamut of questions, many of which were the same questions I asked after our baby Heather left us, after Erin left us, after Scott left. Have I committed some horrendous sin that God would judge me so harshly as to take all my children? Am I just a "showpiece," like Job, that God wants to use to show others He can take everything away and we will remain faithful to Him? Do I even know Him?

A parent's endless warfare never ends. They seek to protect and defend their child until their dying day. It is just something instilled into a mom or dad. When a child dies for whatever reason, the parent is left with this defense mechanism that has no object. I believe that is where the endless questions come from. Why wasn't I there? If only I had done this! Why didn't the doctor try this? Where was the one caring for her/him? Why my child? What if I had been the one driving? Did I love him/her too much? Was I overprotective? Did God think I idolized my child? What did I do to make God mad at me? Did they hurt at the end? Did they know I was there? And on and on, endless questions that flood the mind and soul. Do they ever end? I think not. While, over time, the raw edges of grief soften, the soul-searching endless questions remain with a parent. There is sometimes an abject feeling of failure, even if they have been an excellent parent. There is a feeling that they failed their child in those last moments, even if they tried everything, had the best doctors, counseled with their child, protected them until the last breath! The role of parent doesn't cease just because they have left this earth. There is that innate protection mode that parents keep deep within. Often it turns to protecting their memory. Say anything negative to a grieving parent and see if they will not rush to the defense of their child. They struggle to keep their child's memory alive. You may enter their house and find there are pictures of the child everywhere. I vividly remember after our Erin went to heaven, David told me once not to buy another frame. He had counted the pictures I had hung of Erin. He said there were forty of her and eighteen of him! It had not really entered my mind that I was obsessing over keeping her memory alive with pictures. Now, alas, there are pictures of him everywhere. I haven't counted, but I'm sure his are near forty now too. Some parents create a memorial space in their home where they put pictures, candles, and tokens in remembrance of their child. Some must move, but they are careful to preserve the contents of their child's room so they can create a memorial space in their new home. Grieving parents face accusations from friends and family. If those accusations come at a time of struggle—i.e., special dates or remembrances—it can cause added pain. I would say to those who put forth those things that they must allow a parent to grieve however they must. There are no rules to grief. For each parent it is different, with some commonalities. Until their dying day, a parent will remember and mourn the child who is not on earth with them. There was a story of an eighty-five-year-old woman who, when asked how many children she had, told them she had four, three on earth and a baby in heaven. She never forgot or minimized the memory of that baby although it had been many years past.

DAY-25

······•·•······

Signs

After the initial shock of the passing of a loved one, many look for anything that will "connect" them with that loved one. I remember vividly getting up in the middle of the night after our Erin went to heaven and searching the house for anything, *anything*, that she had touched—a card, a sticky note, some unexpected treasure that I hadn't seen before. And I did find a few. Also, I remember the "visitations," or visions, dreams, or whatever one might call them, when I saw or heard Erin. They were so real that, although my grief for David is forefront right now, I will share them. That is the way you will know the importance of what I'm about to say next.

The first visitation of Erin was only a few days after we had knelt by her beautiful body on her bedroom floor. I was standing in my bathroom, brushing my hair, looking at my teary, swollen eyes. I "felt" Erin tell me, "Mama, I'm okay." Those words brought peace to me. One more vision I had of Erin was where she was wearing a long peach-colored dress, almost like a Victorian-style dress. It had lace around the sleeves, neckline, and hem. It was covered with little pockets. I watched as she would dip a paintbrush into one of the pockets and splash it on the wall of this mansion as if she were painting. But as she splashed, beautiful flowers would appear on the wall and they would be living flowers. These dreams or visions would come at moments when I would be at my lowest. I will share more visions of Erin in a later chapter.

A few weeks after Heather had left for heaven, I had a dream about her. I saw a little girl, maybe three or four years old, standing in a beautiful meadow under a huge spreading oak tree. There were lovely wildflowers all around her. She had shoulder-length curly brown hair, and her long white gown was almost transparent. Her skin was also almost translucent. In her arms was a baby lamb. It was the only dream I had of Heather until Erin made her heavenly journey. The cover of this book will contain this scene, I hope. It is one that is still so vivid in my mind after thirty-five years.

Now, back to the present. Each day I keep hoping for a sign. I had three from Erin in the first few weeks. David was witness to what I experienced. So he knew. But in heaven does he remember? I grasp at the least little thing. Last night we had an unexpected sleet event. I just knew that David was sending us a big snow. He would have remembered that first year without Erin, when we had a huge snow on her angelversary, and I felt it was a sign. But the sleet only lasted a short while and then turned to rain. I keep searching for signs, for dreams, for any connection to my sweet boy. I call him boy. He was twenty-four years old. But in a mom's eyes, they are always little boys, I guess. I sort of expect he will send a huge sign when he does. He would get so frustrated (if one can be frustrated in heaven) with me waiting, searching for a sign, that he would just send a big sign. So I wait. And hope. Is it because I have distanced myself from my best friend, God? Is it because I haven't been able to pray or read my Bible since that fateful day? I don't know.

I don't know why it is different this time. But I have rarely dreamed or had a vision about David. I was taking a nap, which only lasted fifteen or twenty minutes. Just as I woke, I saw David's face. At first, he was lying down, then sitting up, and last he was standing near a building, and I could only see him from the shoulders up. He was wearing the sports jacket and outfit I chose as his burial outfit. The clarity of the vision was what surprised me the most. I only saw the side of his head. But it was as if he were in very bright sunlight. When I got up from where I lay, I walked outside to clean my car mats. I was standing on the carport, looking out over the backyard. David and Berry had given me a huge wind chime one Mother's Day.

It hardly ever chimes because it is so heavy. As I stood beside it, it began chiming. The notes it was playing were very distinct, almost sounding like a song I knew. It chimed for as long as I stood beside it. When I stepped down to work on the mats, it stopped. I decided to step back up to see what happened, and sure enough, as I stood beside it, it chimed again. A friend told me that, as much as David loved music, that was most assuredly a sign he was near. Later, I did have a vision of David sitting on a bench. I saw Jesus come and sit beside him and put his arm around him. David was laughing as they conversed. There was one other dream of David in which he was in a conference room. I realized there were many gathered in this building. He was assigned the task of overseeing the music and had his guitar in hand. He told me to take care of the music in that room while he went to some of the others.

I still long for the dreams and visions. When I have dreams about my children, I awake feeling so refreshed, as if I really had been with them. I hope to have more to share later in this book.

From Valor to Nothingness

I am a woman of faith. I have been called woman of valor by a dear friend and pastor. But today I feel far, far from that. I scanned the journals that I wrote when Erin passed to see how I coped spiritually then. Even though I battled with my faith, I don't think I was then where I am now. You see, God, my Father, and I had a very special relationship. Jesus was my best friend. I belonged to Him. He had "written His name on my forehead," so to speak. He redeemed me from the curse of sin. He bought me with His own blood as He himself suffered unspeakable atrocities to redeem me back to the Father. I received His sacrifice for me when I was a young child. So, my whole life was dedicated to Christian principles.

Lately, even with the challenges of caregiving, I would make time each morning, at least an hour, to spend with God. I'd read the Bible, like Smith Wigglesworth, an old minister from the 1800s, until I had fed my soul. Then I'd go outside and walk and talk with God in the cool of the morning. It was a special time. When David was diagnosed with leukemia, I walked with a calm assurance that everything would be all right. When he went into respiratory failure in 2015 and was in a medical ICU, then moved to cardiac ICU upon respiratory failure with a fifty-fifty chance of living, I went to my knees in desperation, often only being able to cry out "Help!" to Father God. Churches all over the world are praying. My family are all involved in the ministry. Church after church would let me know they had David at the top of their prayer list. During that crisis, my dear friend Alicia Jannings even got some friends to engage in a twenty-four-hour prayer fast until the crisis passed. We got our miracle! God answered those prayers. After that, I told Him that for all eternity, I would stand at His throne and sing that verse in Psalms 34:4 (KJV): "I sought the Lord and He heard me and delivered me from all my fears!" It would be an eternal song to the Father God. Despite what the doctors predicted and them letting us know they would decide whether to "pull the plug" after fourteen days, David pulled his breathing tube out and came off dialysis after five days in the cardiac ICU. Soon we were in rehab, where he regained the use of his muscles, learned to eat, hold a spoon, and swallow again, and slowly began to walk. After about a month, we were released to the hotel. Then a month later, we got to come home at last to continue rehab here. And what joy filled our souls!

So where is God? I wrote the preceding long paragraph so the reader might see my relationship with God and the role my faith has always played in my life. I found my way back into His arms after He took Erin, after He took Scott, and even after He took my baby Heather before I could even hold her in my arms. I found my hope again, my faith. I clung to it like my lifeline when David was diagnosed. I prayed over David, over his hospital room, over all the drugs, blood, and platelets going into that precious body. I went back to the hotel numerous times and either fell by the bed, exhausted, to cry out to the Father or walked the floors praising Him for whatever life was at that moment. I shared the many victorious moments and scary moments on Facebook in a prayer blog my sister Judy had set up to inform our followers of David's progress. People often told me they were amazed by my faith.

Now, nothing! Everything is nothingness! I haven't opened my Bible since February 12, 2016, the day I hugged and kissed my sweet boy after his last breath was taken. I haven't prayed, except to finally bow my knee to say that I know God is almighty, El, the God over all. That's all I can say.

I lay in bed this morning and thought of how we, as humans and as Christians, think we know God. We have the platitudes down pat! We know the right things to say to others. We make our confessions and professions of faith. But does anyone know God? The Bible says He is a God of justice and righteousness. He cannot sin. I know that is true. Even with my questioning, I dare not cross those lines. I remember David told me recently that, although he struggled with hypocritical-so called Christians who were that in name only, and even with his own faith shaky at times, he believed he was like his namesake. I named him after David in the Bible. He said he did fear God. I fear God. But right now, I don't know who God really is. Has He forsaken me, as David in the Bible feared once, as Jesus faced on the cross? Has God, who I thought favored me, decided I was not worth the effort? I had a Bible verse on my appointment board in my bedroom for the last six months. It was Psalm 41:11 (KJV): "By this I know that Thou favorest me because mine enemies do not triumph over me." And another that I had there since David was first treated for leukemia in 2014. One of the first things I did upon arriving home February 12 was to erase all the verses on my board.

DAY-27

•••••••••●●●●●●••••••

Where Are the Promises?

When I woke up, I remembered the other verse on my board. (Memory lapse is one of the side effects of extreme grief!) It was Psalm 108:13 (KJV): "Through God we shall do valiantly, for He it is who shall tread down our enemies." I felt, after the transplant was a success and the one-year mark was met, that this truly was our verse.

I also began to research Job. I just wanted to read the many comments on the internet about him. I found one writer who had a message about why God allows suffering. But after a few minutes into this sermon, I quickly realized he was with Job's comforters, saying that sin brought the suffering into people's lives. Job's friends tried to convince him that his sin had brought the troubles to him. And the book of Job begins by stating that Job was blameless. I had a friend at David's grave site tell me that she had thought on Job's and my similar path. But she knew I was blameless and wanted to share just that with me. Berry and I both have grappled with that very thought, looking to ourselves and how we might have displeased God.

I opened my Bible just now for the first time since February 12 to find the above verse. As I thumbed through the pages of Psalms, a book I had read and almost memorized the whole time I was sitting in the various hospital rooms at Emory with David, I realized I had "claimed" so many of those verses as my own. But now I'm thinking, do we, as we have heard from the mouth of many ministers, have the right to "name it and claim it"? Have we had it all wrong all these years? I look at the author of many of the Psalms, David, who was loved of God. And yet he questioned whether God had forsaken him. Would God let him go down to the pit and not praise Him anymore? He pleaded with God not to take His Holy Spirit from him. I have done the same thing. In the place I find myself now, I am almost afraid to try speaking words of faith and even accessing my spiritual language anymore. Did it work with my David all those times I would write verses at the top of the pages on which I kept David's med lists? The verses that grabbed my heart, which I desperately wanted to believe would come to pass in my own life for David, are penned all over those journals I kept as David lay in the bed beside me. The one I penned most frequently was "The seed of the Righteous shall be delivered" (Isa. 44:3 KJV). I seriously believed that! I even specifically asked God to please not let death be the deliverer. Many say, "Well, he is delivered now." No, he is not! I don't believe that! I do believe he is in paradise and not suffering. But you don't need deliverance or healing in heaven! You need it on earth! And I really, *really*, believed that David would be healed! Here!

Another prayer I prayed most frequently was the prayer the Samaritan woman prayed, "And she said, Truth, Lord: yet the dogs eat of the crumbs which fall from their masters' table" (Matt. 15:27 KJV). She knew she wasn't a Jew and was an outcast when Jesus said that healing was the bread of the children. I even reminded Him that David was His child, so healing should rightfully be his! So the grappling, the struggling with my faith continues on and on! I thought of Psalm 23 (KJV), probably the most quoted Psalm in the Bible, "The Lord is my Shepherd. I shall not want." And yet I want. That *want* means "lack." I am lacking. My children, who were my future, are no more on this earth. *Shalom* means "nothing broken," "nothing missing" in the Hebrew language. Many just think it refers to peace. But *broken* and *missing* describe my life, my family. I don't know what

God is trying to tell me, trying to teach me. I grapple. I agonize. I write thus:

A Mother's Grief

Days are long and filled with dark sorrow.
Tears have made a furrow down my cheek.
Daddy muffles the cries as he reads a poem
Shared by a friend who cares.
A visit to your grave site.
A bundle of fresh daffodils
Placed under your "I love you more" plaque.
Wind blowing wind chimes that don't chime often
Lets us know you are somewhere nearby.

We hide from the future
Because you are missing
From the place where we stand right now.
Your mom cries and breathes a sigh
As others observe to see
If she can really survive.
It's a heartbreaking story,
Your leaving too soon.
Your parents are broken and torn,
Maybe beyond the telling,
Beyond the meaning
Of God's calling you home.

DAY-28

· · · · · · · · ● · · · · · · · ·

Sacred Ground

We visited the grave yesterday, the grave that holds the earthly body of our precious son. This is the body that we held in our arms for the first time May 6, 1991, our little miracle, our God blessing after we had lost four babies. So yes, that body was and is cherished. It was the body that I fought with all that was in me to save. With every sickness, there were doctors' visits, and with this last hospital visit, it was poked, stuck, and prodded endlessly with needles and drills. There were scans and medicines too numerous to mention. It hurt to watch. After finishing his week of strong chemo and not being able to eat for three days, he said, "Mom, I think my hair is about to come out, because it feels dry, like hay." Then the pain that would not stop, the move to ICU, the begging for relief. He didn't think he could even go through all this again after we thought the transplant had been successful. He fought so bravely, much better than I could have. My baby boy in a man's body, but still my baby, nevertheless. Oh, how it hurt to bury him. Oh, how it hurts to live without him being in that bedroom just down the hall, to hear him talking to his friends on the phone in his low, soothing voice. I miss the big hugs each night as we said good night. He was a five-foot-eleven gentle giant, a lover of justice, a kindhearted, loyal friend, a good son in every possible way. David, I miss you so, so deeply.

One of the biggest tasks in my own mind right now is designing the perfect stone for my son. Memories of trying too hard to get it just right for Erin flood back. It took me a few years to even begin. But when I did, all I could do was sit and cry in the office of the company that was handling the design. The lady was very compassionate and told me it wasn't necessary to hurry. She shared that one family had lost a father and husband. They just had to have a $40,000 stone and wanted it ASAP. Later, they told her that they had thought it would lessen the pain of loss. But it didn't. Having already buried three children, I already know many of these lessons in grief. So it doesn't weigh as heavily on me this time. But I still want it just right for a son who deserved life, not death. He deserves to be remembered. Shane and Courtney Rachels, two of his closest friends just before passing, wrote a poignant story in a card they sent us just after the memorial service. It said that if we remembered and kept David's story alive by talking of him, sharing him with others, we kept him alive. That is so very, very true!

DAY-29

• • • • • • • • • ● • • • • • • • • •

When Breathing Is Difficult

My body is fighting back now. The stress of it all is beginning to manifest in the physical. I should remember. I've been here before with our sweet Erin's passing. The toll grief takes on the body is a high price. But it is all the price of love, a love that cannot be measured in words or earthly terms. My love for my children was huge! So, the loss to my earthly existence exacts a huge price. I wish I could coin some of the phrases, like "It is better to have loved and lost than never to have loved at all." But they all seem so meaningless in the face of grief. There are no words! None! The ties that bind a parent to their children can never be severed. When a child dies, that tie is stretched from earth to eternity—a tight rope for sure. There are times it gets so tight it cuts the breath short, cuts the psyche to the core of life itself. I have buried my last child, my last dream, my last hope for life on earth to continue. It's easy for people to say words with no meaning. So many are Job's comforters. They try very hard to paint a picture of survival when they can't understand that many times people can't see a future, much less survival. It's easy to say things like "It will get better," "Time heals all wounds," "They are in heaven now, knowing no pain," "You just need to get out more," or "There are people here who still need you." But do any of these things work? They didn't with Erin. They aren't with David. There are so many days I want to crawl in a dark closet and live out my days there. I did find myself lifting my hands last night and uttering a cry of "Help me!" to God. This is the same God who I felt said no to my last prayer to save David. My body cries out for help too. So, will He say no now? Next chapter will tell, I guess.

Pain in my back and chest as a result from lying on a well-worn sofa for hours. I don't sleep at night well, so I sleep when I can. Sleep runs away from a grieving parent. We chase it, but our efforts fail. Trying to sleep is a challenge. But waking up is more of a challenge. As soon as I wake, I think of David, of Erin, of God.

Yesterday afternoon, I tried to sleep, and a memory crept in and threw me back into the pit from which I haven't wandered far since February 12. I remembered two little moles just below David's right ear. I remembered the dermatologist said he would remove them when David got big enough to shave. But they never changed shape or color, so it didn't happen. I began to cry uncontrollably. I rushed in the kitchen to see what I could find that would help me nap. Nothing! I don't like drugs, so I don't keep them around. But I did take a Shaklee Stress Tab and a Shaklee Mood Enhancer, which is just Saint-John's-wort. I didn't sleep but felt a little better until it began to lose effectiveness, at which point I started crying again as I shared this with my husband. He cried too. Finding answers to unending questions and facing memories is so exhausting physically. There are no easy solutions. Such is the plight of a grieving parent. It never really ends.

DAY-31

•••••••••●•••••••••

Short-Term Memory

One of the things that a grieving person, especially a parent, faces during the weeks and months following the passing of a child is a lack of focus. Memory is a problem even as you face the challenges of everyday life. This morning I have been trying very hard to pay bills, looking through a huge stack of EOBs from insurance companies, sorting through papers, and it's just not getting done. My nerves are all over the place. I wonder how I will ever get through it. I'm a planner. I have everything done ahead of time. But I look at the stacks and just get maybe one bill paid and I'm done! Some days I think my passing would be the only thing that would ease this burden. I listened to TV ministers as I paid bills on Monday, my day for that task. But their words went over my head as they talked of how to pray for miracles, how to get God to act on your behalf. Again, I am pushed back to all the times I fell on my knees for David. Again, I am faced with battling with my own spirituality. So, during bill paying, insurance checking, my mind is in turmoil. My mind is on overload. I stop. I grieve my son's passing. I miss. I long. I weep.

I categorize loss of memory as a layer of grief, for it is very real and is very pronounced the first couple of months. The depth of the love is a big indicator of the depth of the grief. Each layer reflects the depth of grief. Struggling to survive the horrendous nightmare we face as we wake each morning makes it difficult to function at 50 percent! Loss of memory is recognizable in most cases. I experienced this with Erin, and now with David, it is a continual challenge. Organization is one of my attributes. I have always prided myself on my organizational skills, much to the chagrin of my family. They may come in the kitchen, living room, or even their bedroom and find that my clearing and cleaning has preceded them. And oh, how I hear about it! But now I find myself searching for things I have misplaced or coming home from the grocery store only to find I didn't get the items I went for. I set a routine so that I don't miss paying bills but still find myself forgetful with other things like chores I meant to accomplish. I make lists, only to forget to look at the list. When the mind is preoccupied with thinking of child loss, that takes precedence over every other thing! It is not uncommon this time for me to quote Scarlett O'Hara's famous line where she says, "I'll think about that tomorrow," when I am faced with a decision I am not ready to make. It is said that any major decision should not be made by a grief-stricken person for at least a year. I am holding off on any major decision unless it is one that can't wait.

DAY-32

• • • • • • • • ● • • • • • • • •

Slowly Opening the Door

When I first open my eyes each morning, the thoughts in my head set the tone for the day ahead. This morning, after a sleepless night, those thoughts again turned to God. Tears filled my eyes as I realized, once again, that I was far from Him. Sure, I believed He had turned His back on me, forsaken me, not heard my most desperate cries to save my son. But in all this I had also turned my back on Him. You must know me! God was my everything! When I married Berry, I told him up front that God will always be first in my life, even before him. He accepted that and believed that that was what made me the person I was. When my children were born, I passed down my passion for God to them, reading the Bible to them every night at bedtime along with a storybook or a story I invented with their name in it. I prayed with them and taught them the value of prayer in their own lives. As both faced physical ailments before they passed, they asked me to pray over them, and I saw both pray too. Until this last great tragedy happened, I would take long walks every morning and just talk to God in the cool of the day, as I had imagined Adam had. I invited the creation around me to sing with me as I sang songs of praise before I began my prayers as I walked. This was a very special time. I also spent hours in the Bible, often memorizing scripture, whole chapters, to prepare myself for whatever trials life threw my way. So you can see the knowledge of God's love, the Lordship of Jesus Christ, and the ministry the Holy Spirit played in my whole being. And now! Now I really do feel that I am adrift at sea with no sail. And the sea is very, very stormy. My ship goes up to the pinnacle of the huge waves just before they crash over, and I feel I am drowning. The wind is fierce as it howls about me. I look through the fog at others who are safely on the shore with their families, enjoying all that life offers them. They are playing with their small children, helping them get ready for school, going shopping for clothes and toys, getting ready for graduations, wedding, birthday parties, a new baby, a new house, a vacation, and wonderful family events. They are all smiles and joy and hugs and laughter.

I am a childless mother who had all those things once, and now in the winter of my life, I am alone. My husband and I sit and stare at an empty house that is full of memories. There are pictures of all the children on the walls. Almost every toy they owned is safely packed away in the basement and attic, with a few still sitting on shelves in their closets. There are volumes of family pictures that document those happy days. We had plans with them. There were dreams of wonderful family Christmases, with grandchildren running around the house, birthdays to celebrate, a wedding for David, college for Erin, a life! Now, as Job put it in Job 17:10 (AMP), "my purposes and plans are frustrated." Yes, I know He is the almighty God. If He chooses to open the earth and swallow us all, He can. I acknowledge that! But I also thought He would save my children. I often quoted the verses that indicate that. "I will save thy children" (Isa. 49:25 KJV). "No weapon formed against you shall prosper" (Isa. 54:17 KJV). "Thy children shall be like olive plants about thy table" (Ps. 128:3 KJV). "All thy children shall be taught of the Lord and great shall be the peace of thy children" (Isa. 54:13 KJV). I knew many more, and I prayed them, pleading with God to save my children. Now they are with Him and I am left to suffer alone. It's a cold place where I am right now. I told God this morning, through my tears, that I didn't like being separated from Him. It's not a place I chose. It seemed to choose me. Will I find my way back? Can I forgive Him for taking my baby boy after He took my two girls and my stepson? I think I am pushing open the door a tiny bit. But I hurt with the doing of it.

DAY-33

• • • • • • • • ● • • • • • • • •

Have I Lost My Praise?

I woke up at 5:00 a.m. Berry has already left to take his brother in for surgery. So, the house is very quiet. I got up, stripped my bed to wash linens, which was a Wednesday thing to do. I cleaned up the kitchen/living room a bit, made coffee, made my smoothie, and began crying as I went in and sat on David's bed. It is still unmade since the last day he left it on January 29, 2016, as we went up to Emory for what was supposed to be a routine office visit. It turned into an admission into the hospital and the beginning of two weeks of hell as they started chemo right away. He got sicker with each day, even as he fought his way to recovery. It didn't come. I lay on his bed this morning. I wept as I hadn't wept much. I asked God, "Why?" even though I was told not to. I talked to David, telling him how much I missed him, how sorry I was that he endured so much pain physically and emotionally as he reached out for love and found that some people can't return it. He loved his girlfriend with a commitment that many don't have anymore. But it was returned with abandonment, not just once, but multiple times. I told him I wouldn't bring him back to this earth that is so chaotic and filled with pain. But I miss him more than the breath I take.

I remembered years ago, a teen in our church died suddenly after a horrible car crash. Just a few weeks after her passing, one night

I dreamed she was sitting at the foot of my bed. She was a pretty, happy teen, always joking around and enjoying life. Her name was Debbie Goodwin, sister to one of my best friends, Alicia Jannings. And then her spirit was hovering near. I "felt" her tell me that anytime I wanted to see her, all I had to do was enter into praise of God and she would be there too. Praising God puts us in the "heavenlies," so we would be nearer our loved ones. So here I am in the present, wanting so desperately to connect with David once again. I thought I'd try it. Why not? I removed the dust cover of David's keyboard, as I had done many times before. But as I began to try to play a chorus of "Bless the Lord, O My Soul," I found I couldn't! How could I bless God when He had taken my son? I tried another song that I remembered. No. I couldn't play it. I could, but I wouldn't! I began playing a song I had written when I was praise leader in our church. I wrote it when Erin was going through a difficult time as a teen. "He Will Perfect That Which Concerneth Me." It was based on Psalm 138 (KJV). But after a few bars, I quit again. How could I praise God when He had taken my last child? He had taken my future, my hopes and dreams. He had taken David even after all my desperate pleas for healing, after all the hard work of giving 150 percent of myself to David's care and seeing David struggle to fight when He felt hopeless. This is God, who was always my best friend in the good times and bad, who was always there for me. But now I feel I don't know Him. He is, as I read in the book of Job, the almighty, who sits on the throne of heaven and decides who lives and dies. And there is nothing we can do about it! Yes, I know that He has the right and power to do just that! Yes, I know that I am not God. But I also know I am His child. He said He would be near the broken. I clung to all the promises that I could find that were in the Bible regarding the children of the righteous. I am the righteousness of God in Christ Jesus, who redeemed me on Calvary. I had the right to ask that He save my son. The Word says, "I will save thy children" (Isa. 49:25 KJV). It says, "Ask and it shall be given. Seek and ye shall find" (Matt. 7:7 KJV). So how can I find my way back to praising God?

I began to sing an old church hymn that my mom and dad used to sing. It is called "Farther Along" by W. B. Stephens. It is an old song about the fact we will understand it in the "by and by."

Tempted and tried, we're oft made to wonder
Why it should be thus all the day long;
While there are others living about us,
Never molested, though in the wrong.

Refrain:
Farther along we'll know more about it,
Farther along we'll understand why;
Cheer up, my brother, live in the sunshine,
We'll understand it all by and by.

Sometimes I wonder why I must suffer,
Go in the rain, the cold, and the snow,
When there are many living in comfort,
Giving no heed to all I can do.

Tempted and tried, how often we question
Why we must suffer year after year,
Being accused by those of our loved ones,
E'en though we've walked in God's holy fear.

Often when death has taken our loved ones,
Leaving our home so lone and so drear,
Then do we wonder why others prosper,
Living so wicked year after year.

"Faithful till death," saith our loving Master;
Short is our time to labor and wait;
Then will our toiling seem to be nothing,
When we shall pass the heavenly gate.

Soon we will see our dear, loving Savior,
Hear the last trumpet sound through the sky;
Then we will meet those gone on before us,
Then we shall know and understand why.

—Attributed to W. B. Stevens
Alt. by Barney E. Warren, published 1911
Copyright status is public domain

I could play that one. Is it a praise song? I don't think so. It seems more of a song about coping with life, which is what I am doing right now. Have I lost my praise? It seems I have. I won't—*repeat*—won't turn my back on God. He has done too much for me to do that. But I am broken into a million pieces right now. Maybe He will put me back together again and my praise of Him will return and be stronger than ever. Maybe this book is the last thing I am to do on this earth. Right now, all I can do is breathe and believe that hope may return one day. I don't know. I just don't.

DAY-34

• • • • • • • • • ● • • • • • • • •

Picture of Grief

The days are endless. The nights are restless. This headache is throbbing this morning. I got up at 5:00 a.m. and mopped the kitchen and bathrooms. I know the ache in my jaw will come back. It was severe yesterday. Is it my heart? I don't know. TM joint probably. But a grieving mom doesn't really care about herself. I have friends who remind me to breathe, drink water, eat healthy meals, even if it's a little. Berry and I eat one good meal a day. We eat out sometimes just to escape this dark place of grief for a bit. We escape for a while as we busy ourselves with at-home tasks. But there comes a time when you must rest your body. Then it returns, this horrible, sick feeling of sorrow that is so strong it sucks the breath out of your body and soul. It paints a dark picture of loneliness that is inescapable. I read about a woman who painted a picture of her own grief as if her own body had been consumed in a fire. It had scarred and marred her so that she was unrecognizable. But the outside pain wasn't the real picture; it was the inside pain that was the real pain. Grief is not pretty! It is selfish! It is consuming. It changes everything about your life. One day I might feel differently. But it won't be today or tomorrow. I must find my way out of this hole. God, please help me! The tasks of everyday life can be daunting. All the medical bills and EOBs from David's insurance and regular bills keep coming. Grief clouds your memory and dulls your senses. What may have been so important before becomes just a faded task now. But if you are a task-oriented person, it can weigh heavily on you to complete these mundane tasks of life, adding one more layer to an already-overburdened mind. Cooking, cleaning, shopping can also be overwhelming to a person whose energy has been depleted by the soul-searing touch of grief. It has been advised that a person in deep grief should not make any major decisions for at least a year. But no one will tell you that every decision seems a major one when you can barely function. The bottom line is to do what you must and leave the big stuff for later.

If I stay very busy, I can manage my grief. But the moment I stop or see something that associates with a strong memory of David, I sink to the lowest pit. How long can I keep this up? Sometimes I wish I could be more like Berry. He sits and reads things on his laptop, stopping only to eat or take a nap. I have noticed the naps are more and more frequent. He seems to just be able to shut down. But I have also read that depression causes some to sleep more too. I've always had to stay busy, keep my mind and body busy doing something. But I know as I age, I won't always be able to keep up the energy. Even now, my projects get divided into several parts, where, in the past I would finish everything I began. The days go endlessly on, no lessening of the pain each day brings. I'm getting by.

We go through so many of the stages of grief. I think there are many more than the five that the books reference. Even the sadness at times takes different faces. I made my first trip to the grocery store alone a few days ago. Berry has been by my side constantly because he is worried about me even driving. I thought I could make it. I even went to a different Ingles. But the moment I walked in, it hit me! The memories of the shopping just for David, which was a constant, trying to find something, anything that he could eat. I saw all the familiar things, and as I went down the second aisle, my breathing was labored. I finally just grabbed some things to escape the memories quickly.

DAY-36

•••••••••●•••••••••

Sundays

Sundays growing up were sacred days. Mama never allowed any work to be done on those days. It was set aside to go to church morning and night, with a big Sunday dinner in between, often accompanied by visitors who shared our meal. Saturdays were spent preparing for Sunday. There were clothes to be pressed, shoes to be polished and set in a row by the wall, hair to be washed and rolled for the girls, cake to be baked, and food to be selected for the meal the next day. It was a very special family day. We all participated. There were no exemptions. Together, we were united as we worshipped the Lord and fellowshipped with one another and with friends. Since that was important in my background, it became the tradition for my own little family as well. My own children often brought friends home with us after church on Sundays, so there was fun and laughter and good food. As the years went by, though, people began eating out on Sundays since most moms work outside the home now. Then people became more "distant," so home visits became less and less.

We eventually left the church where my children grew up and began a home church fellowship with a few other families. I remember that first Sunday after we had left our church. I was determined that this still be a sacred day, and since Erin was married and had her own home, it was just Berry, David, and myself. Our music was Berry playing one of the songs he had learned on the guitar and David playing "Swing Low, Sweet Chariot" on the trumpet. Then all three of us shared scriptures and prayed together. Eventually, our little group grew to include other families, and we enjoyed the fellowship and worship together, even cooking lunch together. Once a year we would have a bigger meeting with others who shared our Christian faith and meet in a center where we could all have room to fellowship together in retreat for a few days. There were special times of fellowship and ministry that I will never forget. Of course, as with all things good, there was eventually a falling away, a dispersing of the group. We soon found ourselves back to our individual families.

After Erin went to heaven in 2006, we were so broken that it seemed okay that we just fellowship with a small group. We visited a few churches near us and loved the people at all of them. But I missed our group and the intensity of the study of the Bible that we enjoyed. I remembered, after Erin left for heaven, how long and empty Sundays seemed. Coming from my background, I envisioned so many enjoying families that day. That seemed to emphasize the fact that my family was broken. The three of us continued to worship by watching a minister on TV, whoever we could find that was sharing the Bible in truth. But I continued to miss the fellowship with the body of Christ.

A Different Sunday

Now that David has left for heaven, Berry and I are so displaced. We don't really know where our place in life is, much more our place in the body of Christ. We've had groups from both churches that are in our community visit us, bring us food, and support us with prayer and calls. We have begun attending a very small church near our home. But we are in such a downward spiral into despair that each day is like walking in a thick fog. And Sundays are no different. Struggling with my own spirituality right now is as hard as the grief itself. That might sound strange, but it is for me. I depended on God for my very breath! I still do. I just don't know where I "stand" with God now.

I still go back in my mind to those middle-of-the-night, agonizing prayers for David, those knee-dropping cries for help in the hotel as he fought for his life in the ICU just after his transplant. I think of how he survived that horrible time to live just one more year! I remember the stress I felt at hearing the cancer had returned and how I had to take a stress pill because my stress level was through the roof. David said he thought I was more stressed than him at one point! But at the end, he felt he couldn't make it through another few months of chemo. I just wouldn't give up! I clung to God, to the finished work of the cross of Christ, to the healing that I just knew would come!

And now I'm thrown to the ground again, only this time not in prayer but in despair! How do I reconcile with God, who chose to say no to my pleas for healing for my last surviving child? How do I continue with praise and worship to God, who has always been the constant in my life, my dearest friend, but who has now taken all my children back to Himself, leaving me lonely, broken, grief-stricken beyond tears? How do I respond to all the people who have prayed with us over the last two years who are also angry about the outcome? How do I see a future with no dreams, no hope, no posterity, no future generations to carry on the teachings that I spent hours and hours training my children to know?

I feel I am in a glass bubble with so many people everywhere, watching to see how I emerge from this dark place. Yes, it's Sunday. But it's a totally different Sunday from the ones in my past. Berry and I will get up (although I've been awake since two thirty), we will eat whatever we can find since I am not cooking now, we will visit the grave and clear some grass. We will eat lunch somewhere. If we don't feel able to attend church, we will stare at the walls and at each other and shake our heads, wondering how, why, and what happened once again. We may have a visit from a minister and his wife who stop by sometimes. We may not. The visitors that were at our door constantly those first few weeks have almost stopped coming. I guess people think we survived the burial, so we will be okay, not realizing that grief begins after the burial and continues the rest of life. It's Sunday. Will there be a miracle today? Will we be resurrected? Only God knows the answers, all of them!

Sundays continue to be the most difficult weekday for me. Sundays are associated with quiet, restful family times. There is no work to be done. So my hands are rather idle on those special days. But the hours pass by too slowly and allow too much time for reflection on grief, on missing, on what's not here anymore, and on my sad life. The day is difficult. It is lonely. Maybe, in time, I can get back into a better place with God, with faith. I read my one chapter in Job this morning where he acknowledged his search for God. I feel that way too. Job said he searched for God to the north, south, east, and west but could not find Him. He said God's plans are unchangeable. He was terrified of God. I identify with everything Job is saying. Maybe I am as Job, in a way. I haven't lost my health, my land, or my possessions. But to bury all my children has crushed me to powder. I am afraid of God even though I have kept His ways and have honored Him every day. But now He terrifies me. And I cannot find Him.

DAY-37

••••••••●•••••••

Descriptors

It has been said that people shy away from a grieving parent because they can't even imagine themselves in that position. All our lives, if we are good parents, we live to protect our children from danger, from hurt of any kind. When a grieving parent buries their child, it's as if they are living their greatest and direst nightmare. So to those who have never experienced this, here are some descriptors of this journey from stories told in the Bible.

A Job Life

Job, in the Bible, had to bury all ten of his children. As people read this story, they are struck with fear that here was a good man, a blameless man, who had to bury all ten of his children. Then the question of why comes up. The whys often emerge with full force in the new and raw grief a parent faces. People ask why bad things happen to good people. Why did this happen to this child when they were a good child who never hurt anyone, who loved their parents, who did the right thing? The blame game keeps coming up with me, as my husband and I both have questioned whether our sin or our failure or something in our lives was why our children were taken so young. It is probably one of the first things that came to my mind when we buried our baby Heather, our Erin, and our David. We search our inner soul to see if we are guilty. Often, we might not find anything there, as our soul is in such turmoil.

A Moses Life

Moses, in the Bible, was a Hebrew raised as an Egyptian by the pharaoh's daughter. When he grew into a man, he began to see the injustices perpetrated on his own people as they were slaves to the Egyptians. So he struck an abusive guard and killed him. This sent him fleeing for his life into the desert. I have often thought of Moses. Here he was, a prince with all the privileges of the pharaoh's family. And yet he gave it all up to right a wrong. Because of this, he found himself wandering in the wilderness for forty years. I equate this grief journey to that wilderness. Moses didn't know his identity anymore. A grieving parent loses their identity when they bury a child. For twenty-four years, I was guardian, caregiver, and protector to my son. I nurtured him, helped him find his strengths and weaknesses, laughed with him, and cried with him. My entire identity became wrapped up in my daughters and sons. When people socialize, what do they discuss? Their children. When they celebrate Christmas, Thanksgiving, birthdays, who do they celebrate? Their children. When there is an illness or family crisis, it's the family circle that gathers around. When you bury your children, life as you know it stops.

There is no future, no grandchildren to be born, no more birthday parties, no more Christmases or family celebrations or rooms full of young people. It is an empty wilderness, dry, hot, cold, and lifeless. We don't have forty years left as Moses. But even one week in a desolate place is almost too much to bear.

DAY-38

• • • • • • • • ● • • • • • • • • •

A Roller Coaster of Emotions

The coffee is hot as I sip and type. The warmth of the ceramic cup seems to warm my soul. I relish it. I reach and stretch for anything that will bring even a small measure of solace to my broken heart and wounded spirit. Cooking has always been a passion of mine, creating the dishes that my family loves. Erin loved the corn bread dressing I made each Thanksgiving as I tried to recreate the recipe my mom and grandmother always made. David and Erin loved the family recipe for chicken pie passed down from our aunt Jeffie Fitzpatrick. David loved stir fry, ramen noodles, and Hamburger Helper. The last two weren't my choice, because I always believed in healthy meals. But after chemo, David hardly ate anything. So, when he had a taste for something, I made it. These last two things had a lot of salt, which might have been a need. Scott used to love the old-fashioned Southern cuisine after he joined the Army and traveled so far from home. I guess it took him back to a safer place in his life. I was glad to cook for him on his rare visits home. But now? My husband and I just don't care whether we really eat or not. We get out of the house to try to escape the pain of emptiness. The things we loved so much seem gone since we buried our children. But if we can find a moment's peace in a cup of coffee or a meal at one of the down-home Southern restaurants in our community, we seek that.

Days are long for a grieving parent. Nights are longer. During the first few weeks after the memorial service, friends and family are by your side. When they aren't there, they are usually calling to check on you or texting to make sure you are still breathing. When life itself seems hopeless, it is hard to breathe. It's been thirty-eight days for us now. The calls are fewer and fewer. The visits have almost stopped. We still get a few cards in the mail each day. But hey, life goes on for others, right? It reminds me of the lyrics of a song I heard as a teen. It was a song by the Carpenters. Because of copyright laws, I can't write the lyrics. But it talks of why the birds can go on singing, why the world just goes on as if nothing happened. That was how I felt when we had to say goodbye too soon to each of our four children. After Erin passed so suddenly on March 2, 2006, there was a bird outside my bedroom window. And that bird would sing very early in the morning when I first woke to the pain of life itself. I really, really wanted to shoot that poor little bird. And if you could know me, you would know I would never hurt a flea! But it seems so ironic that that bird could feel any joy, that the sun could possibly shine, that the spring days could bring forth new life when my Erin was gone from this earth. And I felt the same way about David and Scott and Heather.

David was still at home. So, we felt that his heavenward going has hit us even harder. He had been there to give us reason to go on when Erin and Scott left for heaven. And now, we can't even believe that he is gone most of the time. All our efforts were focused on helping him get well for the past two years. Every waking moment, we put forth every ounce of energy into helping him beat this leukemia. And he was beating it! The anger rises in me every time I think of all he went through. And it came back! How could it? Didn't I pray enough? Didn't we take him to the best doctors, spared no expense to help him? The anger consumes me sometimes.

Being too well acquainted with grief, I know the stages. I hate them. I hate grief. But I know what is coming. That's the scary part. I've been through grief before with our Heather, Erin, and Scott. I know that you don't just go through five stages of grief. You drift in and out, in and out, around them and through them. Sometimes they go through you. After I put the dust cover back on the keyboard, I had this sudden urge to throw something. My eye caught a beautiful little figurine of a little boy and girl I had sitting on my microwave. I resisted the urge this time!

DAY-39

· · · · · · · · ●●● ● ●●● · · · · · · ·

Night and Day

Sleep becomes a struggle. Last night I had a flashback to that last scene when I kissed my sweet boy an earthly goodbye. As I bent over him after they had pulled all the tubes and IVs, I looked at his sweet face. It was a face of peace now after such a struggle with pain over the past few months. There was no furrow on his forehead. I immediately noticed a tear that had trickled down his right eye and dried en route down his face. It broke me to see this. And last night, as my own tears were flowing uncontrollably after I finally lay in bed, I remembered that tear. It tore at my very soul, my innermost core, to think that my son might have realized what was going on and didn't want to die. Did he know? Even though the doctors assured me he was sedated and felt no pain when they intubated him, did he feel the pain anyway? I watched outside the ICU room as they started what I think was called an arterial line in his femoral artery since they couldn't get accurate BP readings from his arm or the arterial line that was already in his wrist. The horror became worse as I saw another doctor create a sterile field around and just below his knee and then drill a tiny hole there. Later, my niece Amanda Perez, who is a nurse, and my friend Nerissa's daughter, who is a nurse, both explained that if they can't access a vein, they do this to push meds in more quickly. They were trying to bring the acid level in his body down since his heart kept stopping. The horror got worse when the doctor in charge came out to get us and said, "His heart has stopped once. You might want to be in here when it stops again, which will probably happen." Oh, the agony of those moments will never fade from my memory. Did he know? Could he feel? Sleepless nights. Agonizing thoughts. Tears that keep flooding from my body and soul. It is almost as if I am bleeding tears sometimes.

It's 2:24 a.m. on April 22. I woke with heartburn after being asleep one and a half hours. Sleep escapes me if I wake up. I resist taking sleeping pills, although I do take melatonin occasionally. I should have last night! When I wake, as always, I try to be quiet so as not to wake Berry. He stays up very late. I see the light on under the door, so I know he is awake until the wee hours. But he does take naps during the day. I don't. I can't. I know this clock will wind down sometime and I will sleep. Until then, I try to keep my mind busy. The moment I allow it to be still, the grief takes over once again. I cry. I remember. I must face it. I don't want to! I don't want to know my David is not here! How do I escape this horrible fate? How does a mother go on without her children? I've had numerous people tell me they couldn't! How can I? It was an uphill battle to go on after losing Heather! But I did. And with Erin. But I did! And was it only to be slammed down to the pit again? I am talking to God a little more. But the lack of understanding hinders me.

DAY-40

· · · · · · · · ● · · · · · · ·

Fighting to Survive

Grief steals your memory, creates chaos in the mind, and causes loss of focus. When our Erin passed into heaven, one night I grabbed a notepad and felt it urgent that I write down every memory lest I forget any detail of our sweet girl's life. Now I have begun to do the same for David. If I don't, it feels that they will fade into oblivion, which I know is untrue. When I was showering one night, I could almost "hear" David's voice speaking to my heart. He was saying, "Mom, you must not grieve yourself to death. If you die, then I die again too. Remember how you honored Erin in joining MISS and reaching out to other grieving parents? You must do the same for me. If you love us the same, then you must do the same for me!" This affected me so because I had had a death wish. I could see no reason to go forward with a life only filled with loneliness and pain. I think it was then that I got my "fight" back to survive this for my David. I was determined to keep him alive.

One of his best friends, Shane Rachels, sent me a letter just after David left for heaven. He was grief-stricken over David's passing, as was his wife, Courtney. In the letter he shared this: "A friend put something into perspective for me. He said that fifty years is a life. If someone lives for seventy-five years, it's a life and a half. David didn't get to that mark. But if we hold him in our memories for a moment each day, then he gets a little more time here. And if you, I, and everyone here does that, then maybe he'll get enough time to say he got a full life." What a poignant thought! And so true. Even our Lord Jesus said as He celebrated the last supper with his disciples, "This do in remembrance of me" (1 Cor. 11:24 KJV). We must not let our son's memory fade. I fought to keep Erin's memory alive, and I still do ten years later. The same is true for my little Heather and our Scott. And now this is my new fight, to keep David's memory alive. I was looking at the book of remembrance the funeral home gave us. It is a log of people who signed that they had visited. Erin had a few more names in hers than David his. We were in such a fog that I realized later more had come than had signed in. The same was true for David. But we have gotten many more cards for David than for Erin. So many have come forward and told us they were praying for David over the past two years, even total strangers! Some of those people told us about the anger and disbelief that they felt when he didn't survive this fight. Already David has touched many, many lives.

I must get the fog cleared in my mind so I can finish this book, so I can reach beyond my grief as I did with my other children. It's so easy to stay here in this muck and mire! It's much easier to wrap the grief around yourself and close the door to any who tries to pull you back. I may feel differently tomorrow. But right now, I choose to fight!

DAY-41

••••••••••●••••••••

How Are You?

The phone rings or I meet someone in a store and the question immediately comes, "How are you?" How do I answer? Do I say, "Fine!" as I usually do? Or do I tell them my child has died and he was my last living child? Do I go into detail and tell them my current state? If I did, they would probably never ask me again. It makes me think, *do people really care how you are?* Do I care when I immediately ask, "How are you?" Or is it a customary greeting in America? How I would really answer if I told the truth, I'd say this: "I cry myself to sleep most nights. My chest hurts. My jaw hurts. My body functions, but I don't know how. I eat a little and drink fluids just to keep myself alive. There is no joy in the little things like gardening, music, or watching old funny TV sitcoms like there used to be. Heck! There is little joy in anything anymore. My days are mundane, at best. I am simply waiting for God!" I guess that's how I would really answer.

When the calls, visits, and cards stop coming, what do people say when they see us? When they ask how we are, do we say "Okay," knowing that we are not telling the truth? Sometimes it is easier to say that than to explain. When I do tell the truth and say, "I have no purpose in being here anymore, I have no future, no heirs," I hear, "Oh, but God loves you! You will find your purpose." They are telling me that it will get better. I haven't felt people trying to "fix" us this time. They must know that this time it's different. We have lost all our children. What is there to say to us? The platitudes don't work, although I still hear, "You will have joy again." I just can't see it now.

Grief is not a pretty show. It is selfish. It is harsh. It takes the sparkle out of a mother's eyes. It crushes the heart and wounds the soul. The aftermath is that the grieving parent will never emerge from the pit as the same person, ever! People watch to see how they are. They gaze in wonder that that person could possibly be surviving after burying all their children. It almost seems they are watching to see when the end will come. I hate it! I hate being pitied! At MISS (Mothers in Sympathy and Support), some of us call ourselves survivors. I don't know if I have survived or will survive this time.

Others will even project the future for you. They circle the hole. They gaze in wonder and often speak things over you. I've heard, "Maybe this happened so you can help other grieving parents." My response in my mind and even out loud: "Been there, done that! It was like a prison sentence. Don't put that one on me again!" Also, I've heard, "You seem better now!" My response, at least in my mind, is, "I can speak to you without crying this time so I'm better? Go home with me. See me in David's room every day, hugging his pillow, which I refuse to wash because it still has his scent on it. I hug it tightly, remembering all those nights I'd hug him and say 'Good night' and 'I love you.' He would respond, 'I love you more!' Then I sit on his bed and cry. See me when I'm sitting, watching TV with my husband, and someone on a show will remind me of David and my eyes fill with tears. See me when I finally lie down at night with tissues in hand, trying to sleep but only crying." So I seem better? Is it because they want us better? They want us walking in the store with a smile on our face, showing our lives are better. How can it ever be better if we live without our children? What kind of future is it without hope of grandchildren to brag about on social media? It is a future with every year celebrating birthdays and angelversaries with a birthday balloon tied to a tombstone and laying flowers on a cold grave that holds the most precious bodies we've ever known. How can it be better when Thanksgiving, Christmas, Easter, and other special days are filled with only happy memories of days gone by? We watch others make new memories with wonderful family gatherings. *Better* is not a word I use for my life now.

DAY-42

•••••••••●•••••••••

The Longings

Parents dream of the future when they first hold that sweet baby in their arms. Immediately, all their hopes and dreams for the future are changed. They are somehow transferred into this little bundle of joy. As the child grows, those hopes and dreams are tweaked by the emerging personality of the child. The parents' dreams are merged with the children's. But they are still a part of everyday life. When, suddenly, the child dies, those hopes and dreams go with them. When they are buried, the hopes and dreams are buried too.

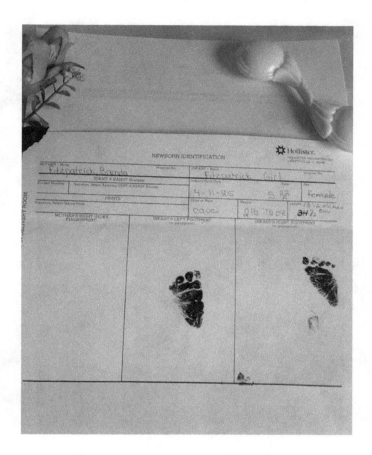

When we buried our second baby girl, Heather Lynn, our dreams were crushed. I had envisioned Erin and her baby sister always being close, as I had been with my own sisters. We wore one another's clothes, shared our own dreams and secrets with one another. I knew there would be a bond that wouldn't be broken. But it was not to be.

Erin never knew her little sister, never got to hold her or see her on this earth. As Erin grew, she became her own person. I had dreams of her taking ballet since she was so tall. But she chose twirling, Girl Scout, softball, cheerleading. She was always social and loved being surrounded by people. And that was fine with me! I loved the big birthday parties and going to events with her to support her.

Then our little David came, and my dreams were that he would fish and hunt and garden like my dad. But he migrated to Power Rangers and martial arts. So, we enrolled him in tae kwon do, which he loved! He stayed with it for seven years, becoming a black belt, and just one month short of receiving his second-degree black belt. He loved music, so he played trumpet in the band in school, played piano after a few lessons with me but picked up on it quickly and soon was playing complicated scores that I couldn't even play. Later, he loved guitar and became quite accomplished in that as well. He loved mind challenges, so he quickly began video gaming with friends from all over the world. That, too, became a passion. He enrolled in trials of games that were about to come out and sent feedback to the company about the games. He preferred the strategy games to the shooter games because it was a challenge.

Scott was only nine when I married his dad. He was a quiet, shy little kid but loved sports. He played baseball and loved to swim. We watched him play football in high school. He loved bodybuilding and did quite well with it in high school. He decided to leave the quiet country life and join the Army. We were so proud when we drove to Fort Knox for his graduation from basic training. He became a tank mechanic, which made his dad proud since he, too, loved mechanics. Soon Scott progressed from being a quiet, shy child to a strong military guy who was tough but made friends all over. He continued with his bodybuilding and won first place several times, once in Iraq in Desert Storm. He was proud when he succeeded in lifting five hundred pounds. We didn't get to see him often when he was in Korea, Fort Hood in Texas, Iraq, and Afghanistan, Fort Riley in Kansas, and eventually in Fort Stewart in Savannah, where he met and married his wife. But he left his mark on the world, just as David, Erin, and Heather. They had their own dreams, and for that, I am thankful.

My longings now are just simply to hold them in my arms one more time. I remember so vividly hugging Scott just before he went to Afghanistan the last time. I looked him in the eyes and told him I wouldn't stop praying for him until he was back on American soil.

Oh, the longing for my children! The longing for the hugs, the kisses, the smiles, and the activity. Life just overwhelms you when you sit in a silent house that once was filled with laughter, music, and fun.

DAY-43

••••••••●•••••••

Easter

Morning broke for me at two o'clock and again at five thirty. As I awoke, I began to talk to God. Although He is silent now, I know He hears me. I told him all the agony I was feeling inside about the silence, about His decision to call David home to heaven. So many emotions emerged in that one-sided conversation as I lay in the darkness and saw what I thought were angel wings fluttering on my ceiling. I thought of Job sitting in silence with his friends for seven days, saying nothing. That's where I should be after forty-three days. And yet I open my mouth and mind to communicate with no response that brings back the peace.

Today is Easter, Resurrection Day, the High Holy Days for all Christians, the Day of Atonement, the day that life was freely given for humans who were doomed to destruction because of Adam's fall from grace. I still respect and honor my Savior, Jesus Christ, and my Father, God. I will not turn my back on Him, even though He may remain silent for the rest of my life. People visit me, text me, call me, meet with me to try to bring comfort. They long for me to find peace again with the Father God. They watch to see if I will collapse and die or get up and be resurrected to a life as a grieving mother who will long for her children if she has breath. This mother will look at pictures of happy families celebrating life's events, hugging grandchildren, and making memories that she longs for herself.

After I made my morning coffee, I searched on the top shelf of my pantry for the egg coloring kit. I bought one each year after the Easter season was over, when it was on sale. Even though my children were both grown, I still would color eggs, just like my own mom did. I made them baskets. I loved making the baskets myself, shopping for months for just the right doodads and little candies. I reached up and found the dusty little box. There are no children here on earth for me today for the first time in thirty-three years, one month, and one day. But I am coloring eggs. I cried when I realized last year David was here. We came home from Emory on March 26, 2015, so it was his first day back home after transplant and almost dying in ICU, then rehab. But what a joy it was for him to be home. Just forty-four days ago, one of the things he said to me while we were sitting in the hospital room was that he just wanted to go home, to eat ramen noodles and just be home. Oh, how desperately I wanted to be bringing him home in the car instead of him being in an ambulance, going to the funeral home. Oh, how my heart cries on this Easter Sunday morning, when so many churches are holding sunrise services right now, eating breakfast, celebrating Resurrection Day. Will I be resurrected again on this earth? No more questions, Lord! No more! I wait in silence for You to speak.

The day is over. We had guests, which helped ease the pain of our first Easter in thirty-three years with no children in this world. My heart aches for my David. Ten years without Erin have taught me to cope with the pain, although I never stop missing her or longing for her. But David's home-going has sent me to the bottom. "David, I miss you! I love you more! Send me a sign! I look every single day for a sign from you in heaven! Oh, how I wish I could have just one more day, just one more hug from you, my sweet son!"

DAY-44

• • • • • • • • • ● • • • • • • • • •

Self-Care

The grief community I became part of when my Erin left for heaven had good advice for the newly bereaved. Taking care of yourself becomes one of the greatest challenges you face. The sage advice includes drinking plenty of water, walking in sunshine, sleeping when sleep will come, eating small meals or trying to eat, journaling to get out the emotions, allowing yourself to cry since that gets the grief out, and taking as much time as you need to grieve. And the last thing but not the least is, there are no rules to grief. Those may seem very simple tasks, but for a grieving parent, it is not that easy. When you have buried your child, your heartbeat, your life seems pointless. Why should you take care of yourself when there is nothing ahead for you? Even if you are blessed to have surviving children, often you feel hopeless and don't care about your own survival. I know, for that was how I felt. The sad thing is that that child or children that are left feel that too. This is another stressor in the mix, another layer of grief. Now, with no children left for me, it is truly a struggle. I did begin eating again as part of my routine. But I eat with no joy or enjoyment. Another bit of sage advice is to have a routine. It does help. It is very, very easy to find yourself isolated from family and friends. My husband would be very content to shut the gate and let no one in. I don't do well with isolation, especially since we are so alone. But I know of parents who sleep much of the time and some who do isolate themselves. I understand!

Scientists have discovered that negative thoughts affect your physical body. Grief is a negative. It's constantly bombarding your mind with the loss. So after a few weeks or months, it's not uncommon for the body to "speak out." The body bears the burden, just as the mind and soul do. I found with Erin's passing, I could only stay extremely busy until I wore myself down. Such is the case today. My body is speaking that it's time to slow down a bit. Staying busy is something I've always done to not have to deal with the negatives in my life. I've been building David's garden and staying busy when I am awake, except for a few hours at night when I lie on the couch and watch TV with Berry. It provides the distraction that the busyness did during the day. But how long can you stay busy until your body says, "Rest"? Mine is speaking that to me now. So today I am answering with a break. It just bothers me because then the grief will try to overwhelm me as my mind is not so occupied. But facing it is the work. Having a face-off with grief taxes the soul. Unless it is done, though, it stays in the recesses of the mind and soul and can cause other, more deep-seated problems. So face it I must. With God's help (and I am crying out to Him, although not really praying yet!), I can make it another day.

Friends and family are still visiting just to make sure we are okay. We know, from Erin's home-going, that eventually that will stop. I think even now the visits are extended a little past the usual time because they see that we are not coping with losing all our children. It's very hard when I feel I have nothing to say. Or if there are endless conversations about politics or stories that don't include David, when they leave, I feel we have wasted his memories. My husband copes by sleeping more than usual and reading articles on the internet. He will stop and watch a bit of TV with me at night. I cope by staying busy. The only thing is that at my age of sixty-eight, even though I am in good physical health, the energy that I had before is not there. I do little tasks just to pass the time. Right now, the grief hits me stronger the moment I sit down to rest. There are days when the aches and pains are magnified, and I think maybe my time is near. And that seems okay. I am not afraid to leave this world of sorrow. Sometimes I wish I hadn't been such a health "nut" and taken such good care of my body all these years. Maybe that "time" would have come sooner, and I could be with my children. But for some reason, God must have a destiny I have yet to fulfill before I finish my course here on earth. So, I will carry on, trying to take care of me.

DAY-45

·············●·············

Reasons

Seeking answers as to why death happens is common for grieving parents. I saw this in myself after Erin left for heaven and in many other parents I met over the past ten years. And even though we knew David was very sick and had a life-threatening disease, my faith told me he would survive. I never entertained the thought that he would not make it. Never! And when it happened, when he breathed that last breath, it took my own breath away. It shook my faith! It blew me away! The next few weeks, I sat with my husband and we would go over everything. Was it an error on the hospital's part? They had type-crossed his blood to give him the first platelets after chemo. Did they get it wrong? Did the ICU team do something that worked against him? I saw them drill a small hole below his knee and was told it was to push medicine in when they couldn't access a vein. It was the place in his leg where the mass was discovered weeks before. Did this do it? Should I have remembered to tell them that his leg might have a growth in it? Those were just a few of the questions that went through my mind as I kept trying to find the reason.

We also wondered if one of us had sinned against God. Did we bring this on ourselves? I couldn't think of anything that was against the commandments of God that we did. But maybe I missed something! I tend to overthink anyway, so this was a constant in me. And it still is at this point. I remember with Erin, I was on this track for at least six months. My husband just got me to focus one day and said,

"We will probably never know the whys until we are in heaven with Erin. And then it won't even matter anymore." Of course, he was right. But here I am again, burying my last child and finding little comfort in the thoughts of my head.

So, what does a parent do with this? We search! We wait! We hope for an answer. But in our hearts, we know that the answers are few and may not even appear.

My chapter in Job today is the one that contains the words of the last and youngest of Job's comforters. He implies that, even though Job boasts of not sinning before God, still there is sin in Job saying that God withheld justice from him. So they all tried to convince Job that he was unrighteous, even though God said in the beginning of the book that here was a man without blame. It's interesting that people try to find the cause of a tragedy in people's lives. They do often want to point the finger and say that that person has sinned and brought this on themselves, although the person is trying to figure that out, too, often without solution.

DAY-46

· · · · · · · · ● · · · · · · · ·

Their Value Is Far More Than Gold

Parents often live out their dreams through their children. It was so in my case. I finished college and was well into my career when my daughter was born. Many of my own dreams had come true. I had married a handsome man, bought property for our first home. We were doing well financially. But when Erin was born and placed in my arms, nothing else mattered. When I was pregnant, I read every book on parenting I could find. I was determined to do this right. Here was this little life entrusted to me and Berry. Since she was such a beautiful child, it was suggested that we enter her in beauty contests, which she refused! She was everything I had never been. I never felt pretty. And she was. I was never social. She was! I did begin to live vicariously through her. Her hopes and dreams quickly became mine. Her sorrows, her joys, her life became so intertwined with mine that I rarely thought of myself. The parties, the twirling, the cheerleading, the sporting events, the school trips, the sleepovers, the church children's activities all became my life. She grew into this wonderful, independent young woman so quickly in just the blink of an eye. She wanted to go to work when she was fifteen. She went to school, then work, then socialized with friends. Life became a blur of activity for her and us.

When Erin was eight, our beautiful baby boy, David, was born. He was all boy all the time! He loved playing outside, ball games, TV, and even school. I still have visions of him in his Superman pajamas, complete with cape, jumping off the bed and running down the hall. He ran everywhere. His little leg muscles were always taut. He quickly found his passion in a show called Power Rangers. He became a swashbuckler, using any stick he could find to pretend sword fighting. We enrolled him in tae kwon do, which became one of his favorite things. When he was about eight, we found his allergies were what had been making him sick so much of his life. Since he couldn't play outside much without getting sick, he migrated into indoor activities and found his passion in video games. He loved a challenge, so he chose games that required problem-solving skills. Our lives quickly intertwined just as it had with Erin. Because he was sick so much as a child, I always knew when he didn't feel well. He would cling to me. There was another bonding. Music was another passion for him. He played trumpet in the band in school and quickly taught himself to play keyboard and guitar. Since I was a pianist, too, we shared that bond. He quickly grew into a gentleman, always caring for others. He was well-mannered and respectful always to any adult who was near. He made me so proud as I would observe his gentle nature. He was tall, handsome, and very intelligent. My dreams were living through his life as I saw him go out with friends and begin to reach for his own dreams. One of his friends told me David was not content unless he achieved "platinum" level on every video game he played. He was never a quitter. He worked through challenges of life with a passion. One teacher of his advanced math class in middle school told me he was brilliant. He made me such a proud mother, always getting good grades and award for achievement in school. My dreams became their dreams, and it was hard to tell where one stopped and the other began.

Scott came into my life when he was nine. I married his dad, and often he would visit us in our little apartment. He loved swimming in the pool and going shopping with me. He was a very shy child, but so much fun to be with. He quickly found his passion in sports, like football and baseball. But his real passion in high school was bodybuilding. He grew up tall and handsome, looking much like his dad. After high school, he joined the Army and began his lifelong career. We were very proud of him as we saw him mature and travel the world. He stepped out of his comfort zone in his rural home setting to live in other states where he was stationed and eventually serve in Korea, Iraq, and Afghanistan. We saw him become a bold, mature man who knew what he wanted out of life and went after it. He continued with his bodybuilding even when he served abroad, winning first place in a contest in Iraq, bench-pressing nearly five hundred pounds. My husband was so proud as he saw Scott become what he had always dreamed. So again, the dreams were so intertwined.

When each of our children left for heaven, our world, our dreams came slowly crashing down. And when our baby boy, David, at only twenty-four left us after such a battle with leukemia, in a moment of time at 5:32 a.m. February 12, 2016, all hope flew out of the window along with our dreams. He became our life's purpose after Erin, our baby Heather, and then Scott left for heaven. He was our only hope for the future, for continued dreams, as we anticipated his own future with a wife, career, and grandchildren.

This morning I thought of a verse in the Bible that talks of God being like a potter who forms the clay into vessels of his own creation. Sometimes a potter sees a vessel is not of his liking or has a flaw, so he crushes it and remakes it. I thought, *Is that what God is doing with us?* But we are both sixty-eight years old. How or why would He start over with us at this late stage of life? We had beautiful, handsome, wonderful children who fulfilled all our dreams. Can we start over as Job did? I can't have a child at this age. There are no answers, at least none that I can see. We are sad, distraught, undone, crushed! Is there anything left for us? Any dreams? Any hope? As of today, we see nothing. Everything around us is ashes. We are Job.

DAY-47

• • • • • • • • • ● • • • • • • • • • •

Interactions

Socialization changes dramatically for a grieving parent. On the one hand, there are people genuinely interested in helping but aren't quite sure what to do or say. On the other, there are comforters who do know. But then how does a grieving person respond? It's a delicate balancing act. And it is different for each. My husband would just love to close the gate to our driveway and seclude us for however long it takes, even for the rest of our lives. I need people, even if they don't know what to do or say. I don't think it's the difference between how men and women grieve as much as our personality or the way we were trained as a child. There might need to be some compromise between family as to the response to others. We have had many come by to visit. Some were strangers who had prayed through their church prayer groups for David for the past two years. They have expressed their own questions as to why he could not be here now. Some were family and friends who just wanted to know we were still alive and coping with this tragedy. There have even been phone conversations with many, some of whom even cry with me as we share the grief over losing David and losing all our children. I have talked to strangers as I have called about the finances associated with David's long illness. These people have been very compassionate as I cried, trying to deal with this when I am not ready. We know they all mean well. But there are times I just don't know what to say, how to respond. I feel my response is shallow, without heartfelt appreciation.

I don't like being that way. One thing that is true about grief is that you change. Even if you don't like the changes, some are inevitable.

I must give credit to a group of people who have been there for us since our Erin went to heaven in 2006. I remember the hours spent searching the internet for grief support groups. I typed with every possible word in the search bar to find anything that might be of comfort. Finally, I typed in "grieving moms" and came upon the site for MISS, Mothers in Sympathy and Support. As I joined and began sharing the huge burden of sorrow I bore, immediately responses were there, multiple times a day, and even in the night hours, when I couldn't sleep. Here was a group of people who were complete strangers, responding to me with open arms and hearts. They all had lost children, so they knew the heaviness I wore as a garment. They eased my sorrow as I plied them with questions about how I was feeling. I visited the website at least three or four times a day. Finally, one of the administrators asked me if I would be a moderator for the site. I thought it was a little early, as Erin had only been gone a few months, but they had lost some moderators and needed help. I began what would be a ten-year journey of sharing, caring, and receiving comfort and help. I soon found that in helping others, I, too, was helped. I never knew the friends I forged on MISS would one day come again to my rescue. But they certainly did. As soon as David was diagnosed in 2014, they were calling, sending meals, sending cards to the hospital, and never left my side. Two of them showed up at the hotel and hospital to support us in person with whatever they saw we needed. What a blessing! And even now, they are here. New members who came just before I had to quit posting two years ago to care for David have been so supportive. I have found that God does send angels among us. I must mention Dr. Joanne Cacciatorie, the founder of MISS, who, out of her own tragic loss of a precious baby girl, Cheyenne, began this group that has influenced families all over the world. She is a role model for us who are grieving. We see, through her, that we can honor our child's memory by reaching out and using our own brokenness to make a difference.

Right now, amid my great sorrow, I don't see how I will ever do that again. How do I find my way out of this dark night of the soul?

But I want to for my David. He deserves to be remembered in a big way. He is my lovely son, my greatest treasure. I want him remembered. I want to share him with others.

CHAPTER 8

•••••••••●•••••••

David's Battle

Here is what I thought would be the beginning of this book, written in the hospital in 2014. I chose to put it here rather than at the beginning.

Meeting God in His Secret Place

Psalm 18:11 (KJV) says God's secret place is in the darkness. Psalm 91 (KJV) has always been a favorite chapter. It begins with "He that dwelleth in the secret place of the most High shall abide under the shadow of the Almighty." I wanted so much to "abide" under the shadow of the almighty. But I never liked darkness. And here I find myself.

March 2, 2006, at 1:10 a.m., our phone rang. I thought it was a wrong number or emergency, so I picked it up. No one was there! Strange. About ten minutes later, a car pulled into our driveway. I woke my husband to go to the door. Our fourteen-year-old son was asleep in a recliner in the living room beside the front door. As my husband opened the door, we saw our son-in-law's dad and mom. Erin's father-in-law said, simply, "Erin's dead!" I screamed from the sheer horror of those words! Total and utter disbelief and shock set in. After we composed ourselves a minute, we asked if we could see her. They said, "Yes, of course!" We quickly dressed and drove the ten-minute drive to Erin's house. Our son David didn't want to go. He was pacing the floor in panic. As we drove over, my husband said, "We are living every parent's nightmare!" When we arrived, there was Adam, Erin's husband, just staring into the kitchen, in shock. He and Erin loved each other so deeply. His world was crushed, never to be the same again.

That night began a very dark, scary journey down paths I never thought I'd travel. I start with this event for it was one that changed me. I know every major event in our lives changes us. They change our perspective on life's stability, the way we view others, the way we view ourselves, the way we view our spirituality, and even our worldview. I read yesterday that the secret place of God is in the darkness. Well, darkness was all around me that horrible night.

Both my sisters, one of whom is in heaven now, have urged me to write a book. So, in honor of Kathryn, who wrote two books before she passed, and my sister Judy, who is one of my biggest supporters, and of course my four children, I decided to begin. It helps to know the author's background, so I wanted to share some of my own. This might allow the reader to understand how I am handling this grief journey with factors that contributed to my strength and, sometimes, lack of strength.

My mom was a WWII bride. My dad was a WWII veteran. Both came from humble families who had little in worldly possessions but who loved and cherished family and God, above all. My older sister, Kathryn, was born a delight to my parents, a blond-haired beauty. Thirteen months later, I arrived, no hair for a year, then curly and red! I was the only one in my family with red hair (but both my grandmothers were redheads). My sister teased me that I was adopted. She loved to tease! Then the life of the party was born in the face of my baby brother, Rabun. Eight years later, our sweet little brother, Tim, arrived. We were so excited to have another baby! He was so pretty people thought he was a girl sometimes. But he quickly followed in Daddy and Rabun's footsteps with all the hunting, fishing, guitar playing, and manly ways! Then, after we moved in to our new home, which Daddy built after work and on weekends (he was a true worker!), our little darling baby sister arrived. Since we were all teens, except five-year-old Tim, we spoiled our little Judy royally! So our family grew into a wonderful circle filled with music, laughter, trips to visit one another, and more love and fun than you can imagine! There were certainly tears and struggles, but we always had one another's back!

Kathryn married and moved away the same year I went away to college. Then Rabun married and moved away, leaving only Tim and Judy at home. Our little circle had grown but had begun to go in separate directions too. What began as being born into a family of great stability, support, and Christian principles and foundation was preparation for the tough times that would surely come for each of us.

Beginning at the Beginning

We had great fun growing up in a serene country setting. There wasn't much money, but as children, we learned to create our adventures. There were always big family gatherings with lots of aunts, uncles, and cousins. The big home-cooked meals, the laughter as the children played outside and the adults talked as they sat in the swings on the porch, were times filled with love and commitment to one another. Once, though, at one of these, when I was only four or five, I was taken to a closet and molested by a relative. This happened several times, and it scared me for years. I was threatened not to share it with anyone. Later, I found out this was happening to my sister and to several cousins and even an aunt. The shame and sheer fear I felt were profound. I didn't really talk about it until I was in college with my roommates. It was then I realized that that happens more frequently than is shared with others. I never told my parents. But as I came to know Christ better, I learned to forgive, which brought a relief to my soul. I was always an A student and loved school. School was easy for me as I loved learning. But as this abuse began, I developed a school phobia and refused to go, saying my stomach hurt. My mom agonized over my state and worked with the principal and teachers until I was able to continue my education. My dad was my rock through it all. He never threatened but encouraged me. I felt safe when he and Mom were near. This abuse was the first place of darkness I walked through.

Places of Darkness

No one wants to walk in the dark places of life. Who would? But everyone just loves Psalm 91. I hear it quoted in all the religious circles. "He that dwelleth in the secret place of the Most High shall abide under the shadow of the Almighty." What a wonderful, comforting scripture! But! Do people really—I mean *really*—know where the secret place of God is? Of course, right? Wrong! It is not where you may think! Psalm 18:11 (KJV) says it is in the darkness! Really? Really? Yep! It is. Let's move on.

I was so excited to be walking across the Sanford Stadium football field at the University of Georgia on a hot June day to be presented with my diploma! It had been a long, hard four years working and studying. But I had arrived! I had to repeat a couple of courses since my grades dropped during the time my fiancé came back from a two-year mission trip to tell me our relationship was over! My education suffered! Dark place number 2: being rejected by my fiancé! It had been a hard four years. I worked all four to pay for my education, working extra hours on weekends and during Christmas at Sears catalog sales. I had been robbed once on campus and almost drowned trying to pass the mandatory swimming class that was added just before graduation. I spent long hours studying at night. But when I met my first love at UGA, got engaged, planned our future move to seminary together when he got back from the Journeyman program in Brazil, I didn't mind all the hard work. I graduated and got a secretarial job to keep me busy until my teaching job started in the fall. But all my plans became ashes when he came back and told me he was breaking up with me. I cried for three days. My mom didn't know how to comfort me. No one did. My dad always lifted my spirits. (Daddy was so proud that I had finished college!) He decided to give me a wonderful gift. They didn't have much money, but he managed to save enough to give me the down payment for my first new car. It was a Mercury Cougar—so pretty! I loved those sequenced taillights on the 1969 sky-blue car!

I finally got an interview at a little mountain town about an hour from home and was hired on the spot! I was off! It was a beautiful little town in the foothills of North Georgia. My classroom window view was of Currahee Mountain and the mountains beyond. All the people at Toccoa, Georgia, welcomed me warmly with open arms. A wonderful elderly woman rented out a room in her house, my first home away from home. It was just a bedroom with kitchen privileges. Since I was accustomed to helping Mom cook for a family of seven, Mrs. S, my landlady, helped me learn to cook smaller portions! I loved our long talks about her children and the folks in her church. It was only a short distance to my school, so it was ideal. Mrs. S's husband had passed several years before, so she was quite the independent woman, still cutting her own grass and driving her very old car to do her own shopping. About two weeks into my new adventure, I came home and found her on the floor. She had had a stroke and died two weeks later! I was devastated! Another place of darkness. But she will forever be special to me. A friend of hers offered to rent me their basement apartment, where I lived the remaining three years in Toccoa, Georgia. I shared the apartment with three other teachers in the time I was there.

My days at the foot of the Currahee Mountain were wonderful. I loved the children there and made so many friends with the warm community, who always helped one another. The principal of our school was a giant of a man who had been a coach. He had a real handle on discipline and was so supportive of the innovative ideas of our wonderful staff. I arranged for the third grade to take a field trip, apparently the first that year, to a pottery. Later, we ventured out farther to Stone Mountain. The principal even arranged for another teacher and me to go to a conference about open-classroom concepts to Denver, Colorado. It was my first plane ride and was quite an adventure. I had never seen mountains as big as the majestic Rockies. We rented a car and drove to Utah. I was amazed when we reached a point above the tree line. My pioneer spirit was soaring!

One cold January morning, as my roommate and I were riding in my beautiful new car to school, I was about to turn left into the school parking lot. I glanced into my rearview mirror just in time to see a Dodge Charger barreling up behind me. Before I could say the words, "Oh no!" he had hit me and my car was spinning 'round and 'round, ending upside down across the road. In total shock, I saw my roommate Marcy's legs only over the console. I panicked until she said something. We tried to find a space to crawl out through the broken window. I was wearing a bright-blue blazer and pleated white skirt. When we got out, I looked down and saw blood running down my leg and on my skirt. People were gathering all around as they put us in ambulances and took us to the hospital. I was praying, wondering if I was dying. I began to shake uncontrollably, and they wrapped me in warm blankets to prevent shock. At the hospital, our principal was the first there, making sure we were all right. Then my landlord and his wife came. My parents came soon and took us home. Amazingly, a few stitches in my knee were all that was needed. Marcy and I were getting glass out of our hair for days. Our little apartment was filled with people from the community, bringing flowers, food, and comfort. Another place of darkness. But God met me there. I looked at the crushed car that I loved. It was gone! I thought maybe I loved it too much. But I was safe, other than a tiny scar. In each of these dark places, though, I have come to know that we can learn something. We must ask God what it is He is teaching us. I learned here that a community of people can make all the difference. So that one visit, phone call, or card might be a lifeline to someone hurting.

The Battle at Hand

Fast-forward to today, May 29, 2014. As I sit here on a hospital couch, watching my precious twenty-three-year-old son, David, battling leukemia, my heart is ripped. I am broken, almost crushed. He is a trooper, vowing to beat this thing, determined to live. The first chemo treatment ends today, with the last of the steroids. We watched his blood sugar skyrocket last night. He reached out for my hand and said, "Pray, Mama!" as the weakness engulfed him. I prayed. He slept. When he woke up, he said, "I feel stronger! Prayer really does work!"

Oh, how I loved hearing those words. After I had seen his questions about God's love when his sister left for heaven in 2006, it made my heart glad to see him reaffirm his belief in the power of God.

Do we have answers? No. Do we know why God chose to take our second daughter at six months, our firstborn daughter at twenty-three, my husband's son, my stepson at forty-one? No, we don't know. And now we witness the affliction of our baby boy being diagnosed with leukemia. Really?

We've been in this hospital, sent directly here from the ER in Athens at home to Atlanta in the middle of the night. But Emory is supposed to be the best. We want that even if the cost is high. We're here for a month, and then during the next six to eight months, one week each. How can we stand to see David suffer? He's a good kid, never causing us concern, always choosing the right path. When he finished high school (homeschooled through high school), he began having some delayed grief-related issues with subsequent panic attacks. We found just the right counselor, who discovered he had unresolved issues relating to Erin's passing when he was only fourteen. But he was doing well. They prescribed a low dose of antidepressants to help with anxiety. He quickly established a good rapport with his counselor. She was helping him to move ahead, choose a career, and take steps to begin again. And now…

My faith in God has changed. I no longer remind God of all the things I've done for Him, like tithing, giving to others, singing, teaching, playing keyboard, leading praise and worship, etc. I just fall on my knees and ask for His mercy. I know it is there for me, for David, for Berry.

Pity! I don't like pity! I didn't even tell many people, because we want, like Jesus, to have the unbelievers out of this. We want people walking with us in this who believe God to heal David. We don't want people just pitying us after we lost three children and have one so sick now.

I believe, truly, that God spoke to me when this began. I have it written down on a deposit slip when we first went to ARMC to have him treated. It reads, "This sickness is not unto death." I do believe that God will be glorified in David's battle. "No weapon formed against us will prosper!" (Isa. 54:17 KJV).

I sit here on the sixth floor of this huge hospital in Atlanta, looking out David's window at the skyline of Atlanta, the tops of huge buildings lighting up the darkening night sky. So many thoughts run through my tired mind as I eat part of a cold deli sandwich and a stale cookie I found in a bag of snacks. David sleeps deeply, the effects of the Benadryl given before the units of blood. He is a fighter, not giving up even once when the weakness was almost unbearable. I witness him staying strong in spirit, reaching out for my hand to pray for him. The middle-of-the-night texts sent to my prayer partners have been constant. "Heart rate up! Pray." "Nausea…can't keep pills down! Pray." "No appetite refuses to eat! Pray." "Weight keeps dropping! Pray!" "Fever! Pray." And on and on they go. Many times, those prayers were answered within a few minutes!

Day 24 in the Hospital

I sit drinking the last of my coffee, which is cold, as I see him sleeping after a rough night. He was given meds the doctor had stopped and has tremors again. I look at his beautiful, almost-hairless head and see gaps where the hair is coming loose from the harsh chemo. Studying his facial features, I compare his eyes, nose, and mouth to those of his sister, who is in heaven now. So similar, so beautiful, and so sad. If she were here, she'd be all over this. She loved her little brother with a passion! He dreamed of Erin one night. He said they were at the market together, filling many carts with all kinds of foods to make something together. He remembered cranberries and cabbage. She told him they were good for him. She sent a message to tell me and his dad that she was okay. What an awesome dream! I almost feel her spirit at times in this hospital room. He does remind me of Erin. He has a strong spirit just like her. I didn't realize that until I saw him fighting this battle.

Its early morning, four thirty. I drag my weary body out of the hotel bed and tame my wild hair. I put on a little makeup to hide the dark circles under eyes that have cried and worried too much. I make a quick cup of coffee in the little pot in the room to help me wake enough to drive. I stop at a popular breakfast restaurant, because that's what my son feels he can eat. I go inside and am greeted by the manager at the register. "Hello, baby doll." He is a very neat, tall, dark-haired man with a ponytail and false eyelashes that are long. As he takes my order, a group of people comes out of a back room. It's obvious the profession the women of the group by their dress and makeup. Ladies of the night often frequent these restaurants, David tells me later, as he and his friends had eaten there occasionally in the wee hours of the morning. So here I sit, alone in a somewhat-shady side of this bustling town as I wait on my order. I'm in the big city of Atlanta, four miles from the hospital, but a world away from my little country home. As I drive the short distance, I see young Jewish families walking to a synagogue on this clear Saturday morning.

Three weeks at home refreshed us, allowing David time to drop low in blood counts but finally recover enough to begin again. Numerous trips to the ER, local oncologist for labs, and fluid infusions took much of our time. On our visit to the doctor one day, David got a text from his girlfriend of four years that she was breaking up with him. What the heck! Right? Why would someone want to marry him one week, check out apartments in the area, only to let him know later that she had to "think of herself." She said they were going down different paths. She wanted to move in with friends and "start her life." He was devastated, once again, by this girl he had committed himself to, who had several times before pulled disappearing acts and caused him great distress. So along with the struggling to beat leukemia and choose life, he had this added load to bear. He said at one point he had almost said, "No more chemo! Let the chips fall where they may!" It brought great distress to me to see this girl who supposedly *loved* him abandon him in his greatest time of need. But he got back up again. And he fought on with his dad and me right alongside him. More importantly, God has this! I know He does!

Sitting here, watching storm clouds hover over Atlanta as I gaze out the hospital window, I look at my son, who is being infused with chemicals so toxic they can mutate skin cells into cancer. And yet they put them in the body to kill the leukemia. When we walked in three days ago, he felt pretty good. Now he describes the pain as feeling as if he were being chewed up inside, feeling too weak to take the daily walk that is part of treatment. I believe in miracles. I know if God would, He could just zap the ills David is experiencing. We wait! We hope! We never give in to the feelings. We are more than conquerors through Jesus Christ, our Lord!

AUGUST 5, 2014

· · · · · · ●●●●● ● ●●●●● · · · · · ·

To the Finish Line

We're back at Emory for the fourth round of chemo. They said it wasn't in remission yet, so different chemo regimen began this time. We keep hoping as David keeps fighting!

He had to learn to fight on two levels with the heartbreak of his girlfriend leaving and the physical fight he is in. He had a great staff, one nurse assistant who spent a couple of hours just talking and encouraging him. He felt much better after talking to him. We have seen strength that God alone can give to our son. At one point, David apologized to his dad and me for having cancer and putting us through this!

He said today he still can't believe all this is happening. First, Erin's passing. And now fighting off this disease! But every day I pray God's Word that says the "seed of the righteous will be delivered" (Prov. 11:21 KJV) will happen here. I do believe that, even though my flesh is weary. Our strength comes from God, our Father; His holy Son, Jesus; and His Holy Spirit, who hovers over us day and night. Thank you, God!

September 8

Back at Emory again! Remission! Yes, I said it right! *Remission*—a beautiful word! A gift from God! He is going through the fifth round of chemo anyway in preparation for the ultimate gift, the bone marrow transplant! Today, we are all "up," and it feels good! We have met some amazing nurses and doctors!

October 8

We were dismissed after the sixth round of chemo. The bone marrow transplant team activated the donor. But since it was going to be five weeks before all was ready, Dr. G wanted David to have one more chemo treatment, since this type of leukemia is so aggressive. He did have added pain from the anal fissure he has endured since August when he was admitted to our local hospital when his counts were so low. But he didn't have to be readmitted to the hospital again. His counts were low, but he was treated with multiple transfusions and platelets.

November 10

Today brought us back to Emory to prepare for transplant. PICC line was replaced with a Trifusion line, which was a very painful procedure. But he was better after three days.

We are sitting here, witnessing a rebirth of sorts as David receives a donor's stem cells, which can effect a cure for the leukemia he was diagnosed with in May. It looks like a simple bag of blood! But it's a new immune system. They basically killed his total immune system. So, this is a new start. The emotions are all over the place. The prayers are being sent up in great numbers from all over the world, literally. God is performing His work in David, in all of us!

SET BACK

· · · · · · · · ●●● ● ●●● · · · · · · ·

January 7, 2015

I'm sitting in the waiting room outside the ICU on the fifth floor at Emory. David is inside on a ventilator. Last week, he was beginning to get critical as his oxygen level was dropping and no machine in the medical ICU on the sixth floor was helping. The tears were flowing as I stood outside, looking through the window at them working with him. After chemically paralyzing him to try to recover his lungs, nothing worked. His O_2 levels kept dropping. His kidneys began failing, so they began dialysis. They finally moved him down to this ICU and put him on a lung bypass machine called ECMO. He is also on dialysis because he was swelling so as he had acute renal failure upstairs. The doctors have given him a fifty-fifty chance of successfully coming off the machine. They let us know from the start that they will give him around twelve days, and they will decide when to turn the machine off.

But God!

He was five days in room 510 in the cardiac ICU; 5 is the number of grace in the Bible. So this is triple grace! He pulled his own ventilator tube out and freaked out all the younger staff. His nurse told us when a patient does that, it is usually time to come off the machine. Now they have taken him off the lung bypass machine and dialysis!

What a miracle to witness! After these days of sheer agony, sleeping on the floor in the waiting room, eating whatever we could find, fasting sometimes, and witnessing family after family in crisis, we had a miracle! It was hard to see some who were crying as their loved ones passed, and others who struggled as we did. But all those prayers that people all over were praying for David were answered. Praise God for His mercy! The mercy of the Lord is from generation to generation. They took him off dialysis yesterday!

And the Story Continues, But God Is in Every Detail

I sit in the ICU waiting room, a large family came in, many crying, some sitting in silence, staring straight ahead, and sadness on every face. Do I dare break the silence with words of consolation? Or do I sit in silence with them as they wait? The pain is written on each face. It was interesting to meet the many people in ICU as we have been in the one upstairs and now are here for two weeks.

Upstairs we were supported by our wonderful family. My sister Judy and her family have been with us from the start in May of 2014. She and her husband, Terry, have come whenever we needed anything from home or just needed them. Her daughter Kelsey has kept in close contact, often helping us with items we needed or ordering food to be delivered to the hotel when David could eat. Berry came back from home once and had forgotten his wallet. Kelsey, on a Sunday morning, found someone coming our way and went to get the wallet to give to this person. My brother Tim and his wife, Sandra, have kept in close contact, taking me to their house to rest, driving me around to find a hotel, coming at a moment's notice when we were in crisis, coming by to pray with David and bring whatever he needed. My nieces Amanda and Heidi were constantly coming up to Atlanta or by the house, bringing food, hugs, and any support we needed. Amanda even came to the hospital in Athens, where she is a nurse, bringing food and checking on David. She was on the phone with me, helping me sort through questions. She even came into the

ICU to listen to the doctors and help us know what was going on. So many others came and supported us: Aunt Carolyn and cousin Melody driving to Atlanta, coming to bring food, money, flowers, or to vacuum my house, trying to be with us. My cousin Sherry and her granddaughter Madison brought home-cooked food to our hotel and visited and encouraged us. My dear friend Alicia was driving all the way up from South Carolina to sit with us all night in ICU, bringing her son Josh, who is a lifelong friend of David's, to see him. She came several times and even started a twenty-four-hour prayer chain for him. Her daughter Heather was so supportive, bringing me tea and even cooking David food that he felt he could tolerate. She sat in ICU once just to give us a break. It was a blessing knowing she worked at Emory and could come check on us. Our friends Sharon and John Fiedler drove all the way up to bring us comfort food, warm soup, and cakes and just to visit and pray with us and David. There were two friends whom I had never met in person but had met on a grieving forum after Erin left us for heaven. Nerissa lived in Atlanta, and when she found out we were there, she came to my side! What a blessing she was. She helped us with our hotel bill, brought food and items we needed living in a hotel. She would rush to my side if there was ever a crisis with David and even came to sit with him, becoming a strong support in our hour of need. When she wasn't with us, she would call to make sure we had no need. She knew we were there in a strange city, alone, at Christmas. She even cooked an entire Christmas meal and brought it to the hotel. Her mashed potatoes were the only and last thing David was able to eat before he was moved to ICU and became critical. She became a caregiver to us during our stay in Atlanta. And the other was J. Marie Shepherd. She came all the way from Cocoa Beach, Florida, to sit with us during David's transplant, and later in ICU. She sat up all night with us, bringing us tea, walking me down to the chapel to pray when the burden was so great. She made sure we had everything we needed for our comfort. She and her husband, Greg, sat with us during those long, stressful hours, caring for us and making sure we were cared for, even slipping money into my purse. Nerissa and her husband and J. Marie and Greg came to the hotel at Christmas to bring the food and just sit with us and talk for a while. It's truly those who are with you in crises that you never, ever forget. That is true friendship!

David woke up in ICU from the deep sedation with terror, as we were forewarned. Berry was with him. But I quickly came to his side too. The first thing he said was, "Can we go back to the hotel now?" Later, we found he didn't remember much of what had happened the past three weeks. He didn't really remember being in the hotel after transplant. But I guess we are protected from traumatic events. It was a long, hard road to recovery. After being chemically paralyzed in the first ICU and deeply sedated in the cardiac ICU, he had to learn to swallow again, learn to use muscles that were not functioning well, and even build the stamina to walk again. So after being back on the transplant floor about a week, he was transferred to the rehab hospital across the road. But he was on the way to recovery. The transplant had been successful, although he had almost lost his life in ICU because of a cold. After being in rehab for a month, we were dismissed back to the hotel for the last month. When David was able to walk into his checkup without his wheelchair, then we could go home at last! He had to go to wound care here and to rehab to recover his strength. But we were home! We were all home!

FAST-FORWARD TO AUGUST 2015

....•••••●•••••••...

The Battle Is Real Again

David began to run low-grade fevers. Since he had allergies so much as a child, I thought it was just sinus infections. But he was very weak. When he went to rehab, he was beginning to have trouble with pain in his right knee. It was dismissed as probably a muscle weakness after the ICU stay. He wanted desperately to be best man in his friend Shane's wedding. So we rented the tuxedo, put him in his wheelchair, and went to the wedding. He insisted on walking down the aisle, even though he was weak. That was how much he cared for Shane and Courtney. Little did we know what was lurking inside him.

On November 18, he reached the landmark date of one-year posttransplant, so we held a rebirthday party for him. The nurses had told us he would have two birthdays from now on. We wanted to celebrate all his hard work in achieving this goal. He told me later that he really didn't feel like having the party, but he wanted to do it for me because it was important to me! Several close friends and family came. There was a cake, and my niece Amanda brought doughnuts since every time she would visit him at the local hospital he'd ask, jokingly, for doughnuts. The party really sapped his strength, causing him to be in bed the whole next day. December brought more fevers and pain in his back that had begun to worsen. The pain radiated up into his neck and right ear, so I tried applying heat. But the pain seemed to be growing day by day. He began asking for pain meds around the clock, which he never did, since he hated taking pain meds. In January, his transplant team began running tests, the first being a bone marrow test, which should have been done nearer the one-year mark. (In hindsight, I wish I had asked for a PET scan at the one-year mark. Another if-only!) The next few weeks, we were constantly going here and there, getting tests run, as spots had shown up on his liver and kidney and a mass had formed above his right knee. The day he got this news was a very traumatic one for all of us. The ride home from Atlanta was a long one as he cried and said, "I'm only twenty-four years old! I don't want to die! I can't go through that chemo again!" Berry was driving, and I was torn to pieces as I sat in the back seat, praying, praying! We stopped at a store on the way home from Atlanta for Berry to pick up something, and I told David, "David, you have to fight this! If you die, I die too! I can't live without you!" He immediately told me he'd been texting his friends and he had decided he would fight! He said, "But, Mom, you know when your time comes, it comes!"

January 29, we were called in to get the horrible news that a mass (lymphoma) was discovered in his back. They were sending him home on steroids at first. But then the doctor rushed back into the exam room and informed him that the leukemia was back. He was admitted that very day as his white cell count had begun to rise. He asked her if she thought he could survive a round of chemo since he was still so weak. She answered that we shouldn't look at this through rose-colored glasses, indicating that it could go either way. After two weeks of intensive chemotherapy, his pain level was almost unmanageable, and his blood counts were very low.

DAY-48

·········•·········

Forsaken?

I decided to skip to the "hospital stay" sections and write about that fateful last two weeks. But after just a paragraph, the memories were too painful, so I stopped for today.

Last night, Berry and I were searching for something to watch on TV, and we began watching an old series called *ER* but had to stop. Seeing hospital scenes is too painful for us now. Life is too painful! Later, after watching an episode of another show, we both sat and cried and talked about how we are coping with loss. Berry said that death would almost be welcome now for him. He cried as he remembered sitting in the hospital room and talking heart-to-heart with David. I cried as I agonized over what we might have done differently to save his life. Long nights, longer days are filled with memories, some sweet, some hard to bear.

I was reflecting yesterday again on spiritual things. It's a constant struggle to make sense of this, although I know there are no earthly answers. I thought, *Am I separating myself from God, and is that sin in itself? Does my broken heart's questions about God's taking David so soon from us separate me from Him?* Every night I put together a jigsaw puzzle online to relax myself. I always play some music from YouTube as I do this. Last night, I decided to try some of the Christian "soaking" music, which I have done before. But on this one, the lady was quoting scripture. Even though I haven't read my Bible but once, searching for a verse, since David went to heaven,

I thought I could listen to this. But as she began reading scriptures about healing and how God would take care of our children, I turned it off. Those were the same scriptures I was praying on my knees at three in the morning nearly every single night when David was so sick. I couldn't hear them! What's wrong with me? I can't fight against God! He who is my greatest comfort seems so far away now. Can I get past this feeling that He has forsaken me? One of the scriptures I clung to after Erin left for heaven was in Isaiah. It says God has regard for the brokenhearted. And yet here I am, feeling so disenfranchised, so lost, like a man without a country! All those scriptures that I had clung to for my very lifeline are somehow foreign to me now. Where are the prophets? Surely, there is a man or woman somewhere who will come to me and tell me what to do! Surely! I'm so tired of people saying this isn't fair. They have no answers! Surely, there is an answer! The only person I can identify with in the Bible now is Jesus when He said, "My God, my God, why have You forsaken me?" Or is it David when he said that his bed was wet with his tears, that God had frustrated his plans?

DAY-49

· · · · · · · · ● · · · · · · · · ·

Routine Days and Exit Plans

This book has become an instruction manual for grieving. Wow! Is that what my life has become? But when you have faced this nightmare four times, you do have extra insight into grief.

I was given much advice from others grieving each time we had to face this dark night. One thing that helps me is having a routine each day, each week. I plan some little something, a small task for each day. But I quickly found that if some unforeseen event comes to upset my routine, then I am unhappy. It must have become somewhat of a security and brought a stability in my upside-down, inside-out life. Grief has, for me this time, been as if I were that proverbial ship on the ocean, waves crashing about me, lost at sea with no land in sight. The term *lost* seems to capture well the picture of a grieving parent. This book, or journal, or whatever it becomes in the end, has become a new routine task for me. I don't sleep well, so often I wake at four or five. I get up, make coffee, start that first load of laundry (part of my routine), and write. Writing has always been a therapy for me, and much more after grief knocked me down. I don't even consider my audience much, but I do wonder who will come after me to read my musings since I buried my sweet son, who was my sole heir.

It's important when grieving to have an exit plan when you do manage to go out. Today, a friend invited me to see a movie. And yes, I broke down when a young lady in the movie talked about getting the news that she was in remission from cancer. I almost ran out of

112

the movie at one point when I realized the last time I was at the movies was with David. A flashback came of him laughing his infectious laugh at one of the previews. Tears started to roll, and I just wanted to run out. I would have, but my inner discipline took over, prompting me that my friend paid for this, so I couldn't. There were times when Erin passed that I did leave my shopping cart and head for the car as I knew a flood of tears was coming. Sometimes you have forewarnings the tsunami of grief is coming. Sometimes you don't. So it's wise to have an escape plan if you go anywhere. Sit near an exit or in the back so you can slip out quickly.

DAY-51

· · · · · · ● ● ● ● ● ● ● ● ● · · · · ·

Responding to God

Knowing God has been my passion since childhood. Even when I married my husband, I told him when he asked me to marry him that he had to know that God would always be first in my life. When my Heather left us at only six months in utero, my faith was first called into question. Berry and I both questioned what we might have done wrong that brought this upon us. I was shocked at God! I was afraid that I had angered Him. But after a few weeks, with the aid of the compassion and prayers of our friends, we found our way back to Him. When Erin passed, my questioning continued for much longer. Again, we questioned what we had done wrong and, this time, what Erin might have done wrong. I could think of nothing, according to all I knew about God, that would bring this kind of wrath on her or us. I remembered a couple in the Bible who, when Jesus healed their forty-year-old son who had been blind from birth, questioned Him. They asked what sin they had committed that their son be born blind. Jesus replied that there was no sin but this happened that the glory of God be revealed to the world. During the past ten years since Erin passed, I have done everything I could to honor her memory and glorify God in it. In no uncertain terms, I have let everyone know that God was my strength after Erin passed. Once, at a meeting, I found myself surrounded by young people as I shared the story of Erin passing and how she "appeared" to me in dreams and visions a few times. I shared how God had revealed His comfort to us. They sat in rapt attention to my story of life after death. Opportunities have come that have given me a platform to share my sweet Erin with people all over the world. I've been able to offer hope to other grieving families because of my own intense suffering after burying my beautiful daughter, knowing I will see her again in heaven. I have spent many hours on my knees lifting others who were in the depths of grief to God so that they, too, could find peace. I will admit, it took months for me to find my hope in Christ again after Erin passed. Anger flooded me that God would take my beautiful daughter, who was the sunshine of our lives. Whatever I do in life, I give myself 100 percent to the task. So motherhood had all of me poured into it. And I made sure my children knew as much as I could share about God and salvation through Christ. They went to church. Every night we prayed together. I read the Bible or Bible stories to them. We had long discussions about our faith, and I saw both exercise their own faith as they grew.

CHAPTER 9

••••••••●••••••••

David's Final Battle

Over the last two years, as I watched David suffer, there were many hours spent on my knees at the hotel room near the hospital and even on the floor of David's hospital room. I never missed an opportunity to pray over his room, over the fluids, blood products, and medicines put in his body, praying over his body, even when he was in ICU, unresponsive. I cried out to God so often and with such desperation on occasions. But I never, ever thought that this would end with David going to heaven and not riding home in the car with us from Emory. Never! I knew the aggressiveness of the leukemia, as we had been told so often by different doctors. But he had already beaten it once, had a transplant that was working 100 percent, we were told! So we thought we were in just slow recovery after almost losing him last year in ICU after the lung infection. When he was moved to ICU on February 11, 2016, I thought it was just to find a way to bring his heart rate down since they couldn't help him on the oncology floor. He had completed the first round of chemo. He mentioned he felt his hair was like straw, so he knew it was about to come out. The plan of action was explained to us in ICU. I escorted the nurses during that last night as they transported him down to get a CT scan so I could sign permission. At that point, David was saying some things that were a little off. They thought maybe he had hit his head when he fell upstairs on the oncology floor as I helped him to the bathroom. The only thing that showed on the x-ray was a blood clot in the lung, which explained the pain he had been having all night and day. But then things escalated so quickly over the course of a few hours.

He was intubated, and his heart stopped. It hadn't stopped last year when they intubated him. We weren't even warned that it might last year. Then we were called in to be with him as they did chest compressions to get his heartbeat back. The epinephrine didn't keep it going for some reason. He was too weak from the effects of two weeks of chemo! Apparently, he had gotten infection from somewhere. What the heck! Why? As my husband and I stood behind the many nurses and doctors working on him, I was in shock! How could this be? The doctor said, "Try again!" Chest compressions. "We have a heartbeat!" This went on a few times. I looked up at the ceiling, remembering reading of people saying as they left their body during NDEs, they floated to the ceiling. I said, "David, please don't die!" Immediately I heard, "We have a heartbeat!" Again, he flatlined. Chest compressions. I said, "David, please don't leave me!" Again, I heard, "We have a heartbeat!" After this occurred six or seven times, as I stood there, I noticed a nurse had left the side of the doctor who was doing the chest compressions, and there was this open space. After this, an amazing thing happened. I knew it was real, because it had happened to me once before when my mom made her "crossing" into heaven.

I sensed very strongly the presence of the Lord Jesus in that ICU room. Not only did I sense it, but I also had a vision standing right there. David was surrounded by doctors and nurses except in this one space. As my vision continued, Jesus walked up and stood in that open space beside the lead doctor. He was wearing a long blue robe, and his hair was shoulder-length. He reached out his right hand toward David as if He were working on him too. There was instantly a peace that came over me that I hadn't felt before. At that same moment, I felt David's spirit come and stand beside me and say, with urgency, "Mom, I have to go! I love you, but I have to go!" Even with that, I felt at peace. After a few more chest compressions and hearing what I thought was a cough from David, I looked at Brie, the PA who was supervising the whole thing, and said, "How many more times will they revive him?" She said, "At least one more." I said, "Then let that be it. Let him go."

She told us later that her staff was very upset over David's passing. They don't usually resuscitate seven or eight times, I was told later. But they really wanted him to live. David's nurse, Abby, was crying as I went to David's side and wrapped my arms around my sweet boy, hugging him and kissing his still-warm cheek. It was then that I noticed the tear that had trickled down the side of his right eye. Several of the young medical staff there were crying with us as my husband came into the room. David's night nurse on the oncology floor came down and wrapped her arms around me as we cried together. The chaplain, who was waiting outside as we exited the room, asked if we'd like them to remove the tubes and lines so we could stay with David. He even helped us call the funeral home near our home and plan for David to be picked up. He said he had even spoken to the staff and they arranged to allow David to stay there on the bed until they came for him rather than being moved to another place. Even that was a comfort.

So...back to God. I am in a sea filled with stormy waves of grief. I am angry at God. I feel He's turned His back on me. That is not true, I know in my heart. But it's how I feel. Jesus said on the cross, "My God, why have You forsaken me?" (Matt. 27:46 KJV). That's how I feel after burying the last of my children, the children I poured my heart and soul into. My children were my reason to live. And David especially gave us reason to keep living after we buried Erin, Heather, and Scott. I used to take hours-long walks and talk to God in the morning first thing. I'd spend at least an hour reading the Bible each day, feeding my soul. Now, I don't. I have cried help to Him once. I wrote Him a letter last night and told Him how I miss our walks. I hear songs of miracles and scriptures read, but they go right over my head. I am afraid of God. I only see him as the almighty God, El, right now. I can't see the loving heavenly Father I once spent hours within communion and meditation. I miss Him. I still love Him and fear Him. But what I thought I knew, I don't know anymore. Only He can help me.

· · · · · · ● ● ● ● ● ● ● ● ● · · · · · ·

Grief Triggers

Grief triggers can be a challenge. They may cause panic attacks, a flood of tears, breath-catching moments, or an outburst of uncontrollable, soul-stirring grief. Friends on a grief forum I frequent have coined phrases like *grief tsunamis* or *grief waves*. These grief waves hit unexpectedly in a moment of time. You are totally unprepared for them. They might cause you to leave a meeting, exit a social event abruptly, cut the radio or TV off in the middle of a program, slam a book shut, leave a full shopping cart to get to the safety of your car, reject invitations for social events, or close off a room in your house filled with memories. They can come as a small trigger that can cause a moment's pain or a debilitating moment where you wail or can't breathe for a time. Some that have affected me were simple things, like balancing my checkbook and seeing the receipt for the last pizza purchased for David, or seeing the dates just before that last day, getting a credit card bill and seeing the last video game or other purchase and knowing I would never buy another gift for my son. Going in the grocery story was very hard since I had agonized over just the right foods since his digestive tract was so affected by the chemo. Also, the store brought back memories of his favorite foods, like ramen, his favorite pizza, root beer, chocolate chip cookie dough ice cream, and so many other things over twenty-four years.

I was searching for something at home and opened a plastic bin filled with unused medicines or half-filled medicine bottles that had been used over the two years of treatment. I haven't moved his current meds off the china hutch yet. I can't. I saw a bag of bandage material that was used to change the bandage around his PICC line and thought of all the times I had flushed the lines and changed the bandage with the greatest of care so he wouldn't get infections. Tears are coming because I write this now. I moved a plastic hospital pan and remembered the times David wanted his hair washed after it grew back. But he was too weak to shower. I had him lie over my bed. We placed the pan on a stool and washed his hair. He was twenty-four, but there were times I had to help him wipe his bottom in rehab when he couldn't even lift his arms, clean up after nausea, help him walk, or push his wheelchair up a ramp and wonder how I would make it to the top. I was right by his side, not even wanting to leave to eat or sleep when he was so sick.

When a mom has cared for a child until adulthood and then, because of illness, keeps caring for him/her, there is a bond that forms ever tighter. She gets to know intimate details about that child even though she thinks she already knows. Because of this bond, the death becomes all-encompassing, affecting every part of her life. The grief also becomes all-encompassing, and triggers are everywhere.

Last night, as I watched TV, a man was making a grilled cheese sandwich. My mind raced back to David and his love for grilled cheese sandwiches. He even became quite proficient in making his own. Tears were rolling down my cheeks as I watched this scene. Even in the everyday occurrences, our child is never, ever far away. Everything they loved and experienced can provoke a trigger to a grief wave. Some things even cause what some have phrased a grief tsunami, sending us back into the pit. We get through one only to experience another soon. They come without warning, suddenly, sometimes causing us to sway, sometimes knocking us off out feet. While we value immensely the memories, they can be bittersweet as they remind us of the joy that was our child and the huge hole in our lives now.

Grief work is hard work, never really ending.

Now the tears are streaming down my face as I remember. Grief wave! Memories, how they flood my soul! Shopping is hard. It was so hard after Erin left us. I always bought for my children, putting my needs on the back burner. Walking in a store brings a flood of memories of days gone by when they were shopping with me, begging for toys, or just shopping for things they liked. I questioned the first time I shopped after David left as to why I was even shopping. What's the point? Why am I still here? Oh, the questions triggered by just a simple walk into a building! Grief is a horrible thing and does horrible things to a soul. There are survival techniques to manage the grief waves, but I will save that for another day.

DAY-53

········●●●○●●●····

Dealing

There are questions, endless questions. If you are grieving, you have probably had a few of these.

- How do I live without them?
- What will the future be?
- What do I do with their possessions?
- Can I part with their possessions?
- Why me? Why them?
- What sin did I commit that God would let this happen?
- What really happened to them? Did someone made a mistake and cause the death?
- Did they know they were going to die?
- Were they afraid in those last moments?
- What could I have done differently to change the outcome?
- God, can we get a do-over?
- Am I going crazy?
- Is life still worth living?
- Will hope ever return?

The questions can drive you crazy if you dwell on them too long at a time! The sad thing is that for many of them, there will come no answers. But the questions will keep coming.

It's been ten years since Erin left for heaven, and I still have questions. I am not as obsessed as I was, but they are still there nonetheless. My husband sits and ponders Scott's passing, and the need-to-know fills his soul as he can get no answers, even though the Army held an investigation. There are too many missing pieces, too many ends left dangling. With David, I find myself trying to blame Emory, trying to discover what really happened, even though there is a clear cause of death on the certificate. Did someone make a mistake that caused the untimely death? I want to know. It fills my soul with agony to think a mistake may have been made. And it is a crushing feeling.

A grieving parent who cared so tenderly for their child and poured themselves into caring for that child even into adulthood needs to know. They need to have these questions answered. But in more cases than not, they will go to their grave not finding those answers. But then, as my husband said, it probably won't even matter. When our child is in our arms at last in heaven, will it matter? I think not!

DAY-54

•••••••••●•••••••••

Finally, the Second Sign

Last night I had the second real "sign" from David. I had one other obvious sign with the wind chimes. They are the heavy set I mentioned earlier that Berry and David got me as a gift for Mother's Day. I have moved them to different locations to try to free them to catch the wind. Now they hang beside my glider on my carport. The first few days after the memorial, all my chimes rang and rang, filling the air with music. David loved music, nearly every genre, except techno. This would be a way he would contact me, if he could. But the strange part is that every time—I mean *every* time—I would be outside and would start to come in and step beside that chime, it would chime!

When we said an earthly goodbye to Erin, I had several signs. David knew all about them as I shared them over and over with friends and family. So I expect him to send something so obvious because of his knowledge of the signs from Erin. I will share Erin's signs in the next chapter, for I want you to know about them too.

But the second sign, I believe, from David was last night. I had been reading everything on his phone, since he kept it by his side all the time! (He might send me an angry sign for reading it all!) But as with Erin, I search for any little thing that connects me to my sweet son. He had trouble sleeping with all the sickness he endured, so he found that page-turning calmed him. Sometimes in the hospital, he would ask me to turn the pages of my Bible or notebook to try to help him sleep. But he eventually found on YouTube a video of pages turning. I went in several nights and would see his phone beside his bed with the video of page-turning sounding gently beside his bed. I have searched and searched for that on his phone, for I was sure it was bookmarked in some way. Last night I decided to update his apps on his phone. I opened the update setting, and there were several apps I hadn't seen before. And right in front of me was the YouTube app. I opened it, and the first few entries were page-turning. But it was the first entry that caught my attention. A symbol I used for Erin was sunflowers, since she loved them and had decorated her dining area with them. There was a picture of an open book with simply a sunflower on the left-hand page! David would have known I would stop for a sunflower picture. I opened it and listened to the soothing sound of pages turning that he probably listened to recently. I received a small comfort, feeling that my David had sent me a sign. I have tears as I know in my heart I would much rather have him than a sign. But I will take whatever I can to comfort my broken heart!

I hope that before this book is through, I will have many more signs from David to share with you. I do believe that our loved ones are just a breath away. I grew up thinking heaven was some faraway place in another galaxy. But since my Erin went to heaven, and now David, Scott, and Heather, I feel they are near. The Bible says that to be absent from the body is to be present with the Lord. Since my children were all professing Christians, they are with Him. Where is He? He is God, and He has no limits in time or space. They don't either. There must be portals where they can go in and out, unnoticed by us, because we are not familiar with the spirit world. It's a mystery to us. It still is to me. But since my heart is in heaven and earth, I connect in a way I never would have before.

Next up, signs from Erin. You will be amazed, as we were!

DAY-55

........•.......

Signs and More

First, I want to believe that David will send me phenomenal signs since he was firsthand witness to the telling of the signs from Erin. If our earthly knowledge travels with us into the spirit world, and I believe it does, then he would know what I would look for. It would be special and big!

Erin was an amazing child! She loved people, parties, getting involved with the lives of all those around her and just living life! She lived life big! So after her passing into heaven, if there is any way to let me know about her, she would be the one to do it! And I feel she did! Let me interject here that this is what I believe happened. There are different schools of thought on whether those who have passed into the spirit world can contact us. There was a minister on TV recently who, when asked this question, said that it was demonic to have contact with the dead. If that is true, why did Jesus say He would never leave us or forsake us? How did He walk and talk with His disciples on the road to Emmaus? If we believe in the resurrection of the dead, then why can't we believe that they might send us signs? There are many trains of thought on the issue, which I will not argue here. The signs I received were so poignant and right on time that I am a believer!

The first sign from Erin was just a few days after she had left for heaven. I was standing in the bathroom, combing my hair, and I "felt" her say, "Mama, I'm okay." It was simple, but after being a wreck for those first few days, I needed that comfort. When I said I felt her speak, there wasn't an audible voice; I just knew it was her. About two weeks later, I woke up early one morning and looked at the white wall at the foot of my bed. There was Erin's face, larger than life, and she was smiling. She said, "Mama, the love Jesus has for me is just like the love you gave us growing up, only much, much, much, much, much, much, much greater! And He's standing right here beside me now!" The next time I had a vision or dream—can't remember which—was where I saw a little paddleboat on a big lake. It was coming toward me, and no one was in it. Up popped Erin's and another little girl's head, peeking out over the boat at me and laughing. As the boat neared the wooden dock, they stepped out in the water and onto the dock. As they did, I noticed they were holding hands. The little girl appeared to be around eight or nine and had brown curly hair. I mused, *I wonder if that could be our little Heather. But she was only a baby.* Erin looked at me and said as if she had read my thoughts, "But, Mama, babies grow in heaven! This is Heather!" Wow! I was astonished! The next vision I had was of Erin sitting in a swing with shorts on and her hair up in pigtails, laughing as the swing rose higher and higher. The ropes had flowers growing up them, and it was so beautiful as the light seemed to bounce off her hair. In life, Erin's pediatrician diagnosed her with a type of syndrome where motion makes her freeze. It is like when you bounce a baby up above your head and they laugh. But Erin would always freeze as if frightened. When we took all her clothes off to bathe her, as she'd lie in her bed, she'd spread her arms and bounce from side to side as if she were frightened of falling. So to see her swinging, which she couldn't do as a child, was amazing. She "communicated" once to me that there was no fear in heaven. It was the first time that she had lived without any fear, and it was wonderful.

David had a few dreams of Erin too. The most recent was a few months into his treatment for leukemia, when he dreamed Erin came and took him to the grocery store. They were filling two shopping carts with all kinds of things. He remembered she wanted him to eat cabbage and beets, both of which he didn't like. We wondered if she was trying to help him. Another sign from Erin was when I was driving down to my mom's to care for her, and as I turned the radio on, I heard this refrain from a song, "Wish you were here! I'm finally free to run with the angels on streets paved with gold, to listen to stories of men long ago, to worship our Master. That's where I'll be when you finally find me." It was some lyrics to a song by Mark Harris called "Wish You Were Here." After caring for my mom, I got back in the car, turned the radio on, and decided to switch to another station, and here was this song again, starting on the same verse as above. This happened every time I got in the car that day. Another part of the song was "Don't cry for me, for I'm finally free." On another day, as I was driving home from shopping, I turned onto our street, and another song began playing. It was "I Will Rise Again" by Chris Tomlin. I heard it for a few days, but each time was when I would turn onto the street we live.

It's been ten years since Erin left us. Not a day goes by without her on our minds continually. We still grieve her loss. But we did learn to live with the pain. David even told me a few weeks before he left us for heaven that he was dealing better with Erin's passing. He said some days he didn't even think about it. The healing from extreme grief was beginning.

DAY-56

•••••••••●•••••••••

How Do I Live without You?

My husband and I are retired. Our parents are gone. Our brothers and sisters all have their families to surround them. We are alone. The things we worked for so hard are around us, except for the most important, which were our children. They became our reason for living and working. They were the focus of our days. So now we are living at the edge of our comfort zone, not really knowing why we are still here. What is there ahead? What is our future? Did God leave us here simply to suffer sorrow the rest of our days? Yesterday, Berry found the strength to go and visit a friend, which I was glad for. I thought it would help him. But after he left the house, I found myself engulfed in a loneliness I had never felt before. It was almost a cold loneliness that seemed to engulf me as I realized David was not in his bedroom, where he had been so much the past two years. The grieving wails started issuing forth from my soul. I let them escape as tears flooded down my face. I cried out to God. My words were strong but disciplined, as I still respect Him as the Almighty. My accusations bordered on the edge of improper as I screamed, "You took David so I could write a book!" I repeated my thought to Him. I was angry! And yet I'm not even sure that a book is the destiny before me. I'm not sure what path my life will take. Some have said that we will use this to comfort other grieving parents. With incredulity I responded to them, "Been there, done that! It was like a prison sentence!" It was not what I had planned after saying an earthly goodbye to our Erin.

I didn't do it because I needed something to do, some validation that I was helping to honor Erin's memory. I began to reach out because I needed help. What came after was a result of that! But now David! Really? This young man who was just beginning to come out of the shellshock of his own grief and starting to live, as was his own confession to me weeks before he passed. He had to suffer so I could do some great work? My last living child, my "seed," my future taken from me, and for what? I walk on the edge of my comfort zone, not knowing if I will fall off into the oblivion of the other side or will find a sure path into some unknown destiny that will surface at some future date. And the price? My children? No understanding! None!

There is a little whiteboard beside my computer that is used to keep weekly appointments and the like. Each night I erase the date and put the next week's date in its place. I have thought since Erin passed that each day passed was one day closer to seeing her again. Now it holds a double meaning as I think of seeing David too! There was one point yesterday that I was almost crying out to God to come quickly and take me to my children. Other grieving parents have said similar things to me. A dear friend, Sarah, who lost her only daughter, Lisa, has talked to me on numerous occasions about wanting to be with Lisa. The Bible states that Jesus will come again to this earth to take the dead in Christ first. Then those who are alive still will go to meet Him in the air. Sarah and I both have prayed that He would come quickly so we could be with our children again.

Each day is a challenge for a parent who has buried their children. If that child was your last or only child, life loses meaning. It's hard to go on. Why plan a future for just yourself? I have advised others that God must have some destiny that they have not fulfilled because they are still here. That advice comes back to haunt me now. I have lived a full life, singing in many churches and on the radio with my family as a teen, speaking at church functions, finishing college, retiring after a teaching career, holding positions as musician and praise leader in church for most of my adult life, traveling overseas and many other places, being a mother to two wonderful children whom I was blessed to see grow into adulthood, seeing my daughter married and in her own home, taking care of my mom in her last years, caring for my grandmother before she passed, owning a home, and just living life to the fullest. Now I am sixty-eight and have buried my parents and children. My husband and I sit and wonder what to do with the days that go by so slowly. I don't know what destiny I have left. Is it finishing this book? Is it some unforeseen miracle that will breathe life back into my broken soul and set my life on a new course? I don't know. But time doesn't stand still. And that it is passing brings a small comfort to my broken heart.

DAY-57

· · · · · · ●●●●● ● ●●●●● · · · · · ·

Overshadowing

When Erin left us, her empty place in our family overshadowed every other event in those next few years. There wasn't a new baby, marriage, birthday party, graduation, or any kind of life event that was not overshadowed by her absence. We discussed this on the grieving forum I frequent. It seems that our lives are defined by the "before and after." Before our child passed, we had a different life. After our child passed, everything changed.

Now we have had another, our last child, leave us for heaven. His empty place is huge, because he was not only the last child surviving but was also our youngest. He was precious in every way and even more so because of the battle with leukemia, which kept us even closer than we might have been. We have faced Erin's birthday, the tenth anniversary of her home-going, Scott's birthday yesterday, and Heather's birthday today. Each of these four events, in themselves, is very hard to navigate. But with David's recent home-going, that overshadows all these. We are still in the pit of despair, the throes of bouts of sorrow, weeping and mourning for our son. And yet we can't let these days pass without acknowledging our other children's lives and preserving their memories. So we pause in our grief to visit their graves, lay fresh flowers, hang birthday balloons, and stand and remember the love and the loss of their precious lives. But overshadowing it all is the fact that David was here with us last year to remember. He knew and loved them with us. And now...he is resting beside

Erin. Oh, the sorrow borne by hearts that ache with grief. We do feel we walk with a dark cloud just above our heads as our hearts mourn our dear son.

As I walked into David's bedroom, still untouched from when he left it on January 29, 2016, I hugged his pillow, noticing the tearstains of the daily hugs for the past 410 days. My mind raced to the injustice. I feel cheated, so cheated. I feel my future has been stolen from me by the horrid pangs of death. But just as quickly, my mind raced to Father God. I saw a program on TV about a mom who was agonizing over the loss of her child. The nun quickly responded that God has lost a child too. As I pondered this, I wondered if God felt cheated too. Did He feel that the fall of the man He created caused the death of His own Son? Of course, it did! So mankind stole from God, a punishable offense. But then, when Jesus died on the cross, it was all inclusive for all mankind. That one sacrifice covered all mankind for all time! The very fact is almost too much for this finite brain to comprehend! When the Bible states that God is touched with the feelings of our infirmities, it rings so true that He, too, knows our feelings of being cheated. He does understand.

The unanswered questions I struggle daily with may remain unanswered the rest of my days. But one day, all these troubles will give way to joy. What a day that will be!

DAY-58

·············●●●●●·············

Faces in the Crowd

David told me he had become more outgoing since he had been in the hospital so much and had to interact with all kinds of new people. All three of us had many opportunities to meet others who, we found out quickly, had their own struggles. Being in a strange city so much larger than our little town here showed us many new faces. Atlanta and the Emory campus are multicultural, international communities. Some faces quickly became familiar to us, as David had to stay a month in the hospital for his first round of chemo. The oncology nurses were very kind and patient with us as we dealt with all the aspects of treatment. There was one young man (and I won't name any of these) who became very dear to us. He was a young nurse and has since left. He added a sense of humor into our daily routine, which was much needed. It seemed every time David had strong nausea, he'd be the nurse on call and get to clean up afterward. I began to tease him about running away when David would throw up. But he took it in stride and kept the humor as David's symptoms even worsened. Once he said that David was his hero, as are all the oncology patients.

Sitting on that couch at David's bedside gave me the opportunity to observe many faces. I decided to give the nurses a "name" to suit their personality. One of our first nurses was the Gentle Instructor, another was Army Sergeant/Comedienne, another was Joyful Patience, and I could go on and on. But there was a couple during transplant that must be mentioned. One was our Number One Nurse of all the stays at Emory. We found out during the ICU time that only two people in the hospital had her name, and one was in ICU. She went above and beyond, caring for David with such a motherly tenderness that we will never forget. I remember when he was so incredibly sick, the chemo doing its dirty work on his digestive track, vomiting and diarrhea at its worst. She knelt by him on the bathroom floor, where he had had an accident, and cleaned him and the whole bathroom around him, being careful that he didn't have to strain to help. She was quick to come check on him and see that he was as comfortable as could be. She came to the ICU when he was chemically paralyzed and left a note for us on the board. When he was sent back to the oncology floor and was being discharged to go to rehab, she brought him a pizza, which he had wanted during transplant but was too sick to eat. We will never forget our special nurse!

I also met many family members of patients in the family kitchen area and around the hospital halls. I even met some at the rehab hospital the few weeks we were there. We exchanged prayer requests for our loved ones and shared things that had helped. There was one lady whose husband had brain cancer. I shared with her about a Bible verse that reads, "Be still and know that I am God" (Ps. 46:10 KJV). A friend told me that in the original language, that verse means "to collapse into His arms." I shared this with the lady whose husband was in rehab. She saw David and me the next day in the hall, introduced herself to David, and told him that, through his sickness, she had received strength by what I had shared with her. She shared that with some other special people in her church group back home, and it had blessed them as well. I kept this family on my prayer list long after we left Emory. When David was in ICU the first time, Berry and I slept on the floor of the waiting room. Being there so long, we had met many people from all walks of life. One lady was elderly and was there with her husband. She was precious, offering us advice as we were new to the ICU area. She said her daughter had dropped her off since she couldn't drive. She was there alone, with a huge suitcase, which she struggled to keep with her. My husband and

I took her to the cafeteria to buy her lunch. We formed a bond the short time we spent with her as we spent long hours in the waiting room.

There was also an ICU nurse who talked to me at length one night when I sat by David's bed, watching him as he was attached to a lung bypass machine and a dialysis machine. The hours were long. The stress was real. But this nurse began to talk to me about God and how, even in our darkest hours, He is ever present. She wanted to share a book with me that was good. She brought it out to the waiting area the next night. It was called *When Heaven Pauses*. It made such an impact on me that I gave it away to someone else who was stressed over a loved one, thinking I could order another copy. There was another couple from New York whose son had to have open-heart surgery. He was a business executive, only forty years old. My heart went out to this mom as I saw the anxiety on her face day by day as they waited. I met a young woman in the vending machine room who was there with her ex because he had no one else. My prayer list kept growing! As I was waiting in the valet parking area, a young woman standing beside me wanted me to pray for her friend who was having a liver transplant. I found some people were just waiting for someone to show compassion as they endured such anxious moments facing life-or-death situations every single day. When our Erin passed, the first time I went out, I went to Walmart. I decided to go very early in the morning to avoid seeing people I might know and having a breakdown in the store. It never occurred to me, as we pass people on the street or in a store, what battles they might be facing. How often have I gone past people, nameless, face-less to me, and yet they might have been at their lowest point in life, just barely able to get out of the house? Facing our own dark night of the soul gives a new perspective on life, on people, on everything!

Here I am, awake since two thirty, writing a book that I don't even know will be published. I'm baring my soul in the hopes that this might touch someone else. If I can help one other grieving mom, dad, sibling, or other family member or friend, then my life of sorrow will have more meaning than just getting out of bed, trying to breathe each day.

DAY-60

· · · · · · · ● ● ● ● ● ● ● · · · · · · ·

New Normal

It has been said that after grieving any loss, you will eventually find a "new" normal. That is a hard statement for a grieving parent, for your life will never be any kind of normal anymore. After burying three children, we did, however, find our way into a new "normal." But it took a very long time. Erin was so full of life and was such a take-charge person that finding a way to go on was very difficult. Christmases, other holidays, and birthdays were especially hard since she was the one who loved parties and "hoopla" associated with cel- ebrations. That first Christmas, I would not have a Christmas tree. But another grieving parent encouraged me to do it for David, to keep making memories for him. When I looked at him, I knew I had to. But the tree, which had in years gone by been so filled with orna- ments there was barely an empty spot, was very sparely decorated, with only angels people gifted to us. Birthdays were hard because any semblance of celebration seemed unfair to Erin. David told me once that he knew he couldn't do what Erin did and yet he felt he had to try. Once in the hospital, he began to bare his soul as we all agonized over his illness, the past, and the uncertain future. He said he had always felt he had to take Erin's place and be what she was to us in addition to being true to himself. It was a very heavy load for a young teen to carry! And yet unknown to us, he bore that burden. I wondered later if that contributed to his social anxieties, and even to his illness. One of his new "normal things" was to fill the huge gap, or try to, that his sister had left. We all had developed a new normal without even trying. For me, here are a few things that changed:

- Cemetery visits added to my routine each week.
- Keeping a journal of memories of Erin. Keeping her alive by preserving her memory any way possible.
- Finding a way to cry without upsetting David or Berry.
- Searching for signs or dreams of Erin.
- Short day trips away to deal with special holidays, like Mother's Day.
- Learning how to respond when people ask how many children I had.
- Learning how to respond when people ask how we were feeling.
- Refocusing from two children to one.
- Taking care of me so I could be here for David and Berry.
- Changing how I had shopped for and with Erin. Finding new stores so the memories would not overwhelm me.
- Dealing with (or not dealing with) Erin's clothes and personal belongings that Adam allowed us to gather from their home.
- Dealing with upcoming life events, like Adam, her husband, eventually remarrying and having a child. Or dealing with seeing others like her classmates having children and living a joyful life.
- Learning to cope with music, places, foods, events that triggered grief waves.
- Learning to cope with the ever-present pain of loss that stayed in my heart all the time.
- Allowing myself to say no to group settings, events that were tough to attend because of the grief, even when people who invited me might not understand. Family gatherings were especially painful because they emphasized who was missing. So I had to only go when I felt strong enough.
- Dealing with "comforters" who had many platitudes to offer that dealt, instead, more pain.

- Learning to cope with the stages of grief, the denial, anger, bargaining, depression, and acceptance, which were revisited many times.
- Coping with fears of another loss or of the uncertain future.

These are a few of the new normal things that I faced.

Now, with David's home-going, I begin this journey again. It won't be as it was with Heather, Erin, or Scott. Each had its maze of emotions, tensions, fears, and lifestyle changes. But this time is unique since David was our last child, our last hope of a future of dreams come true. This time we are older, with fewer years ahead. The future is very unclear right now. In our abnormal existence, is there any time left for new normal?

DAY-61

· · · · · · · · ● · · · · · · · · ·

A Day in the Life

My life is a maze of finding answers, finding comfort, finding places of solace. It is a challenge to control the emotions. Do I let them flow out of control, let the grief out through tears, or suppress the anxiousness welling up inside me? Waking is hard. Going to sleep is hard. A full night's peaceful sleep is a thing of the past. Even my dreams haunt me sometimes. At other times, they grant me an escape to a better place, where my son is still in my life on earth. I go about my day, keeping my hands busy to fill my mind so the grief will not consume me. I mop. I dust. I plant flowers. I scrub. I work until my body can take no more. Then I lie on the couch and watch an old TV show. But eventually, the time comes when the TV is off, the work is done, the house is silent as Berry sleeps and I can't.

Once again, I walk into David's room, which is just as he left it to go to the doctor January 29, 2016. Since we didn't know he would be admitted to the hospital that day, everything in his room is as it would have been had we come home that night. I look at his unmade bed, which I refuse to change. I pick up his pillow, which still holds the precious scent of him. I press my face into it as I do every day. The tears and grief wails boil up in my soul. *I want him back!* I cry out in my mind. It shouldn't have ended this way. He worked and fought so hard to beat this thing! He was recovering! His recovery should have ended well. I worked hard to become a "nurse" to him, doing things I thought I could never do. Flushing the PICC lines that went right into his veins in his chest terrified me! But I took the training. I was so overprotective! I was a germophobe of the nth degree! I sheltered him from any germ, any thought of germs. I washed my hands until they were raw and sore. We went, we stayed, we tried every possible drug to help, and every possible test was run. And yet his weak body could not take any more of that poisonous chemo. He knew it before he started. And yet he did it anyway. All these thoughts are a constant with me now. The whys, the how, the ifs are like little puppies following me everywhere I go, never resting.

Every day I wonder why I'm still here. What was the purpose in my living such a full, rich life and reaching this point only to bury the reason I lived? Some days I hope I don't have to live much longer. I think maybe God is through with me. I said as much to Him when I cried out for Him to spare my son's life. I told Him, if he took David, then He was taking me too. Maybe that was His plan. And yet I am still breathing. I still wake up each day. Every day God is on my mind too. I fear Him. I still love Him with that standoffish kind of respectful love. But I don't understand how His great, compassionate love would allow my world to be so crushed until all that's left is powder of a life that once was and is no more. I want to write a poem now.

Remembering My Son

Your life didn't stop when the last breath was done.
It is now so full and complete.
There is no more pain, and no one will leave
As you walk on those golden streets.
Your sisters and brother must have opened the gate
When you took your flight from this earth.
There must have been hugs and tears and joy
And a peace that you never knew here.
No more pain, no more fear, no more sickness or death
Can touch you ever again.
So, my son, while the tears fill up my eyes,

Yet my spirit is near you each day.
I wait and I long for that moment in time
When for me you will open the gate.
I love you more, my David!

DAY-62

••••••••●•••••••

Keeping Their Memory

The years rolled by after our Erin left for heaven. It doesn't take many weeks after the passing for people around you to go back to their busy lives and quit coming around. The many cards in the mailbox dwindle down to an occasional one. The phone calls and visits come to a screeching halt. You are left alone to suffer through the agony of isolation and loneliness that settles. I have experienced this four times now and have seen it happen to others. It's almost as if the world is screaming, "Get on with your life and let me get on with mine!" I've heard all the voices saying, "It will get better," "You will be all right," "You'll get through this," "They are better off, they aren't suffering anymore." And the one that causes anger in a grieving parent more than all, "God picks the rosebuds too. He gets tired of just old people in heaven!" What the heck! I want to respond, "What if he 'picked' your child? Would you be so happy the rosebud was picked then?" If you don't know what to say to a grieving person, just be there for them. Sit in silence. Hug them. Offer a listening ear, housework, a car washing, helping plant flowers, or anything! But don't offer platitudes that make them think you take their child's death as a passing moment. Let me get off that bandwagon and back to my topic of keeping their memory alive. A parent struggles with the time when no one says their child's name anymore. Even some of those closest to me and to my children will talk about the weather, politics, other people, and a myriad of topics but fail to mention Erin, Heather,

David, or Scott. When you bury a child, it is not the end. Their lives were so intertwined with yours that they are still part of your identity. For people to ignore them means ignoring who you are and feels as if they are burying you too.

I find ways to bring up their names in conversations so that the person has to say their names and remember. Other ways of remembrance are doing random acts of kindness and leaving behind a card with your child's name and that you are doing it in their remembrance, ordering a decal with your child's name and date for your car, finding things that helped you and sharing them with other grieving parents, giving some of their belongings to family members who your child(ren) were close to, using any leftover monies from insurance or gifted funds to present scholarships to other young people, keeping or starting Facebook pages or blogs, joining grief support groups to help others, writing books, starting new family traditions that include their name and memory, having a special table with their picture displayed at future events like weddings or dinners, or giving to hospitals, charities, or local schools in their name.

The first special thing I did that meant so much to me as my grief for Erin was new was to give books away. The first book, I found out about when I accompanied my husband to his doctor. In the waiting room, he read an article about a medical doctor who had witnessed, firsthand, a near-death experience in a child. He, subsequently, interviewed many children who had experienced NDEs because he felt they weren't indoctrinated with the experiences of others or even with spiritual ideas. The book helped answer some of the questions that tormented me, especially about what Erin might have felt in those last moments. So I purchased multiple copies, including Erin's picture and a brief memory note of her on the inside, and gave them to grieving people. I have reordered many times and keep a supply of the books handy. The book was *Closer to the Light* by Melvin Morse. Since then, I have begun a quest of other books on NDEs and become fascinated with the commonalities and differences.

Now I am trying to think of ways to honor Scott and David in the same way.

As we sat and talked with the tragedy assistance team officer from the Army, I suggested that if the Army could do anything in Scott's memory, to please offer more counseling and support for soldiers coming off the battlefield. So many of our soldiers suffer from PTSD after facing the horrors of battle. Scott had been on the battlefield four times, only coming home for a short while between each. In his memory, I joined a group called Gold Star Mothers, which is a support group for mothers who have lost children in the service of our country. We were given gold star pins at Scott's graveside. But I didn't understand the significance until I learned that these are given to bereaved family members of our military men and women who have passed. Sadly, I haven't been able to give the group the attention I should because David went to heaven shortly after Scott, and I was thrown back into the pit of despair. But I hope, in the future, to be more supportive of this great organization to honor our precious Scott's memory and help others.

There are so many ways to bring a child's name to the forefront and keep it there. And my goal for the remainder of my life is for people to know the names I held and hold so dear: Heather Lynn Fitzpatrick, Erin Leigh Fitzpatrick Jones, Andrew Scott Fitzpatrick, and David Lee Fitzpatrick. Never forgotten, always loved!

DAY-63

Moving into Anger

I can tell that Berry and I are slowly moving out of the shock-and-disbelief stage of grief (for now), because I see us getting angry easily. I woke up thinking of how I could probably sue the hospital for neglect. I don't want to do that, nor do I have the energy. It's just how I feel as I remember David falling that last day as I tried to catch him. He had been telling the nurses that he needed to use the bathroom, and they had tried a bedpan, which was too awkward for him. When no one was in the room, he decided to try to make it. But in his weakened condition, he got two steps from the bed and began to go down, his IV pole close behind. I grabbed his arm to make his landing gentler. But I have wondered if he did hit himself on the head as he landed sideways. Or did his landing cause an internal bleeding, which they had told us could happen when the platelets are so low? So many questions. So few answers. Grief drives me to want to know, to continually question every single moment and procedure to find answers.

I have not heard anything from the doctors in charge of his care, even though they expressed fondness for him, one even saying she wanted to "adopt" him. There has not been a card of sympathy, a call saying they, too, mourn for David, or any kind of acknowledgement that there was a connection, though we spent countless hours here in the last two years. That is the focal point of my anger for now. While he was under their care, they were so caring, so attentive to his needs. And when we left the ICU room after kissing David goodbye one last time that morning, we were cut off completely from those who knew him so well there. Not one contact except for bills from the hospital that keep coming. I scream inside, *Please care! Please tell me that you remember him! After all the pain and suffering he endured there, please just let me know you remember!* And the silence deafens me! Since this question kept haunting me, when we met for coffee with David's counselor here (a kind and compassionate woman whom David highly respected), I asked her about it. She said she had worked in a hospital before becoming a psychologist. She remembered from her earlier training in hospitals that some doctors and nurses can view a patient in a "clinical" way. That means they can distance themselves emotionally from the actual person. There are others, though, like the few that cried with us that last day, who do become attached to their patients emotionally. They do mourn even if they don't acknowledge it to you. Berry has his own anger issues going back to Erin, to Scott, and the events surrounding their passing. It's hard to let go of the details, although we both know it won't bring them back.

My mind goes back so vividly to the first Christmas after Erin passed. I remember lying on the couch, watching some "mindless" TV show and looking at my sparsely decorated Christmas tree, wishing I could just pick it up and throw it through the bay window, just throw it with all my might. Recently, I had the urge to throw something glass and break it! I just get angry! I get angry at the least thing or the questions that roll like a river through my mind. I get angry at the unfairness of life! I see some who never seem to have a problem, and yet they don't treat people kindly. They live for themselves. How does God decide who lives and who dies? Why does He take the kindhearted and leave those who are selfish and petty? Why did He take all my children and leave me no hope, no future, no posterity so that when I'm gone every remembrance of me is vanquished from this earth? I do hold back, hold the reins in where God comes into the picture because I fear Him. He holds the power of life and death. He has reasons beyond my ability to understand right now. I sure do wish He could reveal them to me. But I must simply bow before

His power because He is over all. I don't hate God. I want to have a relationship with Him again. But for now, I am just angry at life, at the "plan," at it all. I'm a mess!

I stay cold much of the time. It is cool because it is spring. My coldness might come from inside, from the missing place where David was here on earth in our home and lives. My bones ache, my TM joint hurts, my hair loss is evident. I eat for comfort! At first, I couldn't eat, and now I'm eating too much even when I'm not hungry. I haven't done that before. But it's something I can do successfully (or not!). I try so hard to work in my gardens. But I must limit myself because there is little energy. Even that angers me. Why should I try and care for this homeplace when it will be sold and no one will love the pretty flowers and trees I have labored to plant and care for? Solomon was right! "All is vanity! Vanity of vanities, all is vanity!" (Eccles. 1:2 KJV). The things I loved hold little meaning for me anymore. So will I find a new path of life?

DAY-64

······●●●●●●●●●●●●●●

Flashback

Poignant thoughts are a constant with a grieving parent. These might be sweet memories of days gone by filled with feelings of love and happiness. At first, especially, flashbacks to that last day, those last hours or even weeks invade the mind and soul. Along with those thoughts are intermingled plans of how to change the outcome. That may seem crazy, but for me, I keep agonizing repeatedly, "What if I had done this or that? What if I had questioned, more than I already did, every procedure, every drug used in David's care?" We know at this point nothing would change. We can't bring David back to us, no matter how hard we try, no matter how we agonize over thoughts and plans to go back in time. I try to remember every conversation with David, every detail of those last days or his last days here at home. As I write this, tears still roll down my face as I write the words *last days*. The disbelief that he is gone still pervades my thinking. How can this be? I want to remember the last TV show we enjoyed together at the hospital, the last food he was able to enjoy. I do remember I came in his room to relieve his dad armed with Chick-fil-A nuggets and a milkshake for him at his request. He never even got a chance to eat as he was moved to ICU just a few minutes after I arrived. He hadn't eaten for three days because the chemo had once again "destroyed" his digestive tract and his appetite. His throat hurt, so even drinking was a problem. He was dehydrated in the ICU as they wouldn't let him drink when he was first moved there because of running tests to determine what was wrong. They gave him three bags of fluid, which usually brings the heart rate down. But the doctor said it hadn't worked! Finally, I was so delighted when his nurse, Abby, used a damp sponge to clean the dead skin off his lips and moistened them and the inside of his mouth. Even more delight was there when they said he could have a drink. I helped him hold the little Styrofoam cup as he sipped the cold water, drinking as much as he could to quench his thirst. The little remembrances are a comfort now. That was his last drink! Tears again fill my eyes. A short while later, they had to intubate him, and then it happened. His heart stopped. They gave epinephrine, kept him on life support, did chest compressions—the rest is a blur. It is a bad memory of my husband and I standing at the sidelines, watching the team surrounding his bed do everything possible to bring him back. I was begging him not to die, please not to die! He fought to stay. There was a heartbeat! Then it quit. I pleaded with him to not leave me! There was a heartbeat! Then it quit. Peace enveloped me for a moment as my precious son's spirit went out of the room, out of the hospital, out of this world with his Savior, Jesus Christ. I don't know where heaven is. Is it far away? Or is it near? Jesus said, "I will never leave you nor forsake you." If He is always here, is David always here? That same question taunted me when our Erin left for heaven. Where are they? Where is heaven?

Today I went by Walmart to pick up a few things. As soon as I entered the store, there in front of me were the Mother's Day cards in all their bright colors. The tears welled up, and I quickly wheeled my cart past them onto the cleaning items aisle. David and Erin were always determined that I be remembered on Mother's Day. This will be the first Mother's Day in thirty-three years that there will be no child here to hug and kiss. There will be no "Happy Mother's Day! I love you!" said to me with a hug from my own child. Thirty-three years is a long time to have shared this most joyous day with children. And now… I can't figure out if I am Job or Naomi in the Bible. Who am I without my children? What is my identity? Everywhere I go, I see places that my children went with me. There are the McDonald's playgrounds from days gone by. There is Chuck E. Cheese, where

David loved to have his parties. There are places Erin worked, places I went to eat with her on her lunch break, David's tae kwon do studio, their schools, churches we went to, movie theaters we loved to visit, parks, and vacation spots. What do I do to escape this pain of loss, this huge gaping hole in my life? Do I move away? Or do I stay here and let the "scab" heal over the "wound," only to open back up at the slightest memory? I know the drill! I've done this before. I know all the advice that I gave to others. But this is different. My last child is in heaven, and I am here on earth!

DAY-65

•••••••••●•••••••••

Friends and Family

Support is so vital to a grief-stricken parent. We are blessed to have a rather-large family to support us. Although, as we have aged, the family has drifted apart. But when there is a crisis, it seems to come together. My younger sister, Judy, and her family have supported us from day 1. And even now, Judy calls frequently to check on us, which is a comfort. She was more like my child than my sister. I was fifteen when she was born. Since we were so close, when I went away to college, she was so upset. Later, when I moved back home, I'd take her and my younger brother, Tim, to amusement parks, outings, and special events that they enjoyed. I went to the football games where she was in the flag corps. Someone asked her if I was her mom. Now she is the wife of a pastor, teaches computer training classes (although retired), and enjoys her life with her daughter's family. But she still stays connected with me and is a great support. Berry had four brothers, but only one has remained close. Kimsey has also been there for us from day 1. Kimsey checked on our house and our one little goat while we had the long stays in Atlanta. When we were home, he would visit with David, which meant so much to David. He worried about our children along with us and wanted them to be okay. He was devastated when they passed. He still comes by or calls to check on us. My brother Tim and his wife, Sandra, have been there for us from day 1 also. Tim, who pastors and lives nearer Atlanta, drove me around Atlanta to find the right hotel when David was first admitted and had to stay a month, talking to the hotel managers to get us a better rate. He was always one of the first there if there was a crisis. And his church was praying for David for the entire two years, as was Judy's church and many others. My brother Rabun, who is also a retired pastor, called frequently to check on David and offer advice since he, too, has leukemia. My niece Amanda, who is a nurse, greeted us when we came home after that first monthlong hospital stay, bringing food and comfort. She was always near when we needed anything, driving to Atlanta or visiting us in Athens hospitals. My nephew Burton, who pastors in South Carolina, called frequently to check on us and let me know he was praying, often at three in the morning. He is a prayer warrior, and it made us feel better knowing that he kept David in prayer. My niece Heidi drove to Atlanta and came here to bring food or just to check on us, as did our other niece Paige. My cousin Melody came and brought a special vacuum so David wouldn't breathe dust, and she even cleaned my floors for me. She and her mom, my aunt Carolyn, drove to Atlanta several times to bring groceries and whatever we needed. I'm sure I left someone out, but so many came forward to surround us with support. Of course, there were times that they were busy with their own families and lives and we were alone.

The first Christmas, during David's transplant, Berry and I would have been alone with a very few others in the cafeteria at Emory. But two good friends I met on a grieving forum, Nerissa Mohammed and J. Marie Shepherd, came to the hotel and brought an entire Christmas meal they had cooked with all the trimmings. What a blessing! We ate on that meal for several days. Although David couldn't eat because of the strong chemo treatment, the mashed potatoes they brought became the last few bites he ate before going into ICU the next day with a lung infection that almost cost him his life. It's those little things that you always remember. Like the saying goes, "You won't remember those who laughed with you. But you always remember those who mourned with you." And it is so very true!

DAY-66

· · · · · · · ●●●● ● ●●● · · · · · ·

Decisions

No major decisions should be made the first year after losing a loved one, or so it is said. But what about the little decisions, the everyday occurrences? The first few weeks, even choosing an outfit is a major decision. The memory lapses. Did I do that already? Did I pay that bill last week? I can't cook because I can't focus or decide what to cook! So even the minute decisions are huge for a grieving parent.

There are also decisions that others push us to make. A friend wants us to eat out with them to get us out of the house. We go, but I find myself sinking near the end of the meal as the conversation goes on and on without a mention of my children. Also, we are in a setting surrounded by many others, chatting, laughing, sharing pictures of children, enjoying life. I find myself getting short of breath. I must get out of there! So I nudge my husband and make a feeble excuse to our friends that I feel ill, and we leave. We get home. The phone rings. A dear neighbor is concerned about us and wants to take us out. I make my excuses and hang up. Was I rude to refuse? Am I upsetting my neighbor? Then a bridal shower invitation comes in the mail. As the day nears, I know I must decide. I get a reminder the day before from my niece, who was such a help and blessing to us during our long stay away from home and even here. Will she be offended if I don't come? I agonize over what to do! Yet I know what I must do. I must shelter myself. No one will do it for me. Even if they don't understand, I must refuse. My life has always been about doing the right thing! I often put myself on the back burner so that I could do the right thing. And where did it get me? Where? I'm in agony. I'm not perfect, for sure! But I was always an overachiever. Now look at me! A childless mother. Burying all my children is my reward for doing the right thing! (Sarcasm!)

The anger is boiling up inside me at the unfairness of it all. And then…what if I did make God mad at me and I was just presuming I was doing the right thing? What if all that praying for others was just so He would heal David? Was I bartering and not even knowing it? And here we go again? My lack of understanding. My unanswered questions that haunt me day and night. My husband says I must say what Jesus said in the garden, "Not My will but Thine be done" (Luke 22:42 KJV). I refuse! What is wrong with me? I will *not* turn my back on God. I won't! But I don't understand Him. I thought I did! I thought I had this kingdom thing down pat! I knew how to pray, how to fast, how to send out the word to get others to pray. Multitudes prayed with me. "The effectual fervent prayer of a righteous man availeth much!" (James 5:16 KJV). That is what the Bible says. It was "in my face" yesterday as I looked at Facebook. So what was the result of all that praying? David left this earth! My last child is gone from this earth. So where do I go from here? All my Christian friends are appalled as I tell them these things. They, with all the platitudes they have learned to comfort others, are speechless when I tell them how I feel. I know this isn't about decisions, so I'm off topic. Or am I? I bow daily before an almighty God. He has all power. I acknowledge Him. I don't want to offend Him further. I honor Jesus Christ as my Lord, still. I will not turn away from my Lord and God. But what is my relationship with Him now that He has refused to answer my prayer for healing for my son, even as I poured out my soul to Him for help? Where is He now in my life?

No, I can't go to a bridal shower. I can't sit in a crowd of people whose lives are untouched with the sorrow I feel. Grief is selfish. Grief is cruel. I will protect my fragile self, my fragile emotions, and my frequent outbursts of crying by shielding myself in the only way I can right now. I must say no sometimes. I will keep trying. But for now, I must say no!

David

DAY-69

· · · · · · ●●●●●●● ● ●●●●● · · · · ·

David

Let me tell you about my son, David. A book on grief cannot be complete unless you understand who is being grieved. I will share my children with you. I share David first because he was my baby, my last born, my miracle child. I call him my miracle child because after Erin, our Heather was born still. Then he was born when I was older, with a perfect labor and delivery. Before he was born, we had three others who never made it to birth. They left so early there are no medical records and some might have called them a blob of tissue. But for me they were very real, as I wanted so desperately to have another child.

David was born when I was forty-three. He was perfect. There was only a five-hour labor and no problems during the pregnancy. When David was only three months old, I had to go back to work to help Berry support our growing family. It was not my choice or Berry's. But it was needed. I cried and cried when I had to leave him. But my aunt Joy volunteered at a family reunion when I mentioned I couldn't find a sitter. She had three teenage daughters who adored him. The next four years were good for him. I remember once, early on, when I was driving out their driveway and the tears were starting, I was reminded that God loved David more than me. So He would take good care of him. With that thought came a peace that stuck. Joy was so good to him, loving him as if he were her own. And the girls loved him too. Tierra, Nakena, and Angela fought over who would get to hold him first when they got home from school each day. Joy let them take turns. Soon another little baby joined him at Joy's house, and David and this little guy loved playing together as they grew.

When David was four, Joy decided it would be good if he was in a pre-K program to help him socialize. Plus, I think she needed a break by then! He began at the same pre-K program where Erin had been. He loved it! He always loved playing with other children his age since Erin was eight years older. Erin would get off the bus after school there, so it was a good situation. It was a Christian day care, so he would come home singing and sharing what he had learned. I remember once, we were outside, and he just started singing, "God and God Alone." I was amazed that he knew every single word. His musical talent was showing! Later, he loved the movie *Men in Black*. He would watch it over and over and sing the songs from it, not missing a word or note. Even the minor tones were no problem for him. He also loved to dress in his black Sunday suit, wearing it to school every day for a while, along with an old pair of my very dark sunglasses. What a laugh we had! But he was following his passion! Soon a show started airing called *Power Rangers*. He found a new passion for this new TV show! Soon he began pretending to do the martial arts that they used in the show. A friend had enrolled her son in tae kwon do and told me how great it was. So I took David. That began a seven-year training that he loved with a passion. His instructors were two young Christian men from Korea who influenced so many kids over the years. They were very disciplined themselves and so involved in their students' lives. Many times, one of David's instructors would sit with me before class and discuss David and any issues he had. David finally received the coveted black belt and was well on the way to second-degree black belt when he felt his school studies required so much more time and decided to quit. He expressed regret after he finished school that he hadn't stuck with it.

School Days for David

David loved school. In kindergarten, he quickly made friends and would play so hard at recess that once I had to take a change of clothes when he had an accident after not using the restroom break. Very quickly, his teachers noticed his keen intelligence tested and enrolled him in classes for the gifted students. He always made good grades. He was so meticulous about his work and his handwriting. Big changes were ahead, though, when the county built a new elementary school nearer to our home and David had to change schools. He hated this change! He loved his first school, and this was a tough blow. However, he made new friends quickly and even made a friend who would become a lifelong friend. So good things came out of the change.

David's health was a problem from the time he was six months old. One Sunday, he had been running a slight fever and I noticed his arms were turning blue from the elbows down. I freaked out, and we rushed him to the nearest hospital. They had trouble finding a vein, and his screams were getting straight to my heart, so I went into the hall and just cried. The doctor came by and saw me and told me he would go right in. He managed to get a vein in David's ankle quickly so they could continue to run tests, which he later said was only a virus. But every year David would go to school in the fall, not missing a day for about the first month. Then he would begin to get sick, and it would last through the end of the school year. By second grade, I was taking him to allergists, who ran tests and found he was borderline asthmatic. The doctor encouraged me to not let the asthma diagnosis stand because it would affect his ability to get insurance in the future. So we just said he was borderline, although I often wondered if he really was only borderline. Every year he struggled with being very sick early in the mornings but trying to continue school.

David loved music, moving from trumpet in middle school to piano lessons here to electric guitar later. He would play and sing for hours. He began to enjoy some Japanese artists and taught himself the language so he could sing and play their songs. He was brilliant in math, according to one of his accelerated math teachers. He had potential to be anything he wanted.

Middle school was tough. He was thrown into a chaotic environment with about one thousand kids from all over the county. Discipline was lax in some classrooms, and he quickly began to see the unfairness of life. Once he was out sick for several days and he and I both tried to get his assignments. One of his teachers said he would have to get them from another student. Some of the other boys loved to challenge David, which distressed him because he was not confrontational. He could easily defend himself with his tae kwon do, but his instructors had taught them to only use it in cases of threats against his life. David was confronted by one student who kept aggravating him in the bathroom, so David did defend himself. Once in gym class, a student wanted to fight David. The friend behind David told the student that David was a black belt and he should not start with him. So he backed away. David quickly became discouraged with his efforts, and his grades started dropping.

A Different Direction

Since I had retired from my own teaching career, I decided to pull him from school the last quarter of eighth grade and homeschool him. Some of his teachers encouraged me because they said he could be out a week and still make As on the tests on Friday. They felt confident he would do well. And so began yet another change in David's life.

He quickly developed a love for video games. I had to restrict him until he finished his work each day. We had a good first year, going to the library to do projects, going on field trips, improvising our PE to include our ball games and outside activities, cooking, sewing, and all the projects to make it a well-rounded experience. He was determined to finish the books even after we completed our required 180 days, so he worked a little longer. When we got to advanced algebra and calculus, his dad became part of the teaching team. He finally completed the coursework and took the GED. He was anxious, wondering if he had learned enough to pass. But after the three-day session, he scored very high, above 80 percent of high school graduates. He said he was appalled it was so easy and could have passed in third grade. Some adults in his sessions were taking parts of it for the third time. He knew then he had learned more than he thought. He talked of going to college to study criminal justice, something that interested him.

But there were two cogs in the wheel. One, Erin's death sent him into a downward spiral of depression. The second was a bad relationship with a girl he adored. By the end of high school, his depression had worsened to the point we scheduled an appointment with a stress care counselor, who helped him immensely. He was beginning to come back into the light of life. He even said he was dealing better with Erin's passing. It didn't stay on his mind all the time, and he was handling it better. He was ready to get on with life. Then, suddenly, he was diagnosed with leukemia.

After finishing high school, he didn't really know what career path to take. He had a girlfriend he had met in an online game, with whom he talked for hours every night for five years. She was finishing high school too and wanted him to come for her prom. After arrangements were made, we rented his tux and he went to the prom. She was a beautiful girl, and he had a great time. She lived in a coastal town, and after prom, they and another couple went to a park and out to eat. He said he cried on the way home because he didn't want to leave. He went back to her graduation in a few weeks. But shortly after, they ended the relationship, which left him with his first broken heart.

He made several other friends on the same online game, so he received comfort from them. There were two other young girls who liked him even though he still loved the first girl. He told me later in life that it seemed the girls seemed to find him. He didn't really go looking for them! But he was a caring, loving kind of guy. He loved to help others, even those he didn't know well. Cheridon Tao was a true friend, even continuing to talk to him after his girlfriend left. He wanted to go and visit her. David didn't drive because of social anxiety related to Erin's passing. He had gotten his learner's permit.

But since he wasn't in a formal high school, he didn't have the peer pressure to drive and didn't go anywhere except to friends' houses, so he didn't see a need. But in a way, now I am glad, because it gave us more time with him. We'd drop him off wherever he needed to go.

DAY-71

• • • • • • • • • ● • • • • • • • • •

Friends, Lifelong or Not?

We took David to Florida to meet Cheridon, who had been such a good friend. My husband and I enjoyed the nice town while David spent time with Cheridon and her brother. They went to the park and rode the kiddie rides at night, went shopping, and just enjoyed being together. They carved a pumpkin at her house, talked all night, and played video games. He had a blast. They remained friends until they began to drift apart. But she was still talking to him in the weeks before he passed. When he was just off lung bypass, they talked, and I could tell it cheered him. Cheridon was planning to come up to see him when she saved up the money for the trip, but it never happened. Sadly, she died suddenly, which distressed him to no end. It hurt him so deeply, he told me when I mentioned it, that he couldn't even talk about it while he was enduring the latest round of chemo. She had remained one of his lifelong friends, one that he could talk freely to about anything. He felt she really understood and cared for him.

About a year after he broke up with his first girlfriend, he was talking to another girl on the internet. She was younger than he, but he said she wanted to be his girlfriend. He only viewed her as a young girl who kidded around with him a lot. But she said she had liked him for a long time. As they continued talking and playing the games together online, he finally decided they could have a relationship. David was a person of commitment. If he was your friend, he was your lifelong friend. This young girl would call him every day when she got home from school, and they began long, sometimes nightlong talks. It quickly escalated until they felt they were in love. But the relationship quickly became toxic for him. He began to depend on their everyday talks, and she, him. But with the relationship came some problems. He told me later that he felt she was much like Erin. She became a sort of substitute for his sister, whom he adored. That led to dependency on his part, though. He would get upset if he didn't hear from her, and that happened many times. He quickly realized that she seemed to not be able to deal when they had an argument. She dealt with problems by retreating into herself. The problems escalated to the point many times I'd hear David's voice raised in anger as he was on the phone late at night. Then I began to hear him crying at times, begging her not to leave. Sometimes when they would have conversations, she'd leave and tell him to hang on. But she'd be gone for three or four hours. Later, he would learn, she had gone down to get something to eat and watch a movie with her family, leaving him hanging on! This kind of behavior led to him beginning to lose control of his emotions, often pacing the floor, wondering if she had been in an accident or had found another boyfriend. The peak came when she disappeared for a couple of weeks. He had a friend over that day who, accidentally, looked at her Facebook page and saw she was "in a relationship" with another boy. That broke David's heart. His friend tried to communicate with her, but she didn't respond to anyone. A few weeks later, she called and said her parent told her she shouldn't have treated him that way. She said she didn't ever have anyone else. She just wanted out and that was the only way she knew to quit the relationship. She wanted back in again. David hesitated as he had recovered from the brokenness a bit. He said he knew this could happen again and he didn't really trust her. But he gave her another chance. She did this multiple times, causing him extreme pain each time. He never really trusted her completely after that. He wanted, however, to go up and meet her. So I drove him up one weekend. He had a nice time and felt this was good for their relationship. She was always very attentive at first after a disappearing act. But he knew, as time passed, she would begin disappearing again.

Abandonment

David began having panic attacks again, so I took him to the doctor, who wanted him to go for counseling. He did, and his counselor diagnosed him with abandonment issues related to Erin's passing and his grief. He felt everyone around him was going to die or leave him and he would live out his life alone. This girlfriend's behavior exacerbated the problem. So, the panic attacks continued until he was finally put on low-dose antidepressant meds to help.

When David was diagnosed with leukemia, his counselor said she had done some research in college that indicated that a bad relationship could sometimes trigger the onset of disease. She wondered if this bad relationship he had battled for a few years had contributed to the diagnosis. He really respected his Christian counselor. She was very good to keep the sessions going, even by phone, when he was neutropenic after chemo treatments. After about the fourth chemo treatment, this girlfriend decided she was moving away with friends. She wanted a fresh start in life. She said they were going in different paths. He was battling leukemia, and she wanted to get on with her life and not deal with that! (I guess you can see my sarcasm as I had been a witness to the crushing of my son's heart!) So here he is, battling for his life! And she just leaves!

He never wanted me to put all the blame on her. He said he had issues too. And I knew he had issues that were never resolved dealing with grief at such a young age that affected relationships. He was clingy. He needed someone to be there for him through thick and thin. But this girl was not the one! He just couldn't turn loose! Knowing how badly this hurt him still brings tears to my eyes. I must interject here that I honestly do not hate this girl. David thought I hated her. But I don't hate anyone. I do hate what the relationship did to David. I hate her reactions/responses to him and the effect they had on his life. I realize it was a bad relationship, a toxic one that neither of them could sever. David tried to break up just shortly before he passed. He told me he realized that he needed someone who could 'be there' for him, especially then when he was suffering so. He said he sent her a message saying as much. But she re-surfaced three days later and acted as if nothing had changed. So, he kept talking to her. He just couldn't turn loose, no matter how badly he was treated. But he said that as far as he was concerned, it was over.

David was always a gentle, kindhearted guy, even when he was small. He always stood up for the less fortunate. I remember he even apologized to his dad and me for getting cancer! Imagine! Here was this young man, just beginning life, battling a life-threatening disease, sick beyond imagination, apologizing for being sick! Just a few days before he passed, he saw how tired I was as he battled the excruciating pain in the hospital, and I wouldn't leave him. He said, "Mom, I'm so sorry I am putting you through all this!" Now I have tears! He always repented when he was growing up if we had an argument. He told us when he went out with friends that he'd tip the waiters very well because they probably didn't make much. He hadn't begun college or a job yet because of emotional issues, but when he wanted something and we'd allow him to buy it, he'd look for the cheapest thing because he didn't want to spend too much of our money. Just before he was diagnosed, he said he was ready to get out there and find a job. Three of his friends had already told him they knew of a place he could work. So he was excited about the new beginning. He never threw a friend away. He always put others ahead of himself, going the distance, wanting to get them birthday presents, worrying about their well-being if he saw them drinking, smoking, or doing things detrimental to their health or emotional well-being. If he was you friend, he was a true friend. He was such a good son! I'm just so sorry he endured the pain of loss so much in his young life. I do think it might have contributed to his sickness, which led to him not being on earth today. At least now I know he is with God, where there is no more pain, no abandonment, no fear of loss. There is just peace and joy. One day I will be with my son again! What a day of rejoicing that will be!

DAY-73

· · · · · · · ●●●●● ● ●●●● · · · · · ·

Dreams and Visions

Sometimes it seems David is so near I can almost "hear" him speaking to me. Whether he is or not, I don't know. I've heard that our words live on even when we are not on earth anymore. But knowing David knew of the signs and visions I had of Erin, I feel that he will speak to me if that is permitted from heaven to earth. I have always had a strong spiritual connection to everything around me, even plants and animals. Since my great-grandmother read tea leaves (with a smile, I might add) and my grandmother, her daughter, predicted that Erin would be a girl, and she was, I have always wondered if there might be a spiritual gift from God that was passed to me. When David was dedicated to the Lord as a babe, our pastor, as he held him, said he felt he was holding a prophet. David did have dreams many times, which I wrote down. Often they would come true. So the "gift" might have been passed down to him. Anyway, this morning, as I was showering after working in my garden, a grief wave hit me midshower and I began crying out, "Did I kill David? Did I bring a germ into that hospital room that might have given him an infection?" I knew I had had a slight sniffle, nothing with fever or anything. I avoided getting near him when I had it. Then I had a little rash on my foot, where I thought something might have been an insect bite. But David wanted me there! He wanted me near, as he was in so much pain. But I cried out to God in the shower and agonized over this question, "Did I infect David?" As I began to step out of the shower, I "heard" David (in my mind) saying, "Quit blaming yourself, Mom! Quit! You didn't kill me. You didn't!" Then he began describing heaven. Then he said, "Go ahead and give those cards I valued away and everything! I don't need them. You and Daddy won't ever use them anyway. This place gives a whole new meaning to virtual reality! It's amazing. I'm more alive than I ever was there. This is more real than earth! Earth is not even close to this!" I believe it was David "talking" to me! Maybe it is just my imagination. But I want to believe that he is still close to his mom. Next, I decided to take a nap. As I was just waking up, I dreamed I saw him. He was standing right in front of me, just standing up after bending over to get something. He was in a flowered shirt (which he never would have worn here!) under a big oak tree in the shade. He was so filled with peace as I saw him. He looked younger, nearer to around twelve. I was so glad I dreamed about him! So glad!

DAY-74

· · · · · · · · ● · · · · · · ·

May 1, 2016
It's Sunday, Friday's Coming

This title is reverse of a famous writing by a minister, describing the death of Jesus on Friday and His resurrection on Sunday, which turned death into victory for the believer. Today is Sunday, and so it begins. The week we celebrated David's birth. His birthday is May 6, which is on Friday this year. Two days later is Mother's Day, which was one of the happiest days of the year for me. I am so thankful that I was blessed to be a mom. My children by birth and Scott, who was more like a natural-born son to me, even from a distance, were such a huge blessing and brought such joy to my life that it's almost unimaginable. David was a special blessing because we didn't know if we could ever have another child after our Heather was born still and after three miscarriages. But when we were both forty-three, our little miracle child, David, came straight from heaven into our arms. He opened a whole new world to us with toy trucks, tae kwon do, video games, ball games, swords, and music, which filled our lives with fun and adventure. He was tenderhearted yet could be firm and serious when the need arose. He excelled and did his best at everything. One of his friends told me he always wanted to "platinum" every game he played and before others, if he could. *Platinum* meant the highest rank to achieve in the gaming world.

Erin, on the other hand, was my firstborn. She was a blue-eyed, blond-haired doll from heaven. She brought dolls, frilly dresses, laughter, fun, and such love you could only imagine. She loved with a fierceness that the world is so in need of today. She got "up and personal" with everyone she met. And if she saw a need, she did everything in her power to fulfill that need. She loved people!

Scott grew up a quiet, tenderhearted little guy. He loved coming over to visit Berry and me early in our marriage. He'd stay at our apartment and go swimming and shopping with me. He brought baseball, football, and weightlifting and, eventually, the military life into our world. We followed him as he pursued his dreams traveling around the world to new places, opening his life and ours to new cultures. He never went so far that he couldn't call and talk for hours at a time. He kept his home base alive no matter how far he went. When I was blessed to be pregnant with my baby Heather, our lives were filled with little bumps, kicks, and hiccups as we dreamed of her arrival. Our hopes and dreams of having another little girl gave us hope for the future. Erin would have a little sister. I had loved my own sister, who was only one and a half years apart. We shared everything. And then my baby sister became such a joy in my life. *Now,* I thought, *Erin will have a sister to share with.* But God had another plan. He only allowed us that six months and took her home. We were only allowed twenty-three years and three days with Erin before He took her back. David was given twenty-four years, nine months, and six days before God, at my protest, took him back home. Scott was with us for forty-one years, eight months, and seven days. So here I am. I'm a childless mother, at least on earth. But one of the hardest parts is facing their birthdays each year, facing the day they went to heaven, facing all the special days when we should be celebrating instead of mourning. I thought I had faced this enough with Erin. And now, here I am again, facing Friday, May 6, without my miracle baby boy, whom I raised, who taught me many things about life. How do I face it? How do I get through next weekend with his birthday and then Mother's Day? How do I survive my life without these blessings? Am I cursed? I didn't think so. But where are my children? I read in Job last night. I decided that I would force myself to read at least the book of Job in my lack of understanding of my God. Job said it would have been better if he'd never been born. He begged God to show him his iniquity, which I have done over and over. What's my iniquity in loving my children so greatly? And yet maybe there was something in me. I don't know. My life is a fog.

Silent Retreat

No infectious laughter drifts out through your door,
No ringing the bell I left by your bed
To beckon me near when there was a need,
No phone conversations with friends far and near,
No "Come watch me fight this last boss, please, Mom."
"Take me to Shane's or Josh's tonight." I don't hear your
Voice, though I try with all my might.
The soothing, low tones of a voice I held dear
Ring no more on earth as I shed all these tears.
Oh, how I miss you, my David, my son.
You had all our love and love still lives on.
How do we live in this silent retreat,
Filled with memories of you that were so, so sweet?
They say silence is golden, but this silence is black.
How we long for what was! We just want you back!
Heaven awaits us, it won't be too long!
Then once more we'll hear you as silence becomes
A song!

DAY-76

•••••••••⬤•••••••••

Finding Purpose

Setting goals has always been a priority for me. I'm a planner. When my plans fail, I feel I'm a failure. That's the downside of being a planner. My plans for my children failed. The plan was to have them both grow up, go to college, experience life a little, meet a nice soul mate, get married, and have many grandchildren for me to love on and to be there for the children when my husband and I were gone. It just didn't happen!

Erin always loved visiting my classroom. She wanted to be a teacher or an interior decorator. She put her career thoughts on hold when she fell in love with a local boy, Adam, when she was only eleven. They met at a local church during Bible school. After a relationship that was on and off a couple of years, they finally made peace and decided they couldn't live without each other, so they married. They didn't have the big church wedding I had planned for my only daughter who was living. No! They let me know the night before they were going to go across the state line to marry at a small-town courthouse. So I frantically bought a cake, flowers, and the few things I could organize to make that day momentous. Berry, David, and I met them at the Walhalla, South Carolina courthouse and witnessed the exchanging of wedding vows. This was not what I had planned. But I wouldn't have missed it for the world. Adam, her husband, was like a son to me, having lived with us for a short while after high school. That was how my daughter's grown-up life began.

No college, no teaching job. But she loved her marriage, work, and eventually a small house Adam's grandfather helped them buy. She redecorated the whole place inside and out, loving every moment. Then, after only less than five years, *suddenly* she was gone.

My plans for my own children's future were gone as a thin vapor that disappears so quickly.

My whole purpose in life was my children. I had retired from my own career of teaching. My health was still good. Our home was paid for, no real debts. And now? An unclear future. No heirs. No plans. The nothingness overwhelms my mind. I know what Solomon was talking about now. "Vanity of vanities. All is vanity" (Eccles. 1:2 KJV).

My struggle with my faith is taking its toll. God has always been first in my life. And to live each day without prayer, without my Bible reading and study, is my hardest battle now. I determined last week that I would set a new goal. I would read just one chapter in Job each day. I would get outside early, as I used to do, and walk. I would just walk and be silent, not talking to God as I was accustomed to in days gone by, when David was still here. I had been on my knees continually praying for him and others for as long as he lived. I did that with Erin. I thought I had heard from God. But now I don't even know. I don't know how to find my purpose in life. Or even if God wants me to live.

So how do I proceed? Do I set plans? In Psalm 33:10 (KJV), David said God frustrates the plans of the nations. He did mine too. But He has that right. He is God, and I am not. He knows the end from the beginning. His mighty power, I will not deny. His authority, I cannot question. Only He can give me a new purpose, a new plan for whatever days, months, or years I have left.

Purpose for life changes when we lose a loved one. I don't like to say *lose*, because I know that my children are all in heaven. I haven't lost them. They await me there. Something I heard once was, "When you lose someone you love, it changes everything." It truly does. All the plans and purposes that you had mapped out for your life are null and void. When Erin left us for heaven, I remember reading in the Psalms where David said God had frustrated his plans and purposes. I had to push myself very hard to even pick up my Bible again. But I now have determined that I will only read Job until I find it. Find what? I don't even know! But Job said in Job 27 (KJV), "As God lives, who has taken away my right and denied me justice, and the Almighty, Who has vexed and embittered my life," acknowledging that He had been vexed by God Himself. Such are my thoughts, not having answers to the multitude of questions that fog my mind and soul each waking moment. But like Job, I will continue to speak the truth. I will acknowledge that God alone has wisdom and knows far more than we humans do. That's the only point I am clear on right now!

DAY-77

· · · · · · · · ●●● ● ●●● · · · · · ·

Triggers

Each day, and sometimes each hour, is challenging for me. There are so many triggers to grief. It might be pulling out a cookie and remembering David always asked for a glass of milk with his sweets. Or it might be almost hearing the familiar "Mom" he always called out if he needed something. Seeing the stray kitty and remembering how he loved cats brings a trigger. Sometimes the triggers are intense, like today, when I looked at his clothes still hanging in his bedroom and thinking, *I will never get to buy him another Sonoma T-shirt, his favorite brand.* Tears were flowing at just that thought. I was cleaning his electric razor and saw the fine black hairs from his beard, thinking of the time after chemo when his hair was coming out, often on his pillow, and eventually how he had no eyebrows. Tears flow. I remember his kindnesses, like him asking how my niece's husband was after a heart attack when he, himself, was suffering so. Twenty-four years, nine months, and six days are enough to plant a memory behind every moment. There are tears continually from Berry and me. I'm so thankful for the memories. Don't get me wrong. It's hard having grief waves or even grief tsunamis at any unexpected time from a memory. But if I had it to do all over and knew I only would get twenty-four years, nine months, and six days, I would gladly take it. I would just hug him a little tighter, tell him I loved him over and over, and make life as sweet as I could for him. We had a good life with our children.

The hard part is facing an uncertain future with no new memories to cause waves. Oh, how I miss them!

Tomorrow is David's twenty-fifth birthday, the first in these many years I have not had him beside me. Birthdays trigger an avalanche of memories. Last year, I remember that his friends Josh Power and JM came over to spend time with him. He had only been home from rehab about a month and was still in recovery. They wanted to take him out to a favorite restaurant to eat, but when he said he just couldn't go, they left. He was afraid he had angered them. But he was still weak. I talked to Josh later, and he said they were not angry with him. They just wanted to help him get out a bit. I saw his strength day by day. Some days were harder than others. He eventually did get out and visit, even finally going to Josh's house for an overnight stay. But he fell when trying to navigate the outside embankment to get back to my car. He tried so hard. He fought so hard. A few in the hospital criticized him for not walking more, not getting up more. But I was a witness to his pain, to his weakness. He would sit up at home more the last few months because he didn't want to get another lung infection. He even forced himself to go to rehab here when he didn't feel like going. And what happened? He had to be put back on a ventilator those last few hours. It was his nightmare to be in ICU. And he ended up there again. Why my child? He never caused us any trouble or heartache! Never.

So I must go to the cemetery for yet another child to celebrate a birthday by sending balloons or butterflies heavenward, by laying fresh flowers on a grave. My last child! My baby boy, who suffered more in life than anyone should! And then, in two days, I will face Mother's Day for the first time in thirty-three years without my children here to hug me, to show me the love that we shared. Maybe I will get a "sign." Maybe not.

Berry and I are going away to an island retreat his cousin offered. We will be alone with our grief. I have no choice but to face these days of pain. My heart aches. My soul is weary. I'm reading the book of Job in the Bible because I identify with his pain and loss. He acknowledges that God orchestrates all things. He does. He is the Almighty. He sets people up and causes their demise. He rules overall. And sometimes we have no say in His decisions. They are His and His alone. Such is my lot in life right now. God took David, Erin, Heather, and Scott. I don't know why. I don't understand. But He is God, and I am not.

DAY-79

. . . . ● . . . .

David's Birthday

Today marks one of our "firsts," firsts without our David on earth with us. Or is he? I have always thought that when our loved ones leave, they go to somewhere just past the first star in the heavens. But Jesus said He would never leave us or forsake us. So if they are where He is, it is possible they are just a breath away. I like to believe my children surround me. We face these firsts, which are so troubling for us. But face them we must. I've been crying all week. But for some reason, my heart is lifted this morning. Maybe David is near me.

When I first awakened, I saw a tiny bright light just at the corner of my door. Then I felt I could "hear" David saying, "Mom, you were a good mom. Thank you for 'bearing' me, not just at my birth, but all my life." (I thought, *What a wonderful "burden"! But it was not a burden at all!*) He continued, "Rest easy, Mom! I'm okay. And I love you!" A simple message, but so full for me! Right after the "message," I heard a crash in my bathroom. I ran in to see what fell. It was a little soap dish I had attached to the tub wall. Things falling? A sign? Last night, as Berry and I were watching TV, I heard a strange sound, like a ticking, then suddenly a crash! I jumped up and went to the TV area where I heard it. I searched and searched behind the TV and couldn't see anything had fallen. I had all kinds of thoughts of what it might have been. Then, as I lay on the couch, watching TV, I saw the sound bar over the TV was gone. Sure enough, it was the sound bar that had fallen. Since David loved music, I can't help but feel he is sending us signs.

I send my love to heaven today, wherever that is! I believe it is nearer than we even know!

Facing David's first birthday not on earth and my first Mother's Day without my children was too much. Berry and I went to St. Simon's Island for the weekend. I got up early each morning and went out by the fishing pier and sat, walked, and reflected. There was a cool breeze blowing off the water, which stretched endlessly on the horizon. Its vastness couldn't help but bring God a little closer to my broken heart and soul as I remembered He told Job that only He could tell the waters where to stop on the earth. Birds were flying all around as peace settled over me for the first time in months. On the last day there, Berry walked with me very early. We saw the sun rise, and as I watched the water, I saw the fin of a dolphin as a fishing boat drifted by. Reflection, meditation, prayer, solace hovered near me as I continued to grieve for my children, but in a different place, in a different way.

•••••••••●•••••••••

May 11, 2016
Revisiting Faith

Preserving memories of David is a priority, as it was for Erin. I want people to know his name, to know his character, to know him and not forget! I am creating a memory garden, just as I did for Erin, Scott, and recently converting one for Heather. Heather's is going to be a bulb garden, just as she was my little flower "bulb" with so much promise unrealized on this earth but blossoming for sure in heaven.

Since David was my last child, love of my soul and heart, I want his to be very special. Each morning I get out very early and work on it. Just a plant here, a brick there, a little birdbath, flag, and gazing ball adding each day to its small splendor. Today, as I was watering and digging, my heart began crying out to God. I put the brakes on asking why, because a very spiritual lady once warned me not to question God. Now I feel a warning when I begin. But I come very close as I cry out to Him for understanding.

Today, my mind raced back to my younger years, when I longed for marriage, a child, a home. I prayed and exercised as much faith as I could and had others joining me in faith that my dreams would be fulfilled. This very handsome young man appeared at my back door once, and so began the fulfillment of my dreams. A few years later, joy filled my heart once again when the doctors laid in my arms the most beautiful baby I'd ever seen. Our Erin Leigh, our first true miracle, was before my eyes. As she grew, she glowed with beauty inside and out. Once, a lady told Berry he should enter her in a local beauty pageant, as did a photographer who made her picture once. But Erin would have none of that! Then, two years later, I was overjoyed to know we were having another child. I began to plan for Erin's little sister. But at six months, something went very wrong! She stopped moving! I knew something was wrong, and soon we were having a funeral with a very tiny casket to be placed in the ground. The heartbreak I felt went on for months as I tried to figure out what I had done wrong, what we had done wrong that God would take my baby girl. I knew, at thirty-seven, my internal clock was ticking. But I longed for another baby. Erin wanted a baby brother or sister, as many of her friends were blessed with them. I didn't give up. Faith began to come into play again. I got pregnant. But sadly, it lasted only two weeks.

Twice more it happened, and by this time I was nearing forty. The doctors began to show me all the statistics of what could go wrong. I changed doctors. My new doctor offered genetic counseling. But I refused, and it was okay with him. After I called the 700 Club and prayed with them and others, my faith was finally rewarded with the most beautiful baby boy in the world. I called him my miracle child. I felt my faith was rewarded in, yet another miracle and dream come true.

He grew into a very musical, agile, athletic guy, loving martial arts and video games with challenges. He was very bright and excelled in school. He was kind yet very introspective, careful in every decision he made. As he grew, he began to know pain as relationships turned sour a few times. But he was blessed to have some great friends who supported him 100 percent. He became a Christian, and even though he turned away from God when Erin left us for heaven in 2006, he told the chaplain at Emory when he was diagnosed with leukemia that he came back to God and trusted Him for his healing. I did too.

But after twenty-four years, nine months, and six days, God decided to take David back to heaven. I have read that children are a reward of the Lord. But what if He takes them back? Does the reward get taken away from you? Children are your crown in old age. But mine is bereft of my children. Is my crown bereavement? Is that my reward for exercising my faith? I cry out to God. I don't understand. Did He hear my pleas for David's healing? Did He even hear me? Or did He hear me and turn away? Has He forsaken me because of some sin I've committed? Or did I just presume on His grace and presume I was special to Him? I keep trying to sort it all out as the tears flow continuously for my children. Burying children is not right! It's not! And why all mine? Wasn't one enough? Yes, I am full of questions. But I can't ask them of God. So I ask them of the wind. I ask them of my little goat that watches me outside as I bawl, crying out with the pain I feel inside. I ask them of the great oak trees that will be here when I'm gone. Were my children not as important as that tree? The point is that I stretched my faith and kept trying to have children when most would have given up. And it was rewarded. But only for a few years, and then the thing I had faith for was taken so abruptly away, leaving me emptier than if I'd never had children.

People say, "You've done this before. This will pass. You'll get better." But *no*, I haven't been this way before. I haven't buried all my children before. And no, this won't get better on this earth. How could it? David can't come back to me. I can only go to him. I don't want to have bitterness of soul, but I am skirting the edge of it right now. God, please help me!

DAY-90

•••••••••●••••••••

Good versus Evil

Most of chapter 24 of the book of Job is spent discussing the justice (or seeming injustice) of the prosperity of evil ones. Job went into intricate details about those who perpetrate crimes and still live a life of prosperity. Often, those people prey on the innocent, the poor, and the dejected. And yet no matter how corrupt they live their lives, they still live a long and sometimes-prosperous life, knowing no loss or grief. I identify with Job's feelings. Some have sat in my house and expressed the same ideas of why those who are good and try to do the right thing are hit with affliction after affliction, without cause or reason. And nearby are others who have given themselves to selfishness, greed, and living whatever life they pleased, indulging in self-gratification even if it's drug use, alcohol addiction, pornography, of mistreatment of others. Yet we see them living the life, knowing no affliction, no pain, still prospering on the corporate ladder of success. There is little understanding of why some who are good are taken and others who are not. It is a question that I have seen repeated time after time. Is there justice in this life? Is there equality among men, truly? Of course, many would say that the evil ones will meet their just reward after death. But what about this life? Isn't life a gift from God? If so, then why are some taken and others less worthy left? There are so many questions and so few answers. We know that God sets great store by justice. Somehow, in the grand scheme of things, there is truly an answer. But we may have to wait to hear it when this life is finished.

Job chapter 19 (KJV) says, "And Job again took up his discussion and said, 'Oh, that I were as in the months of old, as in the days when God watched over me, when His lamp shone above and upon my head and by His light I walked through darkness; as I was in the prime ripeness of my days, when the friendship and counsel of God were over my tent, When the Almighty was yet with me and my children were about me.'"

Job longed for the days when all was right in his world. I long for those days, too, when there was such busyness that I stayed tired all the time. I even long for that good tiredness that comes from being busy with my children. I long for the justice of God and for the days when He watched over me and His friendship was so near.

Berry and I went to see a movie today, *The Avengers: Civil War*. David would have wanted to see that one. As I walked out, I noticed the posters for upcoming movies that I knew David would have planned to see. In the movie, I saw the exercise bars that are used in rehab, and my mind flashed back to those days when David was learning to use his legs and arms again after nearly dying in ICU in January of 2015. I remember how hard it was for him to walk, how he struggled with the exercises, like holding on to that bar and trying to make it around it a few times without his legs buckling. He fought so hard to come back from that near-death experience. He was still fighting, still going to rehab here when we got the word that the cancer had returned. It's so unfair. I want the justice for fighting so hard for my children to even know God, taking them to church, sitting and praying with them, teaching them Bible verses, making sure they had every advantage in this life, even sacrificing my own wants and needs so often for them. I don't regret any of it! But where is the justice? Why did I have to bury them before they even had children of their own, my grandchildren, my heritage? What is there now? What is my purpose? How do I go on breathing each day? I mourn! I mourn!

DAY-95

Signs Keep Coming

I went to eat with my sister, her daughter, and her grandson today. Being with her at her big dinner party last week was too much, so I asked for a more private luncheon. It was nice to hold the baby and see the sweet smiles. Judy, my sister, has been a strong support for David, Berry, and me through this whole ordeal. She is the first one we call when there's a crisis. And she always comes. I am thankful to have her in my life. She is fifteen years younger, so she has always been more like a daughter. When she was little, around three, and I'd come home from college in Tennessee, she'd always cry when I left. We bonded at an early age in her life. So no matter how painful, it was important to me to celebrate her birthday.

Driving home, I heard a new song by Toby Mac. David loved heavy metal music, and some other genres as well. But most of the Christian music I loved he felt was much the same. I was surprised when he told me he liked Toby Mac. This song today was the first new one I'd heard from TM in quite a while. It was called "Move." The lyrics begin by talking of heartache and how, sometimes, we go through times when we feel God hasn't heard our prayers or responded. That's how I have felt. As I read Job today, I know he felt that way too. In Job 30:19–20 (KJV), Job says, "God has cast me into the mire, and I have become like dust and ashes. I cry to you, Lord, and You do not answer me; I stand up, but You only gaze indifferently at me." Job had issues similar to what I feel each day now. I keep waiting for something. I don't know what! Some direction must come eventually. But I wait. I don't even say I hope, for that is far from me right now. I search for signs. I wrote a letter to David in my journal two nights ago. I asked him to send me a sign that only he and I knew about. I don't know if it was the song. But Erin used to send me songs that were unmistakably from her. So I felt the song was from him, because the only Christian artist I knew he liked was Toby Mac. So I'll take it as a sign!

The Emptiness
The silence is deafening, the place where you were
I glance in your room as I walk by your door
The TV is silent, there's no music's roar

DAY-101

· · · · · · ● ● ● ● **●** ● ● ● · · · · · ·

Reaching Out

I learned after our Erin left for heaven than when you can reach out, sharing does bring a measure of healing. I have tried desperately to do that now in the early stages of this new grief but have been unable to lift a finger to help someone else, as I am in the throes of suffering so intensely. But today, on Memorial Day, I decided it was time and gave some money, along with a random-act-of-kindness card with Scott's name on it, to a friend in need. As we stood together at the cemetery and she shared in my grief, it felt good to give back. As I was driving away from the cemetery on a small side street in Colbert, something fell from a huge oak tree and crashed onto my windshield. I had to stop the car to see what it was, and it was a huge sprig of mistletoe that had fallen from a high branch. Since it landed on my side of the windshield, I took it as a sign from my children that they were sending kisses from heaven to me. Previously, I had gone by my sister's house to leave some lily bulbs that Erin had planted and wanted to share. Judy presented me with a gift, a beautiful necklace she had found in a shop on a recent trip. It had the little slogan that David said each night when I hugged him good night, "I love you more." Such a treasure! I felt I had been rewarded over and over for finally being courageous enough to reach out to another. This was my Facebook entry for today. I believe in posting the good, the bad, and the ugly. Such is the face of grief. Some days are better than others. I have found that people (and especially the younger generation) really want to hear the truth, unfiltered, just as it is, with no sugarcoating.

Pit day. I ventured out alone to shop. I don't know if it was a mistake or if I needed that time to cry in the car. Passing by familiar places that David and I went together, seeing the Sonoma display in Kohl's, grabbing a burger at Steak 'n Shake because I knew he loved that place, handing the server an act of kindness with a "David remembrance card" for the car behind me. Such is life when you grieve and miss your boy or girl. Tears, memories, life…

DAY-103

•••••••••●•••••••••

Gardens, Distractions, and Hope Deferred

There is something about staying busy that helps me. It must be the distraction from the overwhelming thoughts that race through my mind night and day. I have always loved the out-of-doors. During childhood, I remember following my dad around the fields, woods, and pasture at the homeplace. My dad was an avid gardener, always in the field, hoeing out the crops before and after work. So it must make me feel closer to him since he left this earth some years ago. I find myself humming or singing as I work so hard with my hands in the dirt! It refocuses my attention on something other than the sadness of my existence. And even though I mourn the fact that my children aren't here to enjoy the "fruits of my labor," maybe if I can leave a little beauty behind at my little corner of the world, the work will serve two purposes.

As June approaches today, I know that soon it will be too hot for me to be outside much. Early mornings are still cool now, so that's when I love to water plants and work the soil. But I know all too well that when the day is hot and I must be still, the grief will come and sit by me the rest of the day. It's never far away. Is grief a spirit that taunts the soul and agonizes the mind? I don't know. But I know that as much as we love, that is how much we grieve. It's not something we can pack neatly away in the back of the closet and revisit when we want. Its waves rush over us at unsuspecting times, often knocking us completely off our feet. There is no warning light flashing, no "Danger ahead" signs. It just hits! Sometimes it's a gentle wave, just washing over our soul. Sometimes it is a full-blown grief tsunami that puts us in bed or sends us hiding as we weep and howl. For me, it can be as simple as remembering the tiny little mole behind my David's right ear. Or it can be as soul crushing as refusing to even think of Christmas and the future, even one day ahead, for fear it will totally crush me to powder. It could be the clothes still hanging on the hook at the entrance to David's room, the unwashed bedding that still holds his scent, the Disney coffee cup that he always used, or that half-bottle of shampoo that I used when I washed his hair as he lay across my bed when he was too weak to take a shower. The memories are endless. And I thank God for everyone, even the ones that bring pain. After burying your child(ren), they bring fondness, but they also bring great pain because you want to be making more!

Three hours outside! It wears me out! But it refreshes my soul. It always has. I think I was born to be outside! I replanted my two little rows of corn and one tiny row of green beans. My one large tomato and two small plants are thriving. But the deer have eaten the tops off my few stalks of corn from the first planting and several of my sunflowers. So I will try again! That's just who I am! That's why I had David at forty-three! Brenda, the woman who never gives up! Or does she? How many times do I get knocked down and get back up again? Unlike Job, I buried my children years apart. It didn't happen all at once. Years ago, I dealt with rejection repeatedly. I battled depression. But I always got back up after the pit experiences. But now, after burying all three of my natural-born children and one stepson, is it even worth getting back up again?

As I walked from my veggie garden to my David garden to work on the retaining wall again, I heard a bird singing loudly. I told him, "Keep singing!" I used to walk my yards early every morning, and I'd tell them to sing with me. I'd sing praises to God or quote my favorite "battle" verses during the times David was home from Emory, recovering. I was in battle mode, getting my praise on and arming myself with the Word of God, abiding in Him, as John chapter 15 tells us to. But now I don't sing when I'm out there. If I do, it's an old, old song from my childhood, like "Farther Along" or "No Tears in Heaven." I love the Brooklyn Tabernacle choir's rendition of "I Never Lost My Praise." But I can't sing that honestly now. The words resonated in my mind as I walked today, and I found myself saying them. "I never lost my hope. I never lost my joy. I never lost my song. But most of all, I never lost my praise." Then I reprimanded myself because I said, "It's a lie if I sing that now." I have lost my joy, my song, and my praise. Then I came to hope. Hmm? I thought that if the Bible says, "Christ in you is the hope of glory" (Col. 1:27 KJV), then, as a Christian, filled with God's spirit, which is Christ (which means "anointing"), can we ever really lose our hope? I don't see it. I can't even think of the future right now without a total emotional wreck. So where is the hope? I know it's there somewhere. But it eludes me! It's hard to see hope of a future when you have buried all your children. It's hard to see anything ahead but sorrow of heart and soul, at least in this life. I have hope beyond the grave. But what about hope for this life? Where is that?

DAY-104

• • • • • • • • ● • • • • • • • •

June 2, 2016
Questions

Questions still torment me. Was my faith too weak? I thought I had all the answers. Thinking my faith was strong, knowing God answers the prayers of the righteous should have been enough. But it wasn't! It wasn't! As I read in Job today, I realize God ultimately decides. He brings or allows these happenings. He knows the way we will take. He knows we "shall come forth as gold" (Job 23:10 KJV). Well, gold is tried in the fire until it is pure. The fire for me is very hot right now. Someone once said, "God knows the exact time to bring the 'gold' out of the fire just as those who work with gold do. If it is left too long, it is ruined. If it is not in the fire long enough, it is not pure." So I wait and wait until my change comes.

Years ago, I was told by a trusted spiritual friend that I must not question God. I have been careful about doing that. And yet there are so many unanswered questions that plague me. And many of them are of a spiritual nature that only God can answer. In all my searching for answers, thinking back to what I know of the Bible, I recognize many of the great heroes in the Bible questioned God. I do not question the sovereignty of God, or his great knowledge, which is too vast for a mere human to comprehend. But I do question, when I have done all that I have been taught or know about praying the right prayers or standing on the promises made in the Holy Scriptures to every believer, what happened to my children. If I did it all right, then why was there not more miraculous healings? Why are they not here as a testament of God's holy grace to mankind? Instead, my prayers ended in the death of my children.

As I read the thirty-eighth chapter of Job today, I saw God's answer, His first response to Job's misery. He told Job that his four friends spoke without knowledge, which led me to believe that much of what people may think about our situation is probably said without knowledge. Then he began a discourse that lasted through two chapters. The surprising thing is that the whole of it is questioning Job. So might God be, in turn, asking us questions? Is it true, as some have told me, that God is big enough to handle our questions? Of course, I, along with others, would never want to anger God. I have thought sometimes that maybe it was that I had angered Him that is why I am left with no children, bereft of my heritage on this earth. But again, that would be a question, wouldn't it?

DAY-105

· · · · · · · · ● · · · · · · · ·

Crying Gets the Grief Out

After our Erin left for heaven in 2006, I cried so hard that my eyes swelled shut. My eyes overflowed with floods of tears day after day. After a couple of months, David told me it really bothered him to see me cry so much. So I would often ride to the cemetery and just wail and get it all out and come home until the next wave of grief. It was a plan that helped him, and so it worked. Now it's been 105 days since he left for heaven, and those floods have invaded my soul once again. Only now it's just Berry and me. We often just cry together. When one of us starts weeping, the other is soon to follow. I read once that crying gets the grief out, so it's good to cry. It's a vent for the soul-wrenching pain that is here to stay.

Yesterday my dear aunt and cousin, Joy and Tierra, came by with a bountiful supply of fresh veggies. They have been so good to stand by our side, often making the long drive to Atlanta when David was in the hospital, to transport Berry home, bring things we needed, and even help at the end, help us move home. Tierra volunteered to housesit for us. It was such a relief and comfort while we were struggling. We sat yesterday around the kitchen table, sharing stories and gardening tips, and of course, David came up in the conversation, as he always will as long as I have breath. Somehow, I shared how we used to wash his hair with him lying across my bed when he was too weak to take a shower. Then the flood of tears started. I could tell by the look on their faces that they shared my pain. No words were necessary. Joy kept David from the time he was three months old until he was nearly four, when he started pre-K. She and her girls, Tierra, Angela, and Nakena, loved on David, and he really loved them back. They have a special bond with him. But when I have a breakdown and the tears flow so hard, I feel a twinge of guilt that I am making others sad.

Last night my lifelong friend Janice Henderson Smith called to check on me. She and I spent our young years in church together and doing all kinds of activities that made fond memories. She has always been there for me. She is suffering so with many health problems now. But she takes the time to check on me. What a friend! But as we talked, I shared that last week with David and all that transpired until he left us for heaven. I began weeping uncontrollably as I shared. But you know what? She began weeping with me. She was sharing my pain and sorrow. That's a friend! I know she, too, has known great sorrow. But she is a giver and a blessing in my life.

DAY-110

........•......

The Whisper of God

Grief shakes the very foundations of your existence. It shakes your mind first with the numbing shock of the unexplainable loss. It shakes your body as you struggle with your soul. It shakes your soul to the core of your being as the emotional roller coaster takes you into breathtaking dives after you finally think you might have your bearings. It shakes the spirit, the very depth of who you are, which includes your faith. What you believed is put to the ultimate test. Is it real, or did I believe a lie? If you have had a relationship with God, it is shaken. Many never recover. Some decide to go at it alone without the help of the Almighty because they blame Him for their loss. Such is not my case. I never blamed God. I did question His reasons for taking David after the battle and the many victories won along the way. I did question that since I had given Him my time and was so devoted to Him, loved Him with every fiber of my being: Why would He turn His back on me in that darkest hour? He never turned His back. But I felt that way. I know that God is omnipresent. Had I missed his plan for me along the way? When Erin left us, my faith was shaken. But I don't think it was shaken then as much as now. I wondered where heaven was. All my life I had been in church and had studied the Bible and spent many, many hours in prayer. I knew the scriptures. But I had never been faced with death like this, with separation from those closest to me. A child's death is like cutting off a leg or arm. Where was Erin? Where was heaven? Is it just past a star in the farthest sky? Or is it just a breath away? Because I knew the scriptures, I finally concluded that "to be absent from the body is to be present with the Lord." And where is the Lord? The Bible says He is limitless, omnipresent, beyond our comprehension. Then I realized that heaven is just a breath away. My children are right beside me, probably much of the time. Since Jesus, upon resurrection, could see, talk, taste, walk (even through walls), and feel, then if they are "present with Him," they can do those things too. It's mind-boggling to delve into the spirit realm.

None of this takes away the pain of loss. It does bring comfort. Since I went through this agony with Erin, it seems to be something I don't struggle with concerning David.

I have only permitted myself to read Job. That is my spiritual task. I am starting the book over since I finished the last chapter, hoping to find something I missed. I kneel beside my bed each day and recite the Lord's Prayer. But there are moments when I just seem to cry out of my spirit to hear from God. I haven't "heard" anything until this morning. After I watered all my plants and weeded my garden and was about to go back inside, I felt that whisper of God telling me to go and pick a few blackberries. As I walked to the wild blackberries at the edge of my yard, I passed my little daylilies, which were, surprisingly, blooming. They weren't yesterday. But today they were. I whispered, "Thank you, God, for showing me this beauty." As I picked a few blackberries and ate them, I felt God speak to me. The tears washed down my face as I heard His voice for the first time since February 12. He said, "David's destiny here was finished, complete. It was time for him to go. If I had not given him to you, you would not have survived losing Erin. But that was not the only reason he was here. He was my prophet, there for a season. If you think back on what he said, you will see. Have you ever thought maybe the last girl was not the one for him but he was the one for her? He showed her a love she had never known nor ever will the rest of her life. People come into your life for a reason. Let me comfort you. I have brought more people into your life since David's passing than many people see in a lifetime. I have heard every prayer, saw and recorded every single tear." That was a summary of what I "felt" he said to me. I couldn't remember it all. But maybe this was the first day I was even open to hearing Him, when all the time I felt He did not hear my prayers and have said as much in the last few days. Even though I am still full of questions and anger at what He had to do, maybe I am opening to Him again.

DAY-111

• • • • • • • ● • • • • • • •

Silence

As I ride down the road and gaze all around,
One thing is missing: a single sound.
The sound of my children gone all too soon
Screams in my mind and echoes in my soul.
Life as I knew it came to a halt.
It left me reeling, spinning, and thrown into the dark.
The past vanished as a vapor.
The future darkened with fog.
The present is filled with a fight to survive.
Yes, the silence engulfs me.
The place they once stood.
It speaks to the brokenness
Of grief and motherhood.

DAY-112

My Dad

It might seem strange to mention my dad in my grief story. But to fully understand a person's story, it helps to know something of their past. My dad was an awesome man. His biography would have been one that many would love to read. I could even see a movie made about his life. He came from very humble beginnings, having grown up as one of ten children living by a river. Their only mode of transportation when he was small was by boat to a neighbor's or by foot. I remember, fondly, his laughter as he shared stories of his childhood from his hospital bed when he had to have his heart checked. He said he and his brother had accidentally fried a chicken when they were burning a pile of brush his mom had piled for them. It seems the neighbor, who was an ornery man, owned the chicken and it had wandered into the brush pile before they set the fire. Of course, the neighbor was furious and chased them. So they went to hide for a while till things calmed down, not realizing the chicken had hidden in the brush pile. It was an accident. But it was funny to him just the same. He laughed out loud, something he rarely did.

Daddy had a pioneer spirit. He quit school after the sixth grade because he was tired of walking barefoot the many miles to school in the winter. When he was in his late teens, he decided to leave home and join the CCC camps. He went out West to help build roads. His sisters told me he would send them little trinkets, one being the tail of a rattlesnake! Since the family was very poor, Daddy came home and bought them the first store-bought bedroom suite they had ever owned. My aunt recently gave it to my sister. This story made it a true treasure. Daddy then joined the Army Air Corps, serving in WWII in the South Pacific arena. He told us stories of being shot at by the Japanese on an island there. He also said the islanders' children would bathe in mud puddles and only ate rice and fish. He never really liked rice since they had eaten so much of it when he fought there.

He taught himself to play guitar and was quite good. Often, he'd sit at the foot of our bed (my sister, brother, and I slept in the same bed when we were small) and sing songs like "Mr. Froggy Went a-Courtin'." He'd sing several songs to us at night. There was always music in my home growing up. We had piano and almost every kind of stringed instrument, and yes, we even learned to blow on a comb. Daddy would make whistles for us out of canes growing in the fields. I can still almost hear him whistling as he did when he worked outside with his gardens and animals.

Sundays were always special days growing up. We'd get dressed and go to church, enjoying the company of friends and family. There would be a big Sunday dinner, often shared with the pastor and family, or others who would come to visit. Mama always cooked a big meal, with a luscious cake for dessert. Sometimes Daddy would surprise us with a cake he had made, like his walnut cake made with cracked black walnuts from the big tree outside. Then we would have the afternoon naps, then back to church on Sunday nights. It was such a wonderful day.

When I had my own family, I held on to these traditions. Often, the children would bring their friends home with them from church, or they would go and visit them. Things began to change when people started eating out on Sundays. Somewhere along the way, the big Sunday dinners with visitors got lost by the wayside. We went to a church that was about ten miles away, and we were there for every service, two on Sunday, Wednesday-night prayer meeting, every night when we'd have revivals, and often to help work around the church. We'd fall asleep coming home, and Daddy would pick us up and carry us inside to bed. I remember his strong arms around me, making me feel so safe.

I never worried about danger when I was growing up, because I knew Daddy would take care of anything that came. Once, when we came home at night from a church service, my sister and I were undressing. We still had our slips on, but we saw someone peeking in our bedroom window. We ran and told Daddy, who promptly got his shotgun and slipped quietly out the door and around to the back of the house. One of the neighbor's sons was there at the window, and when he saw Daddy, he froze dead in his tracks! Daddy simply warned him, that he better get on home and not come prowling around again or he might be in jail!

Daddy was an avid hunter and fisherman. He worked very hard doing carpentry work and planting a garden every year. But when he had a little downtime, he could always be found in the woods, by a river, or in a pond. I miss my dad. I used to follow him around the fields and woods, learning the name of every tree and plant, learning how to care for animals and plants. If it was a little muddy, I'd step in his big footprints. When I got tired, he'd carry me on his back. He taught me many things, like the love of the out-of-doors, love of animals, gardening, and family. He taught me how to be close to the God, who created all these things. He taught me of a father's love, which I carry with me to my dying day. My daddy's in heaven now. All my children are with him. Do you see why I long to go there? Do you see why I grieve?

DAY-116

•••••••••●•••••••••

Layers

Grief has many layers. In the next few segments, I will share a few of them.

Unfinished business is a huge layer of grief for a grieving parent. This was an issue when Erin left us so suddenly for heaven. Erin was just starting life. She was a newlywed after just less than five years. They were in their first home. She was beginning to master some great recipes for dinner. She was learning how to shop and be frugal with her spending. No children had arrived, although she wanted them. She had mentioned beginning college just before she passed. She was a protector of sorts for her baby brother, always making sure he had what he needed. She would have been there by his side when he got sick. I'm sure of it!

And now, with David, I think it is even more of an issue since he was still living at home, had not gotten his career started, and was not married. I still am delaying looking through his things. Of course, on occasion I moved something in a room other than his and find something that he alone could have left there. And the pain is so strong, the loss so great! I find I am unable to deal with the grief of it. So I put it away for another time. His clothes still hang where they were, except for the few that we took to the hospital, which are clean and neatly folded in his room. The bed he got out of on January 29 to go for what we thought was only a doctor's visit remains unmade, just as he left it. There are diabetic supplies on the desk beside his bed, the pen and needles just as he left them, a few alcohol swab packets lying on the little bedside stand along with his remote control and gaming controller. His back scratcher is on his desk, along with his antinausea medicine and a few other meds. His PlayStation 4 and accessories are still packed in the bag from the hospital, untouched yet. I did lay one of the long-stemmed roses that were on his memorial spray across his desk. The rose dried and remains after these few months as a reminder of the difficult journey that was filled with love.

Caregiving adds another layer to grief. Some days I think, *I need to make another rehab appointment.* Or *I must change the dressing on the scar on his leg or get another Band-Aid for the scar on his nose from being in ICU in 2015.* I told him these were battle scars, and even if they didn't go away completely, he'd have something to show his friends later. He had a huge scar on his back where there was a hole from being in ICU so long. It had finally healed but was blistering up a bit since he hadn't felt well the last few months. Being a caregiver bonds you in new ways to your loved one. We were closer than ever since I helped give his medical care the last two years. And now it still seems I have unfinished business to keep caring for him, as crazy as that sounds. We fought together, his dad, him, and me! We fought hard to save his life. He fought hard! That's why it makes no sense to me that he didn't win this battle, this last long battle! It seems unreal. It seems he needs to still be here, doing the things he did, living the life that was ahead for him. Unfinished business! It's a prominent thought when your child was so young!

This is a great picture of the two of them at Stone Mountain, Georgia. We loved out little trips with the children. Hearing a child's laughter and seeing the joy on their faces when you travel to new places is priceless. What fun and laughter we had! The past never leaves us. It is indelibly printed on the heart. A grieving mom is often taken back to those days of the past. I can be cleaning and find a toy or a little outfit I saved from their baby days, and the tears will flow as I remember the magical moments. This layer of grief is filled with mixed emotions because, while we love and fondly remember all the days of our child's life, it brings such sadness that there are no new memories being made. I am finding it very hard to look at the portrayal of lives of friends and family on social media and all their smiling faces as they make new memories with their families. I am happy for them. But it reminds me of all that I am missing.

DAY-120

· · · · · · · · ● · · · · · · · ·

Grief Affects Everything

Grief affects the body, soul, mind, and spirit. When the first "knock on the door" or "word" announced that Erin, Heather, David, and Scott had left us for heaven, it seemed my soul or emotional self switched to survival mode. When the doctor told us from Heather's ultrasound that she was gone, I was struck with disbelief! It was so hard to wrap my head around it all. It took weeks to even begin to grasp the reality.

We got a knock on the door to inform us Erin had left us so suddenly, without any warning! As we drove to her house, I didn't shed a tear. When we came home and I knelt beside her bed in her old bedroom, I sat on the floor with a notepad and planned the whole funeral without a tear. And if you know me, you know that is totally out of character for me! I cry at everything. Now I know that I was in shock. I have heard that to preserve yourself, your mind goes into survival mode and the emotions are held at bay for a time. There was no sleep for me for at least seven days. When the tears did start, they didn't stop until my eyes were swollen shut. My friends came and tried to get me to eat, but there was no appetite for some time. At first, I didn't want to eat because I knew Erin wasn't eating. It was weird, the things that ran through my mind. When I finally "crashed" and slept that night, it was a deep sleep. But as I awakened to the bird singing outside my window, the anger welled up inside me. Nights were hard. Going to sleep was hard. Staying asleep was harder. And waking up might have been the toughest because you had to face the nightmare all over again. About two weeks after the memorial, I was sitting in my chair, and suddenly, I felt that I couldn't breathe, couldn't go on, and couldn't live without Erin. It was a strange feeling, the panic attack that hit me so suddenly! But then, as I lifted my eyes, I saw David sitting on the couch and Berry in his chair. I knew then that I had to stay here for David and Berry. So I fought a little harder to overcome the panic and fear of an unknown future.

When we got the call about Scott, my first thought was to get to him! Berry thought we should wait to drive down. But I felt an urgency to get to him. So we quickly packed and drove through rain in the dead of night to get to his bedside, only to see him hooked up to life support. It was a hard thing to see, our handsome, strong son hanging by a thread to life. I kept questioning the doctors, even when they said there was no hope, no brain activity. Keeping hope alive was my goal. Scott's wife was sick and in a hard place, so I wanted to be sure he got every chance that was available. Berry stayed by his side most of the time we were there in the little ICU cubicle. David sat in the waiting room most of the time, not wanting to witness this horrendous sight, even though he cared for Scott deeply. It was hard for anyone to see. Berry questioned everything, too, and wanted the Army to do a full investigation. He still questions the events surrounding Scott's passing. I can tell he has no peace about the way the investigation was held. Scott was my stepson, Berry's second son. But he had been in my life since he was nine, and I loved him deeply. To think he was gone just days before he was to retire from the military took its toll on all three of us! Berry's health declined afterward. He found sleep was a way of escape. But he still gets angry when he thinks back on the events of that day. The Tragedy Assistance Team visited us several times and kept in contact. They assured us that Berry could open a new investigation anytime he felt the need. But he hasn't pursued it yet.

David's passing was different because he had been diagnosed with leukemia without any forewarnings. We had dealt with shock and fear of the unknown on many occasions in the two years of his treatment. He almost left us exactly a year after he was in ICU for a lung infection. He went into respiratory failure then and was given a fifty-fifty chance of surviving. But after much prayer from many people and God's grace, he survived. He came through with many scars, both physically and emotionally. He was in the rehab hospital for three months and in rehab to recover strength at home until the time he passed. He fought. We fought. And yet in all that happened, even the many times they called a code MET, I never believed for a second he wouldn't survive. Never! So when they moved him to ICU just after he had finished that last round of chemo to treat the new onslaught of leukemia, I wasn't alarmed. I knew we had the best hospital and the staff would do whatever it took to help him. I stood by his bed and told him, "I told you'd I'd get you help," after he had been in such pain on the oncology floor and the pain meds weren't helping. Little did I know that just a few hours later they would intubate him, his heart would stop and keep stopping until he was gone to heaven.

There are still days I walk into his room, pick up his pillow with his scent still on it, bury my face in it, and think, *He's not gone! He can't be! How can this be? We did all the right things! We got the best care! He fought so hard! He was so incredibly sick and in pain!* I think I am still in denial after 120 days. He was my baby, even though he was twenty-four. He was all we had left, our prodigy, our only heir, our love, our only surviving child! No, my mind still can't wrap itself around him being gone. I cry every day still, several times a day. I hurt physically to the point that I wonder how long I will be here. It's not a sickness; it's a heartache that affects every part of my body. I do get out of bed, simply because I can't sleep. Some nights I still toss and turn. I work in my garden to ease my pain. I do the routine chores of a housewife. But I don't take pleasure in anything. Like Rachel in the Bible, I refuse to be comforted. And I don't know if I will see comfort again in my life. It will take a true miracle of God to bring peace or comfort to me. If His grace allows, then it will come. If not, then I am done.

DAY-127

•••••••••●•••••••••

June 25
Past, Present, and Future

All parents' hopes and dreams become enmeshed with their children's. The future seems bright as you anticipate careers, spouses for the children, and the biggest of all, grandchildren to carry on your traditions, family name, and values. When I look at the future now, all I see is darkness. I know my Christian friends would reprimand me. But I speak only of the darkness of the future in this life. I know and am certain that paradise awaits every believer. When all your children have been taken to heaven and you are left here, it is a long, lonely road with no clear path ahead. All those hopes and dreams for the future have been dashed to pieces. Then there are all the things you taught your children and looked forward to teaching and advising them in the future that you feel is lost forever. There will be no grandchildren, no heirs to whatever material possessions you have collected and valued, no big family gatherings on holidays, nothing!

Looking at the future is bleak. Looking at the past is a mixed bag. On the one hand, you have a very thankful heart to have been blessed with your child for whatever few years you had. Those treasures and the memories of those days warm your cold existence immensely. On the other hand, looking back brings extreme pain. I can't even view the videos of the children, for fear it will send me reeling into the pit of grief so deeply I can't escape. Berry watched those of Erin just a few weeks after her memorial. He invited me and David to watch. I couldn't. If I had seen her sweet face speaking and breathing and walking, I don't think I would have survived! I really don't. And to this day, I haven't watched, and it's been over ten years. The past holds wonderful memories of a happy family and tons of fun, laughter, tears, joy, everything that a mom could want. But the sadness also brings thoughts that no new memories can be made in this life.

The present is a battleground. Waking up each new day to the reality your child is gone from this life brings pain. Going to sleep at night knowing you can't hug your child good night and their room is empty brings pain. Enduring the day, not knowing what will trigger the next onslaught of grief, brings uncertainty. Trying to find peace in the brokenness is a challenge. Friends calling or sending texts, wanting to help, brings another level of uncertainty. How will I handle it? Will I break down and cry again? Will they offer platitudes that just anger me because they can't possibly understand? Do they even care? Are they doing this just to appease their conscience, or is it to make me know they care? So many battlegrounds in the mind, soul, body, and spirit can send you reeling into confusion unless you guard your mind carefully.

DAY-133

••••••••●•••••••

July 1, 2016
Unconditional Love

I was born the second child of five. My older sister was a blond-haired, blue-eyed artistic, creative person who was very confident. I was redheaded, freckle-faced, musically inclined, and always try-ing to overachieve to make my parents proud of me. My brother, born two years after me, was a bubbly, people-loving person who was the center of attention in any event, loving people and loving life. My brother ten years younger was very introspective, studious, over-achieving, and kindhearted. My baby sister, fifteen years younger, was musically inclined, a people person, cute as a button, fiercely clinging to family and tradition to keep the family together after we all began to marry and leave home. I always felt the odd man out. It might have been the red hair that singled me out, although both my grandmothers had red hair. Or it might have been that I was sand-wiched between my parents' firstborn, whom they adored, and the first boy who was the much-cherished firstborn son. At times I felt I was not special to the family. So I overachieved in school, in music, in forcing myself to get through college. I was only the second one in my extended family to have achieved that goal.

If I was to find my place in life or in love, it came harder for me. Life always threw me a curveball. My first boyfriend joined the Navy and quickly found another love. My second boyfriend married my older sister. My third, in college, joined the Marines and we grew apart. The next one, I met in college and just knew he was the one. We planned to marry after he completed a two-year term in a missionary group going to Brazil. We had even investigated the married housing units in Texas, where he planned to go to seminary when he got back. And you guessed it! He married someone he met there. I fell head over heels with the next one who came along when I was in my first teaching job in a city an hour from home. He was "the one" (again!). But he disappeared one day, and the next thing I knew, I was seeing his wedding announcement in the local paper. Love just seemed to keep fleeing away from me. But just when I had about given up hope and was in my early thirties, a friend introduced me to this handsome young man who, incidentally, had gone to high school with me. We never spoke in high school, and here he was! It was a whirlwind courtship, and he didn't get away! Ha-ha! He always says he rescued me from being the proverbial old maid schoolteacher! He had been married twice before, and this sent my parents into fits! But he loved me and courted me ardently for four months and won my heart.

After three years, we were blessed to have our first baby, Erin Leigh. When the doctor laid her in my arms, I was both amazed and awestruck at this little miracle. She quickly had her daddy wrapped around her little finger. She loved him and me in a way we had never known before, that childlike love that knows no bounds, always forgiving, always there no matter what. She was part of each of us, and we clung together as if we were welded shut! Oh, what love the Lord blessed us with in this little girl! When we found we were expecting another little girl two years later, our hearts were so glad. We'd talk to her in my tummy, and Erin would lay her head on my stomach and feel the little bumps and hiccups. But Heather Lynn had to leave this earth before her little feet ever touched the ground. What heartbreak we felt! Berry said as he drove me home from the hospital that he was doubly heartbroken because she was a little girl. He loved his Erin! And Heather would have been right by his side as well. Then after three miscarriages and age creeping up on me, we were still blessed beyond measure when our little miracle boy was born when I was age forty-three. Perfect pregnancy, perfect boy! He wrapped me around his little finger. And so began another love affair of mother and son, like no love I had known before. Erin and I were forged together. David and I were one spirit. I do believe that. The love of a child is a love that can be compared to no other. It is as if God gives us this beauty to show us His love for us.

When I had to bury each of my children, I buried part of myself. I thought of Mary standing at the foot of the cross. Most people see her maybe weeping for a while and going on with her life. I see her grieving the rest of her life for the loss of her Son, who was God but was also part of her. I see the Father God as He had to turn away from His Son for that moment in time, which must have seemed like eternity. The earth quaked and split apart—so great was His grief. The sky turned dark. It was a dark moment in time when the Son of God bore the sins of the whole world. God Himself can't look on sin, so He had to turn away. To be separated from God even for a moment must have been the cruelest punishment of all, crueler than the whipping by the Romans or the nailing of his hands and feet. So God knew the pain I would suffer when I saw my children leave me for heaven. The love will never diminish. And one day I will hold each of them in my arms. But that love was my lifeline. Now Berry and I are alone. It's as if we are starting over. Only we are too old to start over. We had a wonderful life, a wonderful family full of joy and love. Now we are sad, cold, and alone. I do feel their presence around me. But if I could only wrap my arms around them just once more, tell them I loved them, see their eyes as they responded, kiss their cheeks, or walk with them and be with them, my heart would rejoice. But I wait for the day when my change will come.

DAY-138

•••••••••●•••••••

Cause of Death

It's strange, but it's in the shower that I get inspiration to write sometimes. This morning, my thoughts turned to the causes of all my
children passing. So I want to spend a few paragraphs sharing that
with you. Maybe some who are reading this have or will face a similar
circumstance. My hope is that you haven't or won't. But as I said to a
friend this morning, "Life is too difficult sometimes." And it is!

The second pregnancy was yet another dream come true. All
was well, and my little bump was moving around, hiccupping, letting me know she was there. I sang to her as I had with Erin. It was
a happy time. Erin was only two then, and she loved feeling the
little movement in my tummy. When we found out it was another
girl, my husband was so happy. How he loved his little Erin and
couldn't wait to meet this new bundle of joy as our little family grew.
Then on a Sunday, when Heather was only six months along, I felt
my stomach grow ice-cold. I thought that was odd. I hadn't been
sick. She had had the hiccups early that day. After church, I called
the doctor, and they had me come in. They did an ultrasound. My
youngest sister, Judy, went with me since my husband had to work.
When the nurse looked at it, she went to get the doctor. The baby
was not moving. They tried different angles, and there was nothing. I
felt the fear mount as I saw there was no movement. Then the fateful
words came, "I'm sorry, but the baby is gone!" I couldn't believe it!
How could it be that this little girl was gone when she was so much

214

alive earlier? I called my church and had them pray, still hoping for a miracle. We scheduled an appointment at the hospital to deliver the baby on Thursday morning. I didn't want to do that! If there was any chance she was alive, I wanted to give her that. I told the doctor I didn't want them to take her lest she was still alive! But after much prayer during the Wednesday-night prayer service, my water broke, and Heather was delivered naturally several hours later in the hospital. The doctors wanted to run some tests, only taking a small sample of tissue from the inner leg. But the sample didn't test well, so there was no answer to why my Heather didn't make it.

I was devastated. I didn't want to get out of bed. My husband had to manage all the details of the graveside service while I was still in the hospital. My baby girl was gone too soon.

Erin had, since she was a young teen, had problems with her back. She took OTC medications just to get her through the rough times. But she was a worker and worked after school, often standing for hours on concrete floors in stores and offices where she worked. The pain she endured sometimes sent her to the doctor, where they would prescribe whatever meds they thought would help. (In hindsight, I wish I had insisted they run more tests to find the root cause.) She was prescribed muscle relaxers shortly before she passed. But she had also had a root canal a few days earlier and was prescribed pain meds for that. The coroner felt she might have awakened in pain (her husband had to work late that night) and took her pain meds too close together. The autopsy report read, "Accidental overdose of prescription medications." She had visited our house that very day to use our fax machine for her husband's business. She did complain of her back hurting. But we never realized that that very night she would make her heavenly journey, which left us in shock and disbelief.

David's passing was totally unexpected, although he had battled leukemia for two years. We never, ever thought he wouldn't make it, because he was such a fighter. But after the leukemia came back along with lymphoma in his back, the chemo was just too much for his weakened body to handle. He left us after only two weeks in the hospital and after finishing his first round of chemo. It happened overnight, still suddenly to us. We were devastated.

Scott had been a career military man. He joined when he was just out of high school. He completed basic training in Fort Knox, Kentucky. Then he was sent to Korea for a time, then to Fort Hood, Texas. When the war came in 2001, he was deployed to Kuwait, then in the heat of the battle to Iraq. He came home after fifteen months. He married his sweetheart in Savannah, Georgia, where he was stationed at Fort Stewart. But he was soon deployed again to Iraq, and again a third time after a few months home. His last deployment to Afghanistan was different. He became sick with the flu while there. He also told us later that it was a "different" place to be, with so much uncertainty. There were battlefield missions that he could never talk about and we were careful not to question. When he finally arrived home to Fort Campbell in Kansas, he had to live away from his wife since she was keeping their newly purchased home for him until he was out. He was only a few months from retirement. He called his dad every night that last month but was fearful that they would come up with a reason to send him back overseas. He was also upset that he and his wife had to live apart. They had already made plans to move to Florida upon his retirement and live a good life together. He came home for Christmas, got up on a Sunday morning, and according to the Army's report, shot himself. He lived only a few days. We quickly went down to be with him and spend those last few days as he lingered between heaven and earth. It was so suddenly, so unexplained, so devastating. He had so much to live for. He was only forty-one years old! He was a strong, handsome young man who had accomplished so much in his life. Our hearts were broken in a million pieces as we laid our Scott to rest. We have never understood. Some said it was PTSD after being in the battlefield for so long. But we just can't know what happened to our Scott. We both talked to him on the long drive home the day before. He had made plans to stop by on his way back to Kansas. So there were so many unanswered questions!

· · · · · · · · ● · · · · · · ·

July 10, 2016
Where Two or Three
Are Gathered

Today is Sunday. It is quiet and cooler this morning as I hear the birds singing outside my window. Sundays are set aside for worship in my home. It always has been. But now it is different. I still hold the tenet of not doing any manual labor today as I have strived to honor the day. Even though my faith is thin, I still honor God; His holy Son, Jesus Christ, as my Savior; and the Holy Spirit, who has been my constant, my stability through all I have suffered. Though I fear God, I don't understand Him. Either He didn't hear my prayer (which I don't believe) or He chose to take David and all my children away from me, which feels so cruel and unjust, given all that I did to raise them as I felt He would approve. As Job said, there is no understanding, no wisdom. Only God knows these things.

When we left our last church in 2003, we began meeting with a home church group. Once again, we had the big dinners and fellowship. But even that seemed to fade with time as our little group began to disband. Now, Sunday service is watching a minister on TV and eating whatever we find until we find a new church. I resist becoming a part of a traditional church because I know the conversations held before and after about the children and grandchildren. Even the music makes me cry right now. But I still hold this day in reverence. David often would come in and join Berry and me as we watched the minister and gleaned from the Word he shared. We'd sometimes have lengthy discussions about the shared Word. Now that David is gone and Berry and I are struggling with life itself, we still try to watch a minister, even though we are in a fog right now. We have had visits from local church groups, and the people were so wonderful and kind. Right now, I just can't go to any social event because the tears don't stop, the pain so intense. So I wait. I don't even know what I am waiting for. But I will continue to reverence this day.

DAY-147

•••••••••●••••••••

Clearer Understanding

Sugar water is boiling on the stove as I prepare hummingbird food. I love seeing the little birds come to feed. I lie on my couch and watch the feeder in front of my porch as the many different species of bird come to eat. Since David left us for heaven, there is a new bird who has been coming. It's a small bluebird, so beautiful. Blue jays are a regular here. But I've never seen the little solid bluebirds. I read that bluebirds symbolize happiness. That is so apropos for what David is to me. He brought such happiness into my life. A mother-son relationship is so special and tender. I thank God every day for allowing me to have that wonderful guy in my life.

My thoughts were many as I got up this Sunday morning. As I read my daily chapter in the Bible, which is only in the book of Job now, I saw that God said He created the mightiest of creatures, Leviathan. Can man tame this great creature? Can man overpower the most powerful of creatures? God went on to say that man tries to control what God does when man cannot even control the creation of His hands. No, I don't understand God. My faith has been shaken to the core, but I cling to God. He knows what He is doing, although I do not. I'm holding myself away from Him, just staying close enough that I still feel His mighty presence in my life. But I draw back because I just can't understand what He was doing when He took David.

One of the many challenges for a grieving parent, especially when they have buried all their children, is staying alive. If you spent

219

most of your adult life caring for and raising your children, it became your purpose. When one of them becomes sick and you care for them as if they were a child again, that becomes the purpose for your existence as you struggle through the sickness with them, worrying, praying, seeking medical help, dealing with finances and all the other challenges that do not stop. When David left us for heaven after the long, hard fight against this disease, our lives came to a screeching halt. I heard a phrase on the TV that hit home with me. They said someone was "circling the drain" as they watched that person slowly die. This is a good description of a grieving parent, who is daily trying to find some reason to stay alive. But many days want to go and be with their children. I remember accidentally cutting my finger in those first few weeks after David left us. It was actually a relief, as it took my focus off my extreme sorrow onto a physical pain. This morning, I was thinking on that and could understand why some people might get into that cutting of the flesh. Don't worry! I don't want that for myself. I'm just saying that when you are "circling the drain," there are so many things that are understood by the pain you endure daily.

My understanding has been opened to many things now. I see how my dear friend Sarah, whom I met on a grieving forum, must have felt when her beautiful daughter, Lisa, was shot and passed away that night. Lisa was her only child. Her world was crashing and burning that night. Seeing her devastation in those first few months and worrying if she would survive brought me closer to her, trying to help her through the agony. But now I know I didn't really understand! We had lost our Erin, which turned our world upside down. But it was seeing David and knowing I had to remain here for him that brought me "back." When David left us after battling leukemia for two years, there was no one to bring us back. I knew how Sarah must have felt. The future was a fog, the past was bittersweet, and the present became a challenge for survival. I'm not minimizing our loss of Erin. To lose one child, even if you have ten more, does not make that loss less painful. But now I see the value of David being here for us to refocus. When there is no one left, it's almost like a ship set assail on a stormy sea with no anchor.

220

DAY-163

••••••••●•••••••

Avoidance

Survival depends on the will to face the truth and go forward. A grieving parent sees no "forward" when the future is buried with their children.

I find myself in avoidance mode right now. I am burying myself in endless tasks around my house. I am building gardens in memory of each child. Staining a concrete porch, painting rails, clearing out drawers and bookshelves, going through old movies, and doing any other job I can find is how I am avoiding facing grief. When I finish one job, I immediately make a list of others that need to be done. But the one thing I cannot do is move or clear away anything in David's room. I'm finding it harder to even go in there, except my daily trek to his bed and his pillow, where I bury my face to cry as I still smell his sweet scent, the scent of a body that I know held excruciating pain in the last weeks he was here on earth. I have talked with other moms whose children left this earth too soon. Some told me they simply closed the door to their child's room. One mom, our cousin June Bellew, said it had been eleven years and their child John Michael's clothing still hung in the closet and the room was just as he left it. John Michael was only eleven years old when he left for heaven suddenly during an auto crash.

Those watching us from afar only see us from the funeral forward. Some think we will just "get over it." It's far from that! I look at Facebook and see the big happy families pictured at the beach on vacations, at birthday parties, at their child's wedding, or the birth of their grandchild. I see the delight and joy that life is giving them. That only brings the sadness back, the questions of Why me? Why my children? I lay in bed this morning thinking why God would take all my children. There are no answers. I identified with Job when he rebutted his friends who were trying to convince him that he had sinned and brought this tragedy into his life. Job knew he had not sinned but repented anyway. He said he could, in turn, give advice to his friends. But that would not change what God did or would do. Summing up the chapter I read, Job said that in just a few years he would be gone, and his place would not be known anymore. And yet a spark of hope arose in my heart as I knew that God turned the captivity of Job and he did live a long and prosperous life. God gave him more children and riches. I am past the point of bearing more children. So I don't know how God could do that for me. No child could ever take the place of my sweet children. So I don't even know any plan that would work to breathe life back into me. But I'm not God!

DAY-166

· · · · · · ● ● ● ● ● ● · · · · · · ·

First of Many Challenging Days

My beautician gave me sage advice when I was struggling to design the perfect stone for Erin and couldn't bring myself to go. She said, "Just 'screw up your courage' and get it done." So I did! There were tears during the two-year design planning, but I did it! Today was another such day. I had to go to the dentist. That doesn't seem hard, does it? But for me, it was another challenge to walk into that office where I had gone with David and Erin so often over the past. David had to get a dental clearance just before transplant. So that was my last visit there. Then, when I sat in the hygienist chair, the first thing she said was, "How is your son?" Oh my! I thought they knew! But I told her and shared with her as the tears rolled down my cheeks. I knew they would. We shared much as she cleaned my teeth. Then the dentist walked in, and she didn't know either. So the three of us sat and talked for a while as I continued to cry. The dentist had lost her dad to cancer, and the hygienist had lost her dad, also, to cancer. Later, I found out their dental assistant had recently lost her husband to cancer. She and I later shared our grief when I had to have more dental work done. But they listened intently as I shared those last days and moments with David, interested in every detail.

It was a very emotional day, as I knew it would be. But Berry said I must take care of ourselves and these teeth that have been neglected for two years.

I know there will continue to be events that I cannot avoid in which I will have to "screw up my courage" to handle. As my dear friend Sarah and I have decided, "It is what it is." I will cry. I will mourn. If you happen to meet me in the store, don't worry if there are tears. They will continue until I am where my children are. I can't say now that life is good.

DAY-182

· · · · · · ● ● ● ● ● ● ● ● · · · · · · ·

August 19, 2016
Baring My Soul

Baring my soul. By now you know how I have struggled in my relationship with Father God since He chose to take my last surviving child, with whom my soul was interwoven. I have always been a prayer warrior, often praying for hours in the early morning, in the middle of the night, on my walks with God each day, and on my face as family and friends went through trials. Often in Atlanta, during the horrible days of David's treatment for leukemia, I'd go back to the hotel when Berry relieved me at the hospital and be so tired as I fell beside that hotel bed. Sometimes all I could say was "Help!" as I cried out to God to save my son's life. Many times, David would reach out his hand to me in the hospital and say, "Let's pray, Mama!" And we would. One night I witnessed him crying as I woke at midnight. He was struggling with the whys of having cancer. Then he started praying, which he rarely did out loud. But as he repented before God and even spoke to the cancer at the end of his prayer to leave his body (which it did, by the way!), my heart was weeping as we stood between life and death. I never stopped believing he would be healed, even when we came home between chemo treatments and I administered IVs, took him in and out of ARMC, our local hospital, for blood and platelet transfusions, and all the many tests and visits back and forth. When, after our victory of making it to the one-year posttransplant mark, the disease resurfaced in his back as a lymphoma. But we kept going the distance. And I kept believing, fasting, praying, getting friends to pray, often around-the-clock prayer chains. I sat in many waiting rooms outside different ICUs and offices and shared my faith with others. We never gave up! And yet God chose to take my son and all my children! I am called Job by some and Naomi by others (references to biblical people who suffered the loss of all their children). And I can't say that I don't have some bitterness in my soul. I am at a place where I don't know God like I thought I knew Him. I refused to pray or read my Bible for months after David left for heaven. Finally, I decided, if I was to be called Job, that I would read only the book of Job over and over until I had some answers. And yes, I identify with so much of what Job said.

As I read my chapter this morning, it was Elihu, the youngest of the four friends of Job, who was speaking. He had waited for the elders to speak, as was the custom in the land then. And his discourse was the longest. But one thing I noticed, as he attempted to "comfort" (or condemn!) Job, he mentioned *I*, *me*, or *my* fifty times! I concluded that his discourse was coming from his own education, his own ideas, his own thoughts about God and what, to him, was right or wrong. Like Job, I have concluded that God is God! We can sit with people, offering what comfort we know from our own experiences. But we can't explain why what happened to them happened. And no one can judge another by their own experiences. Job's friends were trying desperately to convince him that his sin had brought all this on him. We know later that God finally spoke to Job and told him that the words of his friends were not His words. Job concluded that wisdom is to fear God and understanding comes from departing from evil. No, I don't have answers. And I am probably judged by what I feel right now. But I do fear God. That's all I know. Still, I'm reading only Job.

August 24, 2016
Who Am I?

My identity is in question in my mind. Who am I? Am I still a mother even though my children have left this earth for heaven? Am I still a teacher although I retired seventeen years ago? Am I still a child even though my parents are in heaven? Does God still claim me even though He has wounded me to the core of my being? All these questions are rolling over in my spirit. It makes me wonder if all human beings' identity is contingent on their relationships, their jobs, their standing with God (of course, I do believe that without question!) or their accomplishments in life. Is this what Christ meant when He said, "Greater love hath no man than this that he lay down his life for the sheep" (John 15:13 KJV), or "He that loveth his life loses it and he that hateth his life will have it for eternity" (John 12:25 (KJV)? Is it all a comedy of errors, this life? Are we really just pawns in a master's hands? I do not believe that! I don't! I refuse to! Life has a purpose, even the bad events! My anchor holds! I've had crazy thoughts that even God had rejected me! I faced rejections early on in life. I always thought my mom loved my blond-haired sister, who was very artistic, more than me or my brother, who was closest in age to me because he was the first boy and was very outgoing, funny, and a real people person. I was the middle child, red-haired, who was shy and didn't really know what my talents were. There were several instances in my life that would exacerbate this feeling of inferiority and rejection that I felt. I eventually focused on my rewarding teaching career. My husband didn't arrive until I had been teaching nine years. We were blessed with a beautiful baby daughter, then another baby girl, who left for heaven before her feet stepped on earth, and then a baby boy, who was our miracle at forty-three! But God chose to take them all home. So my husband and I are bowed down with care now and wonder if our life is cut short and cut off. I could list a few more rejections, but I think that's enough to give you a picture. Has God rejected me? In my spirit I know it's a lie. In my natural man there are days when I feel that way. But I've decided that if my crushing, if my brokenness in losing my children, can produce some hope or help for some other struggling person, then I'll keep breathing

I'm walking down the aisles of a department store. I hear a little boy's voice from the past. "Mom, let's go to the electronics to look at video games!" I hear a little girl as she tugs on my shirt. "But, Mom, if you don't have enough money for this, just write a check!" I zoom past any aisle that has items that bring painful memories. But I can't escape it, the memories that are so vivid in my heart, memories of a mom with children and their friends around all the time, memories of birthday parties, softball games, school events, report cards, movies, church, pizza on Friday nights, and the list could go on to infinity! But I wipe my tears and check out with just the few items in my cart, a pair of socks, some paint for a well-worn lawn chair, a doily to hold one of the flowers from the funeral when I bring it inside for the winter. Such is my life now. It went from spring to winter. I went from an active mom for thirty-four years to a lonely wife whose husband is just as lonely for the children who were the light of our lives. Memories echo of a life full of life, echoes of the past.

DAY-211

•••••••••●•••••••••

Left Here Searching

A cousin stopped by yesterday. She had lost her own eleven-year-old son twenty-two years ago. And yet on the anniversary of his tragic death, she brought us a big pot of mums. I know she struggles with her own grief. Yet she stood in my kitchen and listened as I cried and talked of my children. As I talked, I restated a phrase that comes out of my mouth too frequently now. "Why am I here?" Of all my accomplishments in this life—pianist, church organist, college degree, advanced college degree, singer, teacher, world traveler, and other things—I consider being a mother my greatest accomplishment. I'm not saying I was the best mother. As a matter of fact, just yesterday I felt I had failed as a mother. I thought I had done everything right. I agonized over just the right decisions when our children were growing. When a mother buries her child, her heartbeat, what is left? What is my purpose in life now that my children are in heaven and I am left here? I search for that every day. Is this my sentence for some unrighteousness, to lose all my children too soon? Like Job, I am constantly searching for my sin, for what I may have done to displease Father God so much that He would choose to lay this horrible affliction on me. And I can find none. I'm not saying I am perfect! Oh no! But I can find none of the sins that were rewarded with great punishment. So every day I tarry on, heavy laden with grief and sorrow.

As a Christian, I know we shouldn't grieve as others who have no hope of ever seeing their loved ones again. That's what the Bible says. And yet I do! I even think some days that maybe God is through with me too. I worked for years in various churches. I taught school in underprivileged areas for twenty-six of the twenty-nine years I taught. I gave constantly to those who were in need. I spent hours on my knees, honoring prayer requests from others. I shared Christ with whoever was open to the gospel. I have been privileged to have a full and rich life. And now as I near the winter of my own life, have I done it all? Have I finished my course? Or is there yet another mountain to climb? Is there another fertile valley to dwell in for a season where I might find peace and contentment? Is there another soul who needs me to stay a while longer?

Watching basketball in the Rio Olympics yesterday, I heard an amazing story. The young woman who was helping the narrator was the top Olympian in the world in basketball. I listened as she narrated every move the athletes were making. At one point, she said, "When you are at this point, you must not be looking at the clock! You have to make the play." And she described the play. I got a great message from that. None of us know how close we are to the end of the game of life. And even if we are older, there are still battles to be won, life to be lived. So we must not stop to look at the clock! Play to the very last second with every ounce of strength in us! That's my message for today! I thought it was a pretty profound thought!

DAY-217

· · · · · · ●●●●●●●●●●● · · · · ·

Decluttering with a Busy Mind

After a restless night, I turn over only to feel the awful ache in my shoulder from my recent project of building a garden for my baby Heather. David's garden was almost complete, so I dived into this project, hoping to finish before first frost. Keeping my hands and mind busy helps. So I keep at it even when my body screams, "Stop! Rest!" But now it is almost finished, except for the middle six pavers that will support the little bench Berry and I got Sunday. I glanced at the clock to see it was only 4:00 a.m., and I was wide-awake. I tried to go back to sleep and failed. So I made my way to the bathroom to tame my long hair a bit. I decided to never cut my hair again because the ends of my hair touched David the last time I hugged him good night. Another crazy thing, I know. And knowing my preferences for short hair, I also know I will probably not hold to that promise to myself once my curly hair gets unmanageable (which is anytime now!). I dab on a little collagen to try to calm the deep wrinkles in my face that show the world the grief. Then I put on some work clothes and make my way to kneel at my bedside to recite the Lord's Prayer, which I do faithfully every morning, putting as much feeling into it as I can. I haven't come back to the full hour or two long prayers and walks with God yet. Prayer is still hard for me. I sat on the edge of my bed and read the thirtieth chapter of Job in the New

American Translation of the Bible. This is the fourth time through the book. To add a little variety, I am reading a different translation of the Bible each time through. Another book, called *The Insanity of God: A Story of Faith Resurrected*, is in my cache of daily readings. I guess I was drawn to it by the last part since my faith has been put to the ultimate test! I read a few pages and decided it was time to get moving. I did a few leg lifts and stretches to try to tone my sagging body, then it was off to the kitchen, where I decluttered the table and began my Friday work. Today I take a break from outside work to scrub my kitchen. So outcome the mop, bucket, and broom, and my day begins before 6:00 a.m. Here I am, at 6:30 a.m., taking a break with my cup of freshly perked coffee with hazelnut creamer. I try to move as quietly as I can so as not to waken my husband.

Always, when I am working, my mind is in overdrive. It wanders from the task, although my hands just keep working. This morning, as I mopped the floor near the outside door, the scene in my mind drifted to just a year ago, when my hubby and I had to help David make it to the car parked just outside the door. He was too weak to walk unassisted, and we didn't want him to fall. Then the scene drifted to yesterday, when I found out someone dear to us had gotten a good report that she was cancer-free. She deserved it! She had fought her own battle even as David fought his over the last two years. And she had won. Grief is selfish. I learned that while grieving our Erin. The question popped into my soul, "Why did this loved one beat cancer and David didn't?" How does God decide who lives and who dies? Why would he take a young person and let someone who is eighty or ninety live? I think of former president Jimmy Carter, who was at the same hospital as David. He was in his nineties, had brain cancer, and was put on a clinical trial and completely cured in six months! The unfairness of my son's passing began to overwhelm me as it does almost every day now. While I really want to rejoice with others who win the battle, I am constantly trying to understand the whys.

Yesterday I realized that I was heading into the anger phase of grief. I learned from Erin's passing that there are basically five categorized phases of grief: denial, anger, bargaining, depression, and acceptance. I never bought the acceptance phase. I will never just accept the passing of any one of my children. It's just not happening! And I know, from experience, that you don't just go through five phases of grief and get over it! You never get over it. And you go in and out of these phases, sometimes revisiting them multiple times at random! But yesterday, I was in my bedroom and looked over the little corkboard beside my computer stand where I keep appointment cards, notes to self, etc. There was a paper that said, "The Battle is Won!" I had had it there since David was first diagnosed. I think it came in some envelope from a minister. I held on to that for David, for us! And I believed it was won when David successfully received the transplant, when he survived a lung infection that almost took his life a month after transplant, when he came home, finally, after four months in Atlanta near the hospital after transplant. The battle was won! Or so I believed. Maybe it was just those battles and not the final, big one! I walked over to the little board, took the pushpin out of the paper, and began tearing it viciously into little pieces and threw it as hard as I could. I was angry, angry that David wasn't here, still going to rehab and recovering the strength that the chemo had sapped from his body and soul, angry that he wasn't here beginning a job, starting college, getting married, having my grandchildren, or having a life! I was angry that we had worked so incredibly hard to get him the best medical care, sacrificing whatever we needed to, only to have this horrible disease come back and rampage his body. I was angry that I had lost so much of my life and there is no way to retrieve it!

DAY-230

• • • • • • • • • ● • • • • • • • • •

And Life Goes On

How is it possible to miss someone so much that, at times, you can't even catch your breath? Life goes on. I see it all around me. People are still driving to jobs each day, shopping, partying, getting married, having babies, being grandparents, and getting ready for the holidays. Yet I am looking on at life through a dim window. I see heaven holding my children and all the joys that await me through a veiled window too. How is it possible to be here and not really be here? Can you tell me?

Tomorrow will be my sixty-ninth birthday. I pride myself on accomplishing, with God's help, a successful career, marriage, and beautiful family. I am biased, of course, but my children were very bright and beautiful in so many ways. I witnessed both whom I gave birth to loving the "underdog," going to bat for friends who struggled, worrying about the welfare of their family and friends, and giving sacrificially on several occasions. They were both very attractive people inside and out. I saw their Christian faith put to the test on several occasions. But they never denied it. They always stood up for Christ, and the Christ in them reached out. Never did I think that after all the worries, prayers, unconditional love on both ends, successes, and care of my children, I would be sixty-nine and childless on this earth. Never did I think that I would have no posterity to carry on the things I taught my children. Never did I think I would have no grandchildren to love in my old age. And yet here I am.

God has been gracious in sending friends, family, and even neighbors whom I had never met before into my path bringing comfort. And for that I am grateful.

My Facebook post yesterday went like this:

> *We enjoyed a day trip today to Pickens, South Carolina, with Reuben and Mildred. Although we got lost because of a detour, it was refreshing to get away. I have to say the Pickens Flea Market is by far the biggest and best I've visited. They have everything from plants to homemade furniture to fresh veggies and fruits and the many yard sale items, new and used. And after our long day, we enjoyed a time of just chatting while eating Mildred's homemade pecan pie and sweet tea, of course. Then she loaded my trunk with more of her beautiful, speckled yellow canna lilies to add to my bulb garden. To top it all off, when we arrived home, there at the gate was a beautiful pot of mums and comforting card from the Gordon's Chapel Visitation Team. These ladies share the Christ in them so wonderfully! Also in my mailbox was a lovely gift and card from my dear friend Sarah, my sister in grief. So thank you, my friends, for making this day very special. Even though I grieve every day for my children, God has given me some amazing people who won't let me give up on life!*

Life goes on. We can't stop it, even though we want to stop the world sometimes or make it go away, as the old song goes. "Just breathe," I keep telling myself.

•••••••••●••••••••

October 7, 2016
Birthdays, Special Days, and Well, Every Day

Today is my sixty-ninth birthday. Growing up in the Campbell family meant a great celebration with each birthday. And with seven in the family, that meant there was much fun with all the trimmings. There was the favorite cake, gifts, and singing, maybe homemade ice cream, along with a trip to the mountains sometimes in the fall. All the family was gathered around the table. It was only natural for that tradition to continue in the Fitzpatrick household. The only drawback was that Berry's family didn't celebrate birthdays. So he wasn't used to all the hoopla that comes with it. But I made it happen anyway. And he began to come around, especially when the children were in the picture. Erin really loved it since she loved any occasion to celebrate another person's life, or just to celebrate, period! She took the reins when she was old enough to become the party planner. The downside of that was that when she was suddenly gone to heaven, that went with her. My David, bless his heart, told me once that he was so sorry he wasn't the person Erin was and couldn't make the birthdays special. He didn't realize that he, himself, made the day special! And I realize that full force today as I have my first birthday with him in heaven. Oh, I fully expect there will be a *big* sign from him, as he and Erin, Scott, and Heather are probably up there, planning something special. If there is a way of touching my earth, they will do it! The first year after Erin was gone to heaven, we had a big snow on the first anniversary of her passing. It was odd because it was mainly situated in our little county here. Eight inches! That was rare and could only have been a little gift from her! Yes, I do believe in signs! And *yes*, I miss my David too much to do much celebrating today. Berry and I will probably take a day trip, partly to get away, partly to make the best of this day. It is what it is!

October 7, 2016
My Birthday Prayer

I wish that I could tell you
The feeling deep inside.
But I wouldn't want to load you down
With the pain that I can't hide.
Today is supposed to be a day
To celebrate my birth,
But my heart is heavy, my soul is torn,
There is no sign of mirth.
I read in Job after seven days
Of silence with his friends,
On breaking silence, his words portrayed
The battle deep within.
He rues the day that he was born.
His soul was shattered.
His mind was torn.
So on this day as I think on life
And all the special days,
I will miss my David, Erin, Scott, and Heather
In many, many ways.
So let me mourn, come give a hug,
Or just sit and let me share
The joy I knew, the love still here,
When my children were 'round my chair.

DAY-235

·············●···········

Seeing God for the First Time

It's one thing to grow up hearing about God, feeling that you really know Him. But it's another to experience God, to see Him act. I felt that I was on a spiritual plane that was just a little higher than others. I truly did! Because I grew up going to church, reading the Bible, going to meetings, seminars, conferences, even a Christian college, where we delved into the depths of the Bible and practiced evangelism on the streets of Chattanooga, Tennessee, I had the mistaken feeling that I knew it all! Even in my formative years, my brother, sister, and I were in a Christian singing group, traveling to churches and radio stations all over our area to sing. And when I say what I am about to say, I am not belittling any of those experiences. For I truly feel that was my foundation for the path my life would eventually take.

Since our David went to heaven after so great a struggle, leaving me with no children on this earth, I see God for the first time. By that I mean I am seeing the hugeness, the mightiness, the sovereignty of God in a way that is almost frightening in its magnitude. For the first time in my life, I don't really know how to approach God. Yes, I truly know that Jesus opened the door to the Father God. But now I see that even though I did all the things that I had been taught over sixty-plus years, the Father God chose to say no to all my fervent prayers, fasting, prayer chains, giving, believing, all of it. He chose to leave me a childless mother, grieving without accepting comfort.

He chose to take the dearest on earth to me. He chose to allow me to experience the greatest pain a parent can feel with no end in sight except my own death. He is God! He decides! I know this because I am reading Job and see what he endured. Job wished he had never been born. Job's best friends accused him of sinning to bring all the tragedy in his life. But when we read the beginning of the book, we realize it is all a "deal" between Satan and God. God allowed Satan to touch everything in Job's life. But He did not allow him to take Job's life. So God, Himself, decides when our life begins and when it ends. Job 14:5 (KJV) reads, "Seeing his days are determined, the number of his months are with Thee, Thou hast appointed his bounds that he cannot pass." Job also said, "I have heard of Thee by the hearing of the ear. But now my eye seeth Thee" (Job 42:5 KJV).

The longer I live, the more I realize that we can never really know God in His fullness. He is far greater than we can even imagine or think. He had all knowledge. His ways are higher than ours. His wisdom far surpasses man's finite wisdom. Even the greatest minds on earth cannot attain the depths of the wisdom of God. And with His great wisdom comes the truth that we really don't know Him even when we think we do.

I hope, in time, I will know how to approach Him once again. But for now, the fear is great. I am very aware of His love. I am more aware than ever. But the fear of what I don't know has built a wall. I turn off the TV when an evangelist talks about "getting your miracle" or "giving a dollar and getting a blessing from God." We don't control God. He is God, and we are not!

My relationship with God has changed phenomenally! It frightens me, and yet, at times, it excites me. There are days I think He is through with me on this earth. And there are other days when I feel my story is incomplete. There must be another chapter that must be so wonderful I can't comprehend what He has for me. Maybe He has called me to "lay down my life for my friends" or to "lay down my life for my children gone too soon." The future is a great mystery to me.

· · · · · · · ● ● ● ● ● · ● ● ● ● ● · · · ·

November 18, 2016:
I Love You Mo

I Love You More

Yesterday, Berry and I took a day trip, looking at antique shops for a buggy axle he wants. We stopped in a store in Hartwell so I could search for a lampshade. I've been to Athens, searching for just the right thing for a couple weeks. I need shades for antique lamps I found when I found a beautiful teacart. Decisions are hard, so I had about given up. I walked the aisles of a store while Berry went a different way. My feet were getting tired, and I had just about given up when I was drawn to the Christmas flowers since I want to make poinsettia trees with red cardinals for the graves. As I turned around to continue my search, there at the aisle facing me was a pillow display, and right in the center was a pillow with the words "I love you more." The month before David left for heaven, he would say this to me after our good-night hugs. The week after his service, I found a metal plaque with those words on it. A month later, I discovered at the back of a display a little memory box with the words. I have searched everywhere for something with these words since and, for months, have found nothing. So this is significant to me. It gets better! Right beside the pillow display, voilà, lampshades! And there facing me was just the one I had been searching for, complete with scalloped, fringed edges.

I don't know if you believe in signs, but our loved ones are nearer than we know. Jesus, after His Resurrection, appeared to some disciples on the road to Emmaus. The Bible says we are "surrounded by a cloud of witnesses." Who are they? Perhaps our loved ones, cheering us on in the worst of times. The Bible also says we see through a veil darkly. I think those witnesses are just a breath away.

When Erin left us for heaven, even though I had gone to church and studied the Bible most of my life, I wondered where heaven was. And now I believe I know. To be absent from the (physical) body is to be present with the Lord. I felt His presence stronger than I have in years on February 12, 2016, at 5:32, when He came to take David home. If He is that near all the time, maybe we don't recognize His presence. And maybe we don't recognize that our loved ones are that near either. Where He is, they are. So I think my David helped me yesterday. It says there are ministering spirits who help us. I believe it!

DAY-279

· · · · · · · · ● · · · · · · · ·

November 24, 2016
Holidays—Hurdles Ahead

This is our first Thanksgiving in thirty-three years with no children on earth. The sadness creeps in to take our breath away once again as we try to hold back the flood of tears. This morning, I went back in time to the last moments in ICU at Emory as they were doing CPR to try to restart David's heart for the eighth time. What if, after they had pulled the tubes and let me kiss my sweet boy for the last time, I had screamed for him to come back? Would it have brought him back? Did I want him to come back into a body riddled with pain, with the mass growing into his back and who knows where else? I just miss him.

"David, I know you can hear me. I love you, and Thanksgiving will never be the same without you here. I will cry for your absence until I am with you again. And that day can't come soon enough for me. But I promise I will try to fulfill the destiny God has for me here too. You kept fighting. I will too. I love you, my son! Hug Erin, Heather, and Scott for me and let them know I love them as deeply or more than I ever did. I just miss you!"

The New Christmas

One month from today, a new day will dawn in my life. The day will be filled, no doubt, with memories, memories of last year, memories of Christmases that filled thirty-three years of my life with love, with children, with lights, decorations, food, gifts, joy. The day will be different since the last of my children is gone to heaven. There will be no tree, no lights, no joy because I choose it. I choose to not stay here and cry all day or even go to family dinners, where the empty chair is so big it takes all my energy to hide behind a fake smile. Everything in this house screams of the life that filled it for thirty-three years. Most of the toys are still packed away in the basement and attic. I climbed up to the attic today to get Christmas flowers to make arrangements for the grave. There were the ornaments and Christmas whatnots with which I usually filled the house. There was never a space where Christmas wasn't observed in this home. Years of playing Santa, enjoying the surprised smiles on the children's faces as they woke to find their special toy requests and little surprises along with the box of fruit, nuts, and candy that followed the traditions of my mom and dad. Now Berry and I just look at each other and share the sadness of our present state. So we will skip the merchandising of this season, the decorating, the cooking, all the trappings that seem to bring such joy. Now I know that the real joy was celebrating the birth of the Savior and the wonderful hugs and warmth of a house filled with family, with children. That was the real Christmas. We can still celebrate the birth of our Savior. We can remember and share memories of our children. But the thing we will miss most and long for are the hugs of our children.

DAY-289

········•··••·•·······

December 4, 2016
Avoiding Christmas Memories

It's not hard to spend this Sunday thinking on God. Maybe it isn't given to man to understand Him. The Bible says, "The natural man receiveth not the things of God… They are spiritually discerned" (1 Cor. 2:14–15 KJV). So try as I might, question if I want, search and research, go back to the days of the hospitals, doctors, Erin's health, Scott's mental state after the war, I don't think I will ever in this life understand God's timing or His decisions. And why should I? He is God, and I am not. I have come to that conclusion.

Meanwhile, the seasons have changed from fall to winter. The leaves are almost all fallen. The trees are bare. The sun doesn't shine as long during the shorter days. The chill in the air keeps me inside more. And it seems to make me draw inside this shell in the comfort of the walls of my house. There's too much still time, too much downtime when I'm not up and at 'em as in the days of summer. There's too much time to think, to reflect, to mourn. When Erin left us for heaven so unexpectedly, the state of shock and panic left me desiring winter, desiring bare tree limbs, isolation from the cold. I decided, after years of loving spring as my favorite season, that winter was more like me. But now I resist winter. I don't want to be in this cocoon. For I wonder if I can ever really emerge. I know after this last huge blow in my life, after endless hours of longing for my baby, my last surviving child, who fought a battle no twenty-three-year-old should ever face, I cannot be the person I was even after losing Erin to heaven. I have been wounded too many times. So after the winter, can there ever be a spring again?

Yesterday I went in a store to pick up a few things. I've been avoiding Christmas with no huge display of lights in my yard. There has been no unpacking the six huge bins of every kind of Christmas decoration imaginable, no gift buying except a few things for my brothers and sisters, and absolutely no Christmas music playing. The only salvageable thing about Christmas is that I will continue to cherish the birth of Jesus Christ, who is still my Lord and King. I will cherish the memories that I hold in that locked box in my heart of my children, with eyes wide open, enjoying Christmases of days now long gone. Those two things I will keep. I won't let them slip away ever. But when I entered one store, I passed the aisle of Christmas decor. Automatically, I guess, I picked up a little round tin of bubble gum, thinking, *I need to get that for David's stocking.* I always bought my children gum and those little chocolate foil-wrapped fake coins. Even after my children were grown, I continued to make the stockings full of goodies. So I picked up this little tin, and immediately the tears began as I realized that I didn't need to buy David any Christmas things. I panicked as I couldn't control the flood of tears and the overwhelming grief tsunami that had hit. How close was I to the door? Could I just leave the shopping cart in that aisle and escape to the solitude of my car, where I could just scream and yell and wail? I swallowed hard, pushing the cart as fast as I could to another aisle, where there was just "this and that" not pertaining to the upcoming holiday season. I was still weeping but managed to pull myself together as I met the first person, managing an "Excuse me" as I almost pushed my cart into them. But I quickly focused on the shopping list of mundane, everyday things I needed. I managed to ride the grief tsunami wave to shore once again. I've had too much practice at this! This is not the life I planned. So what about tomorrow? Well, like Scarlett said in *GWTW*, "I won't think about that today. I'll think about that tomorrow" if tomorrow comes for me.

DAY-308

••••••••••●•••••••••

December 16, 2016
Better versus Bitter

Bitterness can be caused by an acrid taste in the mouth. Bitterness of soul is caused by either a traumatic event, unforgiveness, lack of understanding of a life issue, and various other causes that traumatize the soul. Grief can, over time, get sidetracked and change its effect in our soul to bitterness. At the beginning, I found myself being very protective of my emotional state. It is almost like wrapping yourself in a cocoon so people can't see the innermost you transforming into some unknown person. It's a fact that if you open a cocoon before it's time, the transformation process won't be complete and the butterfly will not emerge. The same is true of a rosebud. If the delicate petals are forced open by peeling off the layers unnaturally, the rose will never emerge as the beautiful flower it could become. This makes me feel that grief is much the same way. If we force ourselves to "open our cocoon" too soon, we may be more vulnerable to hurtful comments or may be enticed to go places, interact with groups or events that cause more trauma to an already-fragile soul.

It's so easy to become bitter when your questions go unanswered. Each day you get up and you struggle to find the reasons that your child is not here anymore. You think that God is mad at you. You feel that you have offended God. You feel that for some reason, you have brought this on yourself and your child, or children, in my case.

But every day I struggle to fight the bitterness. I don't want bitterness to be the path for the rest of my life. And I don't want bitterness to alienate me from God. So I struggle to reach beyond the questions, beyond the pain, beyond a longing for my children to be here beside me. I struggle to reach out to others to give to them from the help that I have received from God in the last 1,083 days since my David went to heaven. I struggled to reach beyond myself, beyond my pain, to help others. For I have found that truly in helping others we help ourselves. In helping others, we release the bitterness in exchange for doing something good for someone else, for lifting a hand up to another mom, dad, brother, or sister who is struggling with the depths of grief themselves. So I fight the bitterness. Bitterness can come from unforgiveness of God or unforgiveness of the person who killed our child, if they were murdered, or unforgiveness of the doctors and nurses who took care of our child. Or it can even come from not forgiving ourselves for our perceived failure as a parent. As much as the grieving hurts, it is just as hard or harder to fight off the bitterness. We must find it in our spirit to forgive any who might have had some part in our child not being here, even if it's not true. We still feel that way. Such was today along with some other days recently. I have been fighting the bitterness. Again, I can only trust God to help me to be an overcomer in this battle.

There is a beautiful story in the Bible about a grieving mother. Naomi had left her native country to move with her husband to a foreign land, where he found work. During their stay, they had two wonderful sons whom she loved with all her soul. Life was good. The sons grew up and married beautiful women from the country of Moab. But suddenly, Naomi's husband became ill and died, shortly followed by both her sons. She was left destitute, with no provision, no one to care for her except two daughters-in-law. As tradition would have it, she had to go back to her native land of Israel to find relatives to give her a home. As she left all her familiar surroundings and came back home, she told the people there to call her Mara, which meant "bitter." As she hung her head and became comforted by her nearest kin, she felt life was over for her. The story does have a good ending, though, because one of her daughters-in-law clung to her and eventually married one of her wealthy kin. Naomi then became a grandmother to their children.

I don't want to be bitter. And yet there are days when I feel the bitterness sneaking in the back door. The battle is on once again in my life. Experience teaches us that, in life, there is always one more battle, one more hill to climb, one more lesson to learn, often borne out of hardship.

The term *better* is not one that most grieving mothers will use. Sarah, a dear friend and grieving mother, uses the term *different*, referencing how things change, over time, in grief. We know after burying a child that life will never really be better unless we can have our child back. But the raw, hacking, excruciating pain of loss seems to soften over time. Such was my case after losing our baby Heather and then our Erin. I felt when Erin left for heaven that I would never smile again, that my life would be full of tears and sorrow. But even David told me shortly before he left for heaven that he was coping much better with Erin's passing. The edges of grief had finally softened for him. Sadly, for me, though, my soul would be pierced once again with his passing. How often can the soul be pierced and still survive? When Jesus was prophesied to be born, Mary was told that a sword would pierce her soul also. She learned this just after being told by an angel she would bear the Son of God, who would change the world. She knew grief, as this miracle baby only lived on earth thirty-three years before He was crucified and made a sacrifice for all mankind to come to God. Even though she knew He was resurrected and seated at the right hand of God, she had to have known the soul sword-piercing of grief the rest of her days on earth.

DAY-315

· · · · · · · ● · · · · · · · ·

Grief Is Like Walking Between the Shore and the Ocean

A good picture for those who are unacquainted with grief is walking between the land and the ocean. As you walk on the sandy shore, it is obvious that you are grounded. And yet there are incoming tides that gently wash over your feet from time to time. Then you may get distracted as you turn your attention from the vast ocean to a friend or a pet or a scene onshore. And while your attention is turned away, a huge wave catches you off guard and knocks you down. When you can catch your breath again, you stand up, wipe the salty water off your face, and keep walking.

The ocean is the vastness and infiniteness of the eternity where your loved one has gone. You gaze on it with awe as there is no end in sight, and you wonder what the other shore looks like. The saltwater is the bitterness that constantly barrages you directly in the face to the point that it almost tastes "good" as it becomes familiar. You don't want to leave the place where you buried your loved one, for fear of losing them all over again. But you long to get across the vast divide. However, you know that to go there is certain death for yourself. And while you long desperately to be with your loved one, you feel that you are left here for a purpose yet unfulfilled, which must be accomplished before your journey "home" begins.

The land represents your earthly home. The sand you walk on becomes so hot sometimes it burns your feet. You seek refuge in shoes to protect you, a man-made thing that separates you from the grounding the earth allows. And yet it is more comfortable. You decide being more comfortable is better than feeling the pain, so you set a barrier between yourself and the pain. The wind blows, sometimes so hard it almost knocks you down. Such is life's journey. The winds of trouble often blow so hard you wonder if you can make it back to a safe place before the ocean on your right draws you in. And then there are the objects that you step on that cause pain. It might be a relationship gone awry or a family member who hurt you deeply by comments or a coworker who is unjustly critical. You step on a broken seashell and it makes your feet bleed. In grief, no one really understands why you keep hurting, why you keep crying. They don't feel the pain. They don't see the sleepless nights as the pain keeps throbbing and sleep won't come. Others who haven't walked in grief don't know what's just behind the mask you wear. But you know. You feel the sore that just refuses to heal because you refuse to be comforted.

On the one hand, there is life or ground to keep you upright. On the other, there is the unending flow of eternity where your loved one has gone and for which you long. And you are walking in the middle. You keep walking on the one while longing for the other. It is a path between life and death, between here and eternity.

•••••••••●•••••••••

January 11, 2017
God Never Promised
Us a Rose Garden

I was thinking through a sermon of sorts in the shower last night. That's where I do my best thinking sometimes. I am a Christian. When I became a Christian at an early age, it never occurred to me what my life on earth would be. Some believe that God just gives a blank check for protection, healing, wealth, success, and power over all the obstacles that might come. But not true! Do I believe God protects me? Absolutely! Do I believe He protected my children even though they are in heaven now? Absolutely! So you may ask why God allowed these horrible things to happen in a life that was totally, unreservedly dedicated to Him and tried to honor Him every day. Well, before you judge me, ask some of the biblical patriarchs.

Ask Abraham. He had to make the ultimate sacrifice. God asked him to sacrifice the son that he had waited twenty-five years to bear, the son of promise. I believe that climbing that mountain that day to reach the place where he would build an altar on which to lay Isaac and kill him as a sacrifice, Abraham had already, in his mind and soul, made the sacrifice. God did spare Isaac in the end by providing a ram caught in a thicket. But Abraham had to be willing to do the hardest thing in his life to show his faithfulness to God. What is the hardest thing for you?

Ask David. David was anointed three times to be king over Israel. But the present king chased him fervently, fully intending to kill him and trying a few times. David lived in a cave for a time. Later, after he became king, he was run out of the country but later resumed his full kingship over Israel. He lost three children to death, lost his best friend, Jonathan, and lost his first beloved wife.

Ask Joseph. He was highly favored of his father. He had a dream that he was ruling over his brothers. But what happened? His brothers put him in a hole in the ground in the desert to die, later sold him into slavery, and even presented his bloody coat of many colors to his grieving father. (His father mourned him many years before learning the truth!) He was put in prison for three years. But then he was elevated to the position of power God had predestined for him, saving the very brothers who had sold him into slavery, along with his father and family!

That's only three instances of men chosen of God who had to suffer great sorrow in their lives. The twelve disciples, every one, died a tragic death. John, who was so beloved of Jesus, was put upside down in a vat of oil to die but survived and was exiled to the isle of Patmos, where he wrote one of the most mysterious and talked-about books of the Bible, Revelation. Paul was imprisoned, beaten, stoned, shipwrecked, and almost drowned and left for dead a few times and yet was called the greatest of the apostles. Peter, one whom Jesus loved, was crucified upside down.

Here we are in a land that is free, where we receive no persecution for the cause of Christ. Should we expect a bed of roses in life? Job, in response to his wife's suggestion that he curse God and die, said, "Though He slay me, yet will I trust Him" (Job 13:15 KJV). "Shall we receive good at the hand of God and shall we not receive evil?" (Job 2:10 KJV). Jesus said that we could expect tribulation. He said not to fear, that He had overcome the world. So yes, I am a Christian. Yes, I have lived a life that no one would probably want. But "for me to live is Christ. And to die is gain" (Phil. 1:21 KJV).

DAY-362

· · · · · · · · ● · · · · · · · ·

Tomorrow Started without You

As they laid you in my arms
so many years ago,
the sparkle in your eyes set this mother's heart aglow.
Five long years we waited, hoped, and prayed
for the miracle of you, and in my arms you lay.
My miracle child, I called you, as you were an answer to prayer.

Our family grew, and you did too, as we watched you grow and thrive.
A little boy, a mother's dream, the love between us grew.
I saw you fly in your Superman PJs and in your life as well.
There was tae kwon do, then trumpet, piano, guitar, swords,
little cars, bright-red wagons, school events, and more.
New friends to make, new songs to sing, and
new adventures right and left.
You filled our home with music and laughter,
and there were some tears there too.

You became our heart song over the years,
and your life became ours too.
Everything changed when your sister left for heaven.
Our home became so dark.
But your sweet smile and the love you gave made life not seem so stark.
You struggled, too, to find a way to live without your sis.

You found ways to cope with your parents'
grief and even to help yourself.

And just when the days seemed a bit easier
to bear, you faced another giant.
But you fought with courage and kept up the fight to the end.
I never thought when they laid you in my arms
that tomorrow would start without you.
And it really has not, for I know where you
are in the arms of our loving Father.
But my heart is grieved, my arms are bare, our home is dark again.
But knowing our God has the strength that we need,
we keep going just as you did.

And one morning fair we will move through
the air to the paradise that awaits.
For we know that among the loved ones up
there, you will meet us at the gate!
Our love for you continues to grow, your memory we will keep alive.
We will honor you, by doing what you'd do,
helping others and lifting their load.
For we know you are near, right now and right
here, as we know that we never really die.
For our Lord conquered death, and at your last
breath, He breathed His own life into you.
I love you more!

DAY-374

••••••••••●••••••••

Year 2
Time Stood Still

My David, the day came and went, the day that you left this earth one year ago, February 12, 2017. There was no stopping it, just as there was no stopping the horrible drama in the ICU room one year ago. There is no stopping time or events that must, by the will of God, take place. We can try! We can give it our best efforts. But we can't stop the plan of God. We can't stop the time continuum. So we keep breathing.

As with our Erin and Scott, my mind raced back to that day, that week, all the moments, the last words, last events, days leading up to my life coming to a screeching halt as David's heart stopped and mine was crushed to powder. The horror of a mother continuing to live after burying one child is unmeasurable. The sheer, shocking brokenness after burying all her children is something about which books are written and movies are made. And yet here I am, still breathing, still doing life, if that is what it could be called. I keep getting out of bed, often after sleepless nights, going to the bathroom, brushing my teeth, getting dressed, washing clothes, sweeping floors, cooking, scrubbing toilets, all out of sheer habit, all with no real purpose other than keeping my hands busy. I try to pray the Lord's Prayer each morning. I read out of Job or the red letters that mark the words of Jesus. (I have added one more thing.) Each morning I listen to three songs by the Brooklyn Tabernacle Choir, praise songs. I keep hoping that hope will go higher than just a flicker in my heart again. I keep trying to get my praise back. I keep crying. I keep not understanding. I keep breathing.

Now, I have not just grief but complicated grief. When we were struggling with David in Atlanta, I put my grief for my sweet Erin on the back burner. I suppressed it. I wouldn't allow it to surface lest I fail in my care for David. I knew I couldn't do both. It would overwhelm me. It would kill me. So for two years, I refused to let myself think on my beautiful Erin. But now, as I sit here and look out at a gray day, I know that I must continue to grieve for her. Her birthday is coming the twenty-sixth of February. She would be thirty-four this year. But she is forever twenty-three. How can that be? How can it be that I see her friends on social media getting married, buying or building houses, announcing the joy of the arrival of their babies? How can life be so cruel as to deny my children these wonderful events?

Then my mind races back to a scene in my living room. I would dance with my babies. I always wanted to be a ballerina. So I would turn on one of their little music cassette tapes and we'd swirl around and around, often hopping up on a footstool and down again as the room would fill with their sweet laughter. My mind races back to our new house and the kids playing "McDonald's drive-through" on the carport. They would open the living room window, which did not have the screen yet, and one would sit in here and the other would drive the tricycle by the window to place "the order." Erin loved her little kitchen set. I was surprised one day when I walked in to see her dad sitting in one of the little chairs, having tea with her.

I see Erin's eight to ten girlfriends as they had one of their numerous slumber parties. They slipped outside in the middle of the night when it was raining, leaving telltale muddy shoe prints on the kitchen linoleum. Even changing linens on the beds brought fun. I'd thrown the sheet into the air, and one of the kids would climb on the bed under it and the laugher would ensue. Oh, the memories! They are so precious and so bittersweet at the same time.

It is almost like living in the past or dreading what the future might hold but being unable to endure the present. There might be a term for it, like *grief time travel* or *memory revisit episode*.

So I enter year 2 of my grief for David, year 11 for my Erin, year 4 for Scott, and year 32 for my baby Heather. It's not the life I would have chosen for myself. But then, I didn't have a say in that matter. The future is unclear. Will there be more sorrow? Will some miracle of joy come wafting back into my life? How could that even happen since I buried my heart four times already? But life isn't over. We shall see!

DAY-384

•••••••••●•••••••••

March 3, 2017
Seasons of Grief

I shared with some ladies last week about the "season" of grief. Having become all too familiar with grief, I find there are many things I have learned that might help others. One is, each year on the anniversary of the death of a loved one, there is a "sinking" feeling that may come, even subconsciously. Spring was always my favorite season of the year, with the birds singing and signs of new life everywhere. But alas, spring now has become different for me. The first daffodil brings back memories of Erin, our firstborn daughter, picking those first two or three daffodils each year. I'd ask her to wait until there were more, but she just had to get a little bouquet to put on our kitchen table. Eleven years ago, she picked that first bouquet, along with some little cuttings from my budding almond, and made that yearly bouquet for our table. That Sunday, her birthday, was a good day as we celebrated with her favorite pizza and delicious cake. Then, after opening gifts, she and her husband headed off to the movies. It was just three days later, on Wednesday, that she stopped by to use my fax machine for Adam's business. She told me how badly her back was hurting that day. As she got in her car to leave, I remember the hug was a little longer than usual and her bright smile up at me as she closed the door. I didn't realize that would be the last hug and smile before she left for heaven that night around midnight. The horror began for us at 1:10 the next morning as Adam's parents came and knocked on our door with the worst news we'd ever had. The hard part during the next few weeks was waking up each morning. The birds were singing. I wondered why. Spring was here. But it was winter in my soul. Thank you, my dear friends and family, for remembering our Erin with us. She was our joy and song and the sunshine of our lives. She is forever part of who we are. Spring will never be my favorite season again!

Backtrack to April of 1985. Erin was only two. We were expecting our second little girl. She had the hiccups that day in my tummy as I felt the familiar little bumps. Then later that day, she stopped moving. It was a Sunday. Wednesday night, she was born sleeping. A heartache that knew no bounds entered my soul! It was April 11, springtime. She wasn't due until July. Spring brought sorrow once again.

Fastrack to February 12, 2016, we never, ever would have imagined that our baby boy, our last surviving child, would not survive his two-year-long struggle with leukemia. Again, the daffodils bloomed. But this time I didn't even notice. I was in total shock and disbelief. I don't even remember the birds singing last year. It's all a blur and a fog. That fog hasn't lifted much yet, as each day is still filled with pain. Spring came again with a vengeance.

When David was fighting his battle, I refused to think much on Erin and the grief. I think my mind was protecting me from overload. But this year, the day has rolled around again just as it was in 2006. It was Sunday when her birthday came. And Wednesday is tomorrow, and that's the night her heavenward journey began.

Think about it. Do you feel a sinking when a certain month or even season comes around that was the month you lost someone dear to you? It was a season, a season you will never forget, even though you might not be mindful of it. I think it is deep within the recesses of our soul. I began calling that time of year my season of grief.

DAY-399

· · · · · · · ● ● ● ● ● ● · · · · · · · ·

The Day My Faith
Will Be Resurrected

There have been many and varied comments as friends, family, and even strangers have tried to comfort me. Some referred to my situation as these: "I don't know how you can stand it." "I don't know what I would do if that happened to me." My response would be, "I don't know how I stand it and don't know what I will do." I say this with the numbness that is still there after 399 days. Life is something that I am looking on at, almost as a visitor. I can't see a future yet.

I say that to let you know why part of the title of this book will be called *Faith Resurrected*. I fully expect that that day will come, although right now I have no clue how that can even happen. When we buried a little girl many years ago, a sweet little baby girl who weighed two and a half pounds and was thirteen and a half inches long, the first thing I thought of was how I must have displeased God that He would allow my baby to die. What sin had I committed to receive this tragedy at His hand? I agonized for days on end, not even wanting to get out of bed, hurting in ways I had never hurt before. My faith was the first thing in question. And this was an ultimate test of the anchor of my soul. After many months, I did venture back to God, as I found my need for Him greater than my questioning His motives in taking my baby back to Himself. As my Erin, who was only two at that time, grew and my days and years were filled with the wonder of raising a little girl, I seemed to stash any questions I had in the back of my spirit, neatly tucked away in a little folder labeled "Deal with Later." Five years later, our little miracle, rainbow child was born, David Lee, who became my little buddy. As life became even fuller with Erin's twirling clubs, cheerleading, baseball and David's tae kwon do and school/church events, a wonderful life emerged. I still had my Heather in my heart and the questions packed away. Never did I think that I would have to revisit the faith issue so soon.

When Erin was twenty-three, we got the dreaded knock on the door in the middle of the night. So began a deeper soul/spirit searching that still has not ended. For six months, this time, I searched. The questions were more poignant. The fears of failing a God I had developed an even deeper relationship with haunted me day and night. I sought answers that kept running just ahead of me, never catching them. My faith was stretched to the breaking point. Could I still believe in a God who was supposed to be my best friend and Savior, but who would take from me the most cherished gift He had ever given? How could I reconcile with Him on any level? At Erin's memorial service, a friend whom I had met through church but had never really had a friendship with came to our side. Over the next few years, Sharon Fiedler kept up a faithful relationship with me, my husband, and David as we struggled with life and with the haunting questions. She and her family cried with us, met us at the cemetery on all the special days to place flowers and memorials on the graves. She embraced David, praying for him and offering whatever support he would accept. She remembered Erin, placing her picture on her own dining table. But the greatest gift were the prayers for us that never ended. Sharon's brother Jack Paxton, who lived in Florida, would call often just to check on us and sent a generous gift to help us pay for Erin's service. Sharon and her husband, John, held meetings in their home, and so began a spiritual connection that would not let us go. They, along with others, propelled us toward God, even with us having the brakes on. Though the answers were not there, I knew I had to reconnect with the one who was almighty, who knew my name, who felt my pain. Over the course of the next few years,

I did. My husband and my son also formed a bond with these people and felt the comfort of God as they ministered to us and slowly brought us into God's presence once again.

DAY-400

· · · · · · · · · ●●● ● ●●● · · · · · · · ·

Quest for Faith Continues

Then, when the unthinkable happened, when we got the next call about Scott, the three of us drove to Savannah in the middle of the night. When we found that Scott was at the point of death in a hospital there, once again the tears flooded and the question envelope resurfaced. How could it be that this young man, who fought in a war far away and survived four tours overseas in war-ravaged lands, would be dying of a self-inflicted gunshot? I remember getting up in the middle of the night, lying on the floor, crying out to God to protect him when the war raged in Iraq in 2001. We had no warning now that there was any problem? How could God again let this son of ours be drifting slowly off to heaven when our hearts remained crushed from the last blow? Faith! God, where are You? Why? How could this be? Yet as time passed, our friends and family surrounded us with prayer, and comfort came again to soothe our wounded souls. The questions were tucked back into the growing envelope. One year and three months later, our twenty-three-year-old youngest son and our last surviving child, whom we had turned all our attention to after our other children went to heaven, was diagnosed with leukemia. Another blow! But we three closed the circle tighter as we vowed to fight this thing together. And fought we did! We had to move to a city about an hour and a half away as David began treatment that was so horrible it almost crushed his already-wounded soul. But he kept fighting, he said, for us. He knew his dad and I had suffered so from grief already, and he was determined to beat this thing. He gave it his best and fiercest effort. After a successful bone marrow transplant, he got an infection that almost took him from us. Prayers were being held around the world for his recovery, and it happened. We got our miracle! Oh, the joy that filled my heart when, after four months of rehab, we could bring our boy home and continue rehab here. When we drove out of Atlanta, I was a happy mom who had seen faith bring a miracle to our lives. But it was a short-lived season of joy as he began to weaken just few months later, and we were told the horrible disease had come back. When he had to start over with chemo, I think something died inside him. Although he still vowed to fight, his body was too weak. February 12, 2016, just after the first week of completing chemo round one, God came and took him back to himself.

Now the question envelope is just too full! It won't close anymore. Does God even love me? Some days I think He might. Others, I don't. The one whom I used to walk with in the cool of the early morning and have great talks with seems to have turned His back on me totally! As the psalmist said, "He frustrated the plans of the nations" (Ps. 33:10 KJV). He killed my dreams. What is left to dream for when your children are all in heaven and you are sixty-nine years old? Can I have another child when I am past childbearing age? Can I start over in the later years of my life? My husband and I cry together, almost daily. We breathe, and that's about it. I'm fighting bitterness that the enemy of my soul wants me to embrace. I refuse to turn my back on God. He did bless me with thirty-four years with my children. For that I continue to be thankful. But I am left empty, much like Naomi in the Bible when she lost her two sons and husband. So where is faith? I reach for it, and it evades me. I have refused to pray for others since my own prayers were answered with no. But I did utter prayers when a few have gone through trials. Did it do any good? Did God hear me? I read Job over and over. I am reading it for the ninth time now, hoping to glean some understanding, to find out where I went wrong, or just to find answers. After a few months of our David leaving for heaven, I heard a song by the Brooklyn Tabernacle Choir called "Total Praise." Its lyrics speak of times in life when we turn away, when we can't find the words to pray. The first time I heard it, I cried. It ministered to my brokenness. I listen to it daily, along with "Thou, O, Lord" and "He Is Faithful," all by the Brooklyn Tabernacle Choir. I guess I hope it will bring me back. It's a start. It might not take care of any of the questions in the envelope, but it's a baby step toward a resurrection of faith. When God took David, it seems it was the "straw that broke the camel's back." It just seems too much for this mom to bear. I don't have any answers. I just keep breathing. Jack Paxton told me that he saw a flicker of hope in me. It may be.

DAY-415

• • • • • • • • ● • • • • • • • •

Heaven, Where Is It?

Church. I grew up thinking of church as my second home because we were there, literally, every time the doors swung open. From birth I was taught about God and heaven. We all anticipated seeing this beautiful land one day in the "sweet by and by." I consider myself a Bible scholar, having not only attended church often but also having attended a Bible college before transferring to UGA. Hardly a day has passed that my Bible has not been opened, with me often reading several chapters in one sitting, along with several commentaries, books, and information shared by spiritual leaders. I consider myself well-schooled on the idea of heaven being a real, solid place where God dwells, and now His dear Son, Jesus Christ, ruling by His side. It would be hard for anyone to convince me otherwise.

The background is now set for you to know what happens when a Christian is faced with life-altering circumstances that lead them to question everything they knew to be true. When my baby Heather left for heaven before I could hold her in my arms, it never crossed my mind where she was. All babies go to heaven, right? Of course! When Erin, whom I had held in my arms and who I was always near, tending to her every need when she was growing up, watching her grow into an independent young woman with the world at her feet, left for heaven, it was completely different. It struck me that here was my precious daughter, whom I had gone to extreme lengths to protect all her life, even when she was grown, gone! Where was she? I was in shock! How could she be "not in this world"? Where is heaven? Can I see it? Can I find it? Is it one star past the moon? Is it way off beyond the farthest solar system, out of my reach? I can't get to her. What can I do? How can I find her? My mind was a plethora of questions, of searching that didn't end when I went to bed or even when I was distracted. Where was my firstborn? And so my quest for heaven began in earnest. We think we have all the answers as Christians. We know so much, only to find we know so little. Isn't that what Job discovered? At the beginning of our searching, there is God. At the end of our searching, there is God. God is God. But where is He? "Heaven is his throne" (Isa. 66:1 KJV), the Bible says. So if I can find out where God is, I will know where Erin, Heather, Scott, and now my David are.

Where do we usually look when we speak of heaven? We look up into the vast sky above us. But it's all relative. The earth is spinning. So are we looking down or up? Scientists have discovered a new solar system. They have also discovered that there are many universes, not just one. So can we look far enough to see God. The Bible references heaven as paradise (Jesus talking to the man on the cross beside Him). The rich man in a parable was said to be in hell, while Lazarus was in "the bosom of Abraham," referencing the place Lazarus had gone at death of his earthly body. Jesus said, "I go away to prepare a 'place' for you" (John 14:3 KJV), referencing where he would go. But on the other hand, Jesus told his disciples, "I will never leave you nor forsake you" (Heb. 13:5 KJV). God walked with Adam and Eve when He first created the earth. Did He leave His "throne" (heaven) to pay them a visit? Or was heaven with Him as He walked with them? Did we lose heaven when they sinned and broke fellowship with God? Was Eden heaven? So, so many questions!

Experience has taught me to look past all my theology, all my natural thinking, and go right to the Spiritual. I capitalize *Spiritual* for it is the Holy Spirit of God, Spiritual, and not a human or dark spiritual. There was a wonderful gift that I received after my children crossed over into that heavenly realm. I had visions and dreams of all of them. Since the Bible says that "old men shall dream dreams and young men shall have visions" (Acts 2:17 KJV), this is not crazy or out of the realm of possibility. The dreams comforted me in a way no words or human acts could. There have been many times that I have "felt" their presence. I can't explain how I knew. I just knew. People mention often feeling the Lord's presence in church services. Since our loved ones are with Him where He is, why should we not feel their presence.

My conclusion, which put an end to my agonizing search after my Erin left for heaven, was that heaven is right beside us. Heaven is just a breath away. Heaven is another realm that we just can't see. I do believe they can see us. But because we look "through a glass darkly," as the Bible says in 1 Corinthians 13:12 (KJV), we have not yet attained to that spiritual place, where we can see them clearly. This "veil" of flesh hinders our spiritual vision. The Bible, in Hebrews 10:19–20 (AMP), reads, "Therefore, brethren, since we have full freedom and confidence to enter into the [Holy of] Holies by the power and virtue in the Blood of Jesus, by this fresh (new) and living way which He initiated and dedicated and opened for us through the separating curtain (veil of the Holy of Holies) that is, through His flesh." As I read this, I know that the dark "veil" has been made transparent by Jesus. So can we see into heaven? God is omnipresent, omniscient, and all powerful. He can be everywhere or anywhere with no time continuum. Didn't Jesus appear to His disciples in the upper room without walking in through the door? Didn't He come walking across the water to Peter and the disciples on the boat? He was in paradise and on earth, no limits of time, space, or matter. Heaven is where He is. He prepared this place for us. What a day that will be when the bonds are gone. That's where my children are. That is heaven.

DAY-423

······●·······

April 11, 2017
The Case for Life

Thirty-two years ago, a baby girl was born to us. For six months, I had the joy of feeling her kick, feeling her move in a gentle fashion in my tummy, and experiencing the wonder of carrying a baby for the second time in my life. We anticipated with great joy Erin having a little sister. It was on a Sunday that I felt my little Heather Lynn have the hiccups as the little bumps kept going in my tummy. That night after church, I was lying in bed and felt this icy coldness in my tummy. I thought maybe she was warm and the body was compensating. I had heard the womb had its own temperature control. A strange dream happened that night. I was standing on a dirt road, and three women were headed toward me. I recognized them as my dear grandmother, who had passed when Erin was six months old, her sister, my great-aunt Winnie, and my great-grandmother beside her. They all had their hands extended as they approached me, as if I were to give them something. The next morning, when I awakened and began to get dressed for school where I taught, I noticed something was wrong. So I called my doctor. He told me to put my feet up and do nothing to see if I felt better. The little bit of bleeding stopped. I did that for two days, but the bleeding worsened, so I went Wednesday for him to check. My youngest sister went with me because my husband needed to work and take care of Erin. My greatest fears were realized as the ultrasound technician quickly went to get the doctor and he told me that Heather was gone. My baby dead! How could this be? Two days later, Berry and a few family and friends gathered around a tiny cemetery plot and buried this precious baby girl. I was still in the hospital, surrounded by the nurses and doctors, who kept coming by my room. Nearly all the nurses on the floor stopped by to tell me how beautiful and perfect my little Heather was. I plied them with questions as to how she looked. They said she was perfect, with five fingers on each hand and five toes on each foot. The only thing was, she didn't have eyebrows yet. My doctor came and sat on my bed to talk to me and sent me a beautiful bouquet of flowers. The nuns at the hospital came by to check on me. One sat at my side at 4:00 a.m. when I couldn't sleep. As I cried and told her Heather's little feet would never touch the earth, she cried with me and said she knew I would survive this because my faith was strong. She prayed with me and continued to visit. I never got to see or hold my baby girl as the doctors and nurses told me it would be unwise, as she had turned blue. But I wanted to hold my baby. It was all I wanted. My mother, who was in the waiting area, wanted to hold her, too, and bring her a little dress. But back then in 1985, I guess they didn't think any of that was necessary. All I have of my baby girl is a little card with her tiny footprints and her measurements. It doesn't even list her name but only "Baby Fitzpatrick." I still mourn that to this day!

For thirty-two years, I have wondered what she looked like, what her life would have been, how her life would have been intertwined with Erin's, David's, Scott's, and ours. I had a dream once that she was standing, barefoot, in a beautiful, flower-filled meadow near a huge oak tree. Her skin was almost transparent, and she wore a beautiful long white gown. She looked as if she was eight or nine years old and was cradling in her arms a little lamb. Her reddish-brown hair was curly, like mine was as a child. There was a big smile on her face, and she was filled with joy. I clung to that dream as I'd visit her grave each year to put flowers on her grave for her birthday.

The one thing that keeps me going during all the tragedies is my belief that my children are still alive. By that, I mean for a Christian life doesn't stop at the grave. Babies, who have never been old enough to make decisions, in their innocence, must go to heaven. I believe they are back in the arms of God when they leave so soon. Children who are older and have made the decision to accept the sacrifice of Jesus and become followers of Christ have the way opened for them to enter heaven also. All three of my other children, including my stepson, made that decision. I witnessed it myself. Jesus told the Pharisees, when they used Abraham, Isaac, and Jacob as a point of argument, that "God is not the God of the dead, but the God of the living" (Mark 12:27 KJV), referencing Abraham, Isaac, and Jacob. And they had all been gone from this earth for many years. So this also proved the case for life beyond death. The death of the physical body does not mean the death of the spirit and soul of a person. Just because we had to bury four very precious bodies of our children doesn't mean that we buried "them." They are alive eternally. They are all around us. They are with Jesus and with the Father God. As I mentioned in an earlier chapter, God is omnipotent, omniscient, and can be everywhere at once. Our finite minds cannot comprehend this. But it is truth. Jesus said, "I am the Truth, the way and the life" (John 14:6 KJV). "He that believeth in me, though he were dead, yet shall he live" (John 11:25 KJV). I had that engraved on Erin's headstone. My children are alive.

The mourning that I do is for myself, for my husband, for my future. But as deeply as I mourn, it doesn't change the fact that my children are alive in paradise. I will see them again one glorious day.

Today, I remember and mourn for my little girl Heather Lynn Fitzpatrick. I continue to wonder how her life is intertwined with mine. I know it is. It has been for thirty-two years. I mourn for her, but I look ahead to one day when I will have her in my arms. She is my daughter. I am her mom. I love her as much as a mom can love a child, although I have never seen her. God has her in His keeping. I have her in my heart. Happy birthday, my baby girl!

DAY-434

•••••••••●••••••••

A Living Spirit

Yesterday, while cleaning out a drawer, I came across a journal from 2006, the year that changed us forever, the year our Erin left for heaven. As I began to read and see the agony, I found this little paragraph:

> *David said something profound today. He said that while his dad and I are crying a lot, he sees Erin as being a living spirit. He's right. We should too.*

What wisdom coming from our fourteen-year-old at that critical time in our existence! He shared later his own struggles with the untimely passing of his dear sister. But he had a grasp on the spirit world that we didn't see through our tears.

As I reflected on this later in the day, I thought on the biblical account of what happened when the ladies went early in the morning to treat the body of Jesus with the prepared spices, as was the custom in their country. They were in deep mourning as hope had vanished for them when the one who they believed was their Messiah was so cruelly put to death on the cross the day before. As they neared the tomb, they saw the stone had been rolled away. A man standing nearby asked whom they were looking for. When they told him, he said, "Why do you look for the living among the dead?" (Luke 24:5 KJV). I can imagine their thoughts as they stared at the man who, they thought, must have misunderstood them. But this statement is so profound and so true. I kept thinking on this one thing.

I spend much time at the two cemeteries where our children's bodies were laid. Having attended many interments over the years, I've heard different messages about interment. One minister said the dead just changed houses, referring to the body as a "house of clay." Often, I hear the phrase "Dust to dust, ashes to ashes." But for a mom, that house of clay was and is precious, even if it turns to dust. That was the body we cared for so tenderly, so agonizingly, over the course of the child's life. How can we just bury something so precious and never return to where it was placed? I remember so vividly visiting Erin's site two or three times a week at first, crying, wailing, bawling as I couldn't wrap my head around her leaving us too soon before her life was completed. I spent much time kneeling, sitting, worrying over the grave. But after eight or nine years, I realized she wasn't coming back, at least not in the way I had hoped. With my precious David, I still visit at least once a week. But it is different.

Each loss has its own story. And each one is dealt with in a different way. Maybe it was because David was still living with us that his room is now a memorial. We have left it just the way it was that last day we left for the hospital. And maybe that is why I don't visit his site as I did Erin's. The loss is, in a way, even more profound than Erin's because he was our last living child. After reflecting on David's statement back in 2006 and thinking on what Jesus (whom the women thought was a gardener) told Mary as she neared the grave, now I know I don't have to visit the grave so often. Why am I seeking the living among the dead? There is absolutely no doubt in my mind that my children are alive in eternal paradise! None! Can I see them? Only in visions or dreams the Lord allows. But I do believe that one day there will be a resurrection of all our loved ones. I believe they will be resurrected an eternal body that only God knows how to build. The Bible says we will know as we are known. So it must be a body like that one we lived in on earth since we will know them. What a day that will be! I expect to see them here since His kingdom will be here. He will set up His kingdom, and we will rule and reign with our Lord forever. No more tears! Only life forevermore!

DAY-465

· · · · · · ·●●●●●●●· · · · · · ·

May 23, 2017
Separation Anxiety

We had a butterfly-release ceremony for David's twenty-sixth birthday celebration at the grave site. Several friends and family joined us in releasing these beautiful creatures. Butterflies depict change, metamorphosis into something totally different. We believe that our David has been changed into a pain-free, unencumbered, spiritual being that knows no limits and is loved by those who have gone on before him as he awaits our change.

We, too, have known change. The change happened when our Heather was born still. It changed everything. It enlightened us to our own immortality and to life's fragileness. Then, when our Erin left for heaven so suddenly, our world changed dramatically. I questioned everything about life, about spirituality, about our family, about each day without her by our side on earth. When Scott left us for heaven, I saw the dramatic change in my husband, the daily searching for answers, for comfort. This was his second-born son, a son in whom he had such pride, a son who had grown from a shy little boy into a bodybuilder, leader in the Army, and world traveler. My husband talked of him with such pride and joy. But then, in a moment, the joy left my husband's life. I saw him struggle with daily tasks, daily breathing. But when our David had to leave us so soon, it broke us beyond repair. We don't ever really expect to be mended. Our baby boy, our only child left, had been called back to God.

The toughest part of grief, for me, is not even burying my children. (I know your mouth dropped open when you read that sentence.) Let me assure you, burying my children was my worst nightmare, my horror, my worst moment. But even worse than that is the separation I now feel from God. Yes, I said it! I feel separated from the one who gave His own life for me. I feel betrayed by the one I prayed to daily, hourly at times. Can I dare say that? I did. Before you slam this book shut, please hear me out. I have not turned my back on God. I reach out for Him in the early hours of the morning still. I search for Him daily. I force myself to listen to praise music, now sung by others when it used to be me singing. I find myself still singing the old hymns when I am working. I have advanced to reading other passages of scripture than Job. This was a big deal for me as I have read the Bible every day, twice a day for most of my life! How could I pray to a God who said no to my prayers over my children? How could I pray to a God that I was convinced gave promises like "The seed of the righteous shall be delivered"? I set all those promises in my mind and claimed them every day over my children. I wrote them and posted them in prominent places in my house. I listened to ministers as they instructed me in ways to pray over my children, to claim those promises that would not fail! And yet my children, my joy, my posterity, my hope for the future are all in heaven, in a place where I can't hug them anymore, at least not while I am still on earth. I have started trying to pray again. I pray the Lord's prayer every morning. And sometimes I pray for others, those short pleadings that I wonder if God will answer because it is I that is praying. Since He didn't answer my prayers over David, does He hear me? Does He care? In my spirit, I know He does. But my flesh and soul are in an all-out war with my spirit.

I wanted the theme of this book to be about a woman, a grieving woman, who had lost all her children but had had her faith restored. It is a struggle for a woman of faith to have that very faith, which she thought was so strong and solid, be shaken to the very core. My hope is that before this book is complete, before you have read the last sentence, you will see that hope, that faith emerge once again as a powerful force in my life. That is my hope. I reach for it daily.

God is God! We don't tell Him what to do. We don't plan for Him. He plans for us. His wisdom is far beyond what our finite minds can even grasp. With that knowledge, hope's flame still flickers in my heart. I heard Dr. Robert Schuller say once, "God will have the last word. And it will be good." So hope still waits.

DAY-530

•••••••••●•••••••••

Facing Mortality

When faced with the loss of someone so close to us, for the first time in our lives, we must accept our own mortality. Living life when all is well and the family events seem to keep going forward like clockwork gives us a sense that we will continue that way forever. We think everything will just fall in place and life will be good and just go on and on. But after facing the loss of children, we know that life is so very, very fragile and everything—*everything*—can change in a split second of time.

I remember so well the first real loss in our family. We were very close to our grandparents, and when our grandfather lay in ICU at the point of death, the family gathered around him. I was a young teacher and quickly left my classroom and went to be with my mom, who was there alone. But when my grandmother passed just a few years later, it really hit me full force that life is fleeting. It might have been when they began to clean out my grandmother's house, a home that I loved visiting with its warmness and the love that my grandparents had for us. To see things being hauled out and the house eventually being torn down was such a blow to me. It was then, when I was still a young woman, that I knew this life and all its trappings were only temporary. I saw that material things didn't really matter.

Fast-forward to now. Each day since we buried our last child, our David, my husband and I arise each morning seeking a purpose for the day, a purpose for even continuing with a life that is empty.

Our children were our purpose. So we are constantly asking the question within ourselves, "Why did God leave us here?" We don't fear death. We even welcome it at times when the grief is so great and the missing of our babies overwhelms us. But we know we will not leave this earth until our destiny is fulfilled.

Facing our own mortality can be daunting. But facing life after the loss of children is even more daunting.

The longer I live, the more certain I become that "neither death, nor life, nor angels, nor principalities, nor powers, nor things present, nor things to come, Nor height, nor depth, nor any other creature, shall be able to separate us from the love of God, which is in Christ Jesus our Lord" (Rom. 8:39 KJV). Facing the hills and valleys of life, the longer you live, the more you experience, which gives you opportunity to become an overcomer. The Bible also says that "if God *be* for us, who *can be* against us?" (Rom. 8:31 KJV). So does death stand against us? No! If there can be any positive thing in child loss (and I don't say that lightly!), then it is that we lose our fear of death. The Bible clearly states, "Therefore, since [these His] children share in flesh and blood [the physical nature of mankind], He Himself in a similar manner also shared in the same [physical nature, but without sin], so that through [experiencing] death He might make powerless (ineffective, impotent) him who had the power of death—that is, the devil—and [that He] might free all those who through [the haunting] fear of death were held in slavery throughout their lives" (Heb. 2:14–15 AMP).

Our freedom from the power of death came at great price to Jesus Christ. And yet many who are of the Christian belief still live in fear of death their whole lives. There is a freeing from fear of death to a parent who has buried the dearest on earth to them. We live with "one foot on earth and the other in heaven." But ultimately, our freedom came through Jesus Christ and His own sacrifice on the cross. We don't have to live in fear of death.

What, then, can separate us from the love of God? I say, absolutely nothing!

DAY-550

••••••••••●•••••••••

Dreams

As a child, we have dreams. We dream of growing up, getting a really good job, getting married, having kids, seeing our grandkids and the wonderful life that we earn by working so hard. That all came true for me except the grandkids. It seems my dreams stopped before that. They came to a screeching halt right at the fulfilment of all the previous dreams.

I have had a good life. I received a good education, which led to a good job, met a handsome man, built a great little house with acres for gardens and livestock, had beautiful children, and retired just in time to help care for my aging mom and homeschool my youngest child. I saw both my children grow up, Erin marrying her childhood sweetheart. It all came together so beautifully. But one by one my children left for heaven. This left me in my senior years with nothing but crushed and shattered dreams. My dreams seemed to vanish with my last child, who was my heartbeat. I saw no hope of having a future. With David's passing, I found myself at a loss to even know what to do when I got up each morning.

I am surrounded by things in my house that my children would inherit one day. There were treasures passed down when both sets of parents went to heaven. And in the end, I am feeling like Solomon, who, in all his great wisdom, said, "Vanity of vanities; all is vanity" (Eccles. 1:2 KJV). Several times that Solomon spoke of accumulating treasures on earth that would be passed to people who might not even have known us. My worldview has changed dramatically in the last year, four months, and sixteen days. The things that mattered so much before don't matter anymore.

So where is the dream? What do I dream for now that the most precious things I had are gone from this life? I have been told more than a few times that I must move ahead, move on. My question is, Move on to what? I want to say to them, "If you bury all our children, what would you want to move on to?" But I keep my lips tightly sealed. The Bible says, "Without a vision, the people perish" (Prov. 29:18 KJV). The vision is looking ahead. But what if all you see ahead is nothingness?

Everyone has dreams. Right? Well, maybe they don't. I have always had dreams, dreams of getting married, having children, having a successful teaching career. But after those dreams were wonderfully fulfilled, thanks be to God, now I find myself searching for another dream. I just can't seem to find a single one. My children are in heaven. My husband and I are retired. But what is there to dream for if your children aren't here completing that proverbial circle of life. What if the circle of life is broken, crushed to powder? When I meet a friend or family member, the first question is usually, "What have you been doing with your spare time?" It's hard to frame an answer to that one. While they may be involved with their job or children or other fulfilling engagement, I don't want to say, "I scrub my floors, cook, clean, plant, reorganize, or do some other task that fills the time in my days." And yet that is what has become my life as of today.

Maybe tomorrow I will find a dream, something to live for or breathe for. But today I haven't.

Whether a parent loses one child, their only child, or sadly, like us, all their children, there are crushed and demolished dreams that will never be fulfilled on this earth. As I thought on this when I made my journal entry last night, I decided that I will pray. I don't pray as much now, and I'm not even sure why. I know He hasn't left me, and I refuse to turn my back on Him. But I will pray that He give me one more dream to finish out this life. A new dream birthed in me is the one way I can survive. So where is the dream? It is now in the hands of God.

DAY-562

· · · · · · · ● · · · · · · ·

Those Who "Get It"

Our first Christmas was one I just couldn't handle. So our dear friends Jack and Rene Paxton and J. Marie and Greg Sheppard invited us to Florida to spend Christmas with them.

Jack's house was our first stop. Jack and Rene cooked us a fantastic Christmas dinner, complete with prime rib and all the trimmings. Then they presented us with the most amazing gift. They had made a huge collage of pictures of all our children, even getting beautiful, rare frames for some they chose as special. They just covered us in love and compassion, offering no condemnation for however we chose to grieve. It made the "season" more bearable.

Then we drove to the Sheppards' home, and they welcomed us with open arms, sharing our sorrow as we shared theirs since losing their beautiful son Mathew a few years earlier. We spent hours on the beach and sitting up late at night, just talking, sharing, and offering compassion to one another. The exchange students who lived with them at that time joined in our conversations at times, adding youth, life, and fun to our time together. It was a beautiful time of reflection, sharing, and caring that we will never forget.

Recently, I attended a national conference for bereaved parents at the insistence of J. Marie, my dear friend. My husband didn't feel up to the eight-hour drive, so my aunt Carolyn and my friend Sharon went along to help drive. It was the first venture, alone, out of my secluded existence. There were seven hundred in attendance, which alone should have been a signal I was in over my head. But the sessions beckoned, and I screwed up my courage and went. The primary reason I went was to get more information on publishing this book. So the sessions on writing, publishing, and blogging drew me in. But since we tried to fill each day, there were slots in between the writing sessions that needed to be filled. I tried to find those that most related to my own grief. The first one I tried was "Multiple Loss." Big mistake! The thirty or so in attendance were asked to say aloud the names of their children. I swallowed the huge lump in my throat as my turn came. Quickly I called those names so precious to me, along with their ages. As we went down each row, the stories became more and more intense as people shared stories of murder, drunk-driving incidents, child abuse leading to death, drug overdose, and almost every kind of death imaginable. Their emotions were very strong, and soon the whole room was filled with intense grief. My empathy meter was on overload multiple times over. That was added to my own suffering. As I left the room, I quickly texted my friends to let them know I had gone to a more secluded area upstairs to "crash." They came to me, worrying that it might be too much. And it was! They had similar stories of their sessions. But once again I screwed up my courage and plowed through. The writing and publishing sessions were the best. I rushed to get an autographed book by one of the panel members who impressed me. She was very warm and caring as she sat and listened to my story, coming from behind the table to give me a hug and words of encouragement, asking me to stay in touch as she handed me her card. It was the best thing I would take away from the three-day conference. Later, I did protect my fragile emotions when I attended one session on "daughterless mothers." It was intense as the first mom to speak told of how difficult it was to shop without her daughter. Tears flowed as she shared it had been years since her daughter passed. Those same emotions were felt by me right after my Erin left for heaven. I just couldn't deal with the emotion, so I left.

The trip was not a total loss. My dear friend Jutes, who encouraged me to attend the conference, invited us to spend a few days at her home on the beach. It really refreshed my soul to dip my feet in the splashing surf of the ocean, to ride in an airboat in the backwaters of the Everglades, to feel the salty wind in my hair as Greg steered the boat across the waters, taking us to view birds who lived on an island, and dolphins as they fed and played nearby. She and Greg had several dogs and a macaw, who loved on us and entertained us. Jutes's service dog, Kane, who helps her cope with her own grief, seemed to sense my hurt and stayed near me often, even giving me a big doggie kiss once, which she said was a rarity. Those three days boosted my spirit to a level it had not seen in about three and a half years.

Leaving the security of what's left of my world was tough. But I found venturing out beyond the pit is necessary, even if it takes your breath away. There is always a retreat when you come back to "hunker down at home." It's called survival. It's what grieving parents do.

DAY-577

· · · · · · ●●●●● ● ●●● · · · · · · ·

September 13, 2017
A Barefoot Walk

After yet another sleepless night, I read my devotionals, my Bible, my Jesus Calling daily devotion, my Amish devotional, and a few more chapters in Dr. Joanne Cacciatorie's book *Bearing the Unbearable*. As she shares story after story of grief that others experience, I find myself in those pages. I see struggles I didn't even realize coming to the surface. Today I acted on a suggestion I found there. I went outside and took a barefoot walk. I felt the sharp stones occasionally, along with the smooth, soft grass. I stopped to look up at a clear blue sky and the swiftly moving, bright, fluffy white clouds. The seventy-to eighty-foot-tall pines, oaks, cedar, and sweet gum trees caught my eye as the sun shone on me and the gentle wind blew. I looked down at the newly fallen orange persimmons laying on the ground, already being discovered by some little bees and ants. I felt the Creator and wondered, like Job, how I could ever question the one who created all this amazing creation. Still, I wept as I asked Him once again, "Why would You take my children?" He reminded me again that they weren't really mine at all. They were just loaned to me for a short time. (I wept as I remembered the joy of them.) They were in His heart before the foundation of the world. I said, "But what is my purpose in still being here when they are with You?" He said, "Feed My sheep." I said, "I don't have anything to say." He said, "Keep talking.

Keep sharing. Keep reaching out even if it's just to one or two. They need what you have to give." So I took a deep breath, wiped my tears on my sleeve, and headed back to the house.

There have been so many times since my precious David left for heaven that I really wondered if my life was over. Maybe this was the last thing I had to do before my own time had come. On one such occasion, I remember God whispered in my heart, "Your story isn't finished yet." Maybe that isn't what I wanted to hear because, without my children, who am I? And yet lying in bed last night, I kept hearing those words over and over. I began to formulate this dialogue between myself and others.

Your story isn't over yet. You may have been a baby six months in your mom's womb when your story was over. You may have been twenty-three, twenty-four, or forty-one, as my children were when their story was over. But if you are still breathing, it isn't over yet. There is yet another person whom you might be here to lift out of the mire of life. You might be here to plant another flower, to sit with an ailing mom or dad, to be a light to someone who walks in darkness, to encourage a person who is on the "edge," to help someone who has just been diagnosed with cancer, to help your child through a coming crisis, to be a listening ear to someone who can't deal with their problems anymore, or to just give a hug to a hurting soul. What is your story? Why are you still here? Maybe you, like me, don't know why you are still here. Maybe you, like me, have felt like giving up, giving in, just stopping life. But…maybe you, like me, have an unfinished story. You might be twenty-three, or you might be sixty-nine, like me, and think that you've done it all, you've accomplished your goals in life, you have "finished your course." But if we are breathing, our story isn't finished.

What is the rest? What is the next chapter? Sometimes it is just a fog. But when we step into it, it becomes a clear, cloudless day. So for now, I just keep breathing. I keep getting out of bed each day. I keep living.

• • • • • • • • ● • • • • • • • • •

January 2, 2018
Turning the Page

Here I sit, turning the page of another month, another year, 2018. The days turn into weeks, the weeks into years, and I wonder, *How long?* How long will I miss, long for, and cry for my children? The answer is always the same.

When Erin went to heaven, turning the page from January to February always brought a sinking feeling in my heart. Now, as crazy as it sounds, I feel almost a joy as I turn the calendar page to another month, another year. There is this anticipation of the joy that awaits me when heaven is a reality for me. Then my children will be in my arms.

I haven't quit living. But I breathe with the expectation that I will see them again. That belief has allowed me to free myself enough to begin to participate in life events again. We did celebrate Thanksgiving with my sister and a few family members. And although I refuse to display a tree, lights, and decorations, I allowed myself to have Christmas dinner with my sister Judy, her family, and a few more. While I still have grief waves and even grief tsunamis without warning, I have found I can venture out of my safe zone if I limit the venture to set parameters.

I still carry my grief for my children. It is ever present. When I shop for groceries in the same store I have gone to for years, I still quickly go past some of the items that my David loved. Sometimes the tears flow even though I try to stop them.

I had a pinched nerve after doing some heavy yard work a few months back. My husband drove me to the ER, and as they hooked me up to IVs and began to run tests on my heart, I told the doctor I knew what was wrong. Even though he thought it was my heart, I said the only thing wrong with my heart is the brokenness after burying my children. He mumbled something about that being a real medical diagnosis now. So they ran all the tests, only to find there were no artery blockages and my physical heart was okay. Finding the pinched nerve sent me to physical therapy for a few weeks.

As I walked in PT each time, I remembered all the times I took David to therapy to recover his strength after almost dying in ICU. My mind does race back to the days spent with my dear boy as he spent countless hours in hospitals and rehab. I even, to my horror, thought of how they take a deceased body out of a hospital as I drove past the ER after therapy. As I recalled those last moments, tears raced down my cheeks as I quickly drove away. The grief moments still come. No longer do I try to suppress them, but I embrace them because they bring my children close to me in thought, all of them. Not just the good, gentle, happy, joyous times, but the hard times as well.

......●●●●●●●●●●......

January 18, 2018
Home

In her book *Seven Lessons from Heaven*, Dr. Mary Neal tells of her NDE, where she encountered an out-of-body experience. She said the thing she felt so strongly was, when she saw Jesus, she knew she was home. And she didn't have much spiritual training. In other books of NDE (near-death experiences), people felt much the same way. After pondering that this morning, I am feeling strongly that this earth is truly not our eternal "home." We live here for around seventy years, build families, and work most of our lives for material things. But as life gets complicated and hard, often we feel we are not really connected to Mother Earth as we were when we were young.

Loss and grief open eyes to truth, to real issues that we may have kept hidden. Often, as I look on at life now instead of living the busy, complicated, fun, happy, sad, and sometimes-stressful life I used to live, I can see how many people are "spinning their wheels," putting so much effort into things that aren't eternal. And sadly, they are delaying dealing with what is eternal. Building upon spiritual values anchors the soul. When faced with life's stormy seas (and they will come for everyone), having no anchor means that there is a real danger of drowning, of letting the storm take one down into the abyss of a dark sea.

I can say with an honest heart that I truly believe my children are at home. Even though they all faced life's storms, even my baby Heather in the womb, they all had that anchor, Christ Jesus, our Lord. Erin and David were dedicated to God as infants. Later, when they were old enough to understand and make decisions for themselves, both accepted Christ as their Lord and made a commitment to Christianity. Scott called me, excitedly, once when he was just a teen from a Christian retreat at Myrtle Beach. He said he had made his own commitment to Christ. The knowledge of my children being "home" brings so much comfort in my struggles and sorrow each day.

DAY-685

••••••••●•••••••

I Am

A great challenge for any grieving parent is facing the past and the future. When our Erin went to heaven, I was so very broken that I could not view, at my husband's request, videos of Erin's childhood. The pain of hearing her sweet voice and seeing that little girl who was our everything was too great. With our Scott, many of our hours-long conversations when he was in Korea, Iraq, and Afghanistan played over and over in my mind. I saw his bright future in retirement and saw it whisked away so suddenly. So often I imagined what my little Heather would have looked like. Would she have had curly hair like mine? Would she have been very attached to her little brother, David, and helped him grieve after Erin passed? And David, ah! My baby boy, who was taller than me and didn't like me calling him Dave. I wondered what he would eventually do. I knew whatever career he chose, he would give it his all. He always wanted to do the right thing. He hated injustice, cheating, or stealing. And now…we look ahead and see only blackness, only questions, only pain as we face an uncertain future with no grandchildren, no children.

These are some ways I stay "connected" to my children. With Erin, I'd often get up in the middle of the night, just searching for some handwritten note from her or a card she had signed with a note. And when I found them, I put them in a special place to read and re-read. I kept most of her things, especially clothes that still, after ten years, contain her sweet scent. David's room is still untouched and just as he left it. I go in once a day and bury my head in his pillow or touch his clothes, capturing his sweet scent. Keeping a little memory box for both near my couch presents me with opportunities for continuing connection. Erin's has the last earrings she was wearing, a little note she wrote to me, one of the scrunches for her hair, a beautiful hair beret she wore to the prom, and a card she so lovingly gave me for Mother's Day. David's box has only a few things as yet: his guitar pic, a swatch of his favorite pajamas, which became a dust rag after he wore them to tatters (he liked to keep his clothes until they were nearly threadbare!), a parking ticket from Emory (although I think we would all like to forget that experience!), and a rare Pokémon card from his youth. I will add more things later as I find treasures that he also treasured. Staying connected to the past is important to me to preserve their memories.

But as I remember Bible passages, I recall God telling Moses that His name is I Am. When I think on that, I see that it sends a huge message about being in the present.

As a moderator on a grieving forum, we had training on mindfulness. *Mindfulness* is a term being referenced frequently now. But it's true. And for a grieving parent, it takes effort to live just in the day, in the moment. At first, that is all you can manage, a moment at a time. But as weeks and months pass by, it takes real effort not to look ahead or to look back. Focusing on today and what it brings is becoming my way of life. If dealing with my pain means this is the way I must live, then so be it. On my bathroom mirror, for years I had a little poem posted. It was a thankfulness poem that said, "Thank you, God, for this day, for what it will bring, for what it will take away." It's so true. One day at a time! Just one!

· · · · · · ●●● ● ●●● · · · · · · ·

February 5, 2018
Ring the Bell

There is joy in celebrating victory. At the Winship Cancer Clinic at Emory, when a patient is declared cancer-free, they can ring the bell in the clinic. When I first witnessed this, it was amazing. All the patients and families sitting in the many waiting areas of the huge clinic clapped in celebration of that person's victory. The nurses gathered around to take photos. It was truly a wonderful sight. My great desire was to see the day David could ring the bell. After his transplant, subsequent ICU near-death illness, rehab, and slow recovery, I remember that day, June 2, 2015, when his doctor came in the examining room beaming, declaring him cancer-free for the first time since his diagnosis a year and a half before. It was truly a day of joy. I don't know why they didn't ask him to ring the bell. I should have insisted.

This morning, I thought that maybe that was only after a person survived five years. But I just wanted to see him ring the bell! As I did my morning chores and these thoughts came, I could almost hear him say, "But, Mom, I did ring the bell in heaven!" Immediately my thoughts raced back to those first few months here in this lonely house as my husband and I struggled. I remembered the first "sign" I got from David. He loved music with a passion, just as I and his Campbell ancestors before him. Whenever I would step out of my kitchen onto the carport, the huge wind chime would begin ringing. If our loved ones can communicate with us, this would be a way David would! He found his release in music after Erin's passing, after a breakup with his girlfriend, and just getting through long days of chemo. We even brought both his guitars to the hospital. Music was his way of speaking. So, David, I do believe you have rung and are ringing the bells now.

Death has no hold over the believer. David does have the victory. It wasn't even the cancer that took his life; it was an infection. But...nothing can really take the life of those who are in Christ. He conquered death and the grave. So if you are reading this, no matter how hard your life is now, no matter how difficult the battles you are facing, ring the bell! You are victorious! "For me to live is Christ. And to die is gain" (Phil. 1:21 KJV).

When my mind races back to David's illness and the insufferable pain he endured, I think of him in heaven. Where is heaven? I'm not exactly sure. I do believe that it is wherever God is. And I believe with all my heart that David, Erin, Scott, and Heather await me there. As I thought of heaven today, this came to mind:

No more tears.
No more sorrow.
No more fears.
No darkness.
No lies.
No pain.
No anxiety.
No questions.
No unanswered questions.
No uncertainty.
No rejection.
No fretting.
No loneliness.
No abuse.
No racism.
No limitations.
Freedom.
Life.

I could probably sit here all day and night and keep writing the list.

The grand thing is, that's where my children are. They are experiencing all that and more than my finite mind can imagine.

I used to tell them that life, as we know it (seventy-year average life expectancy), is but a grain of sand in terms of eternity. They were encouraged to make their own peace with God so they would be prepared for eternity with Him.

That brings me peace today, even when the tears of loneliness for them overwhelm me. I do know that I will see them again one sweet day in heaven!

DAY-708

•••••••••●•••••••••

February 11, 2018
The Day Before

This is the day before the anniversary, or angelversary, as some call it, of the day David left us for heaven two years ago.

I take you on this journey so you can feel or get a glimpse of the pain of child loss. If you are a grieving parent, you already know.

The anticipation seems to grow each day as *that* day nears. Will I be able to bear it? Will I have flashbacks of that fateful day? Will others think I have gone mad? Am I posting too many pictures of him on social media? Do they think I should just move on? These are a few of the questions that roll over and over as the day nears.

I've been through this more often than I want to think. With our Erin, this year marks twelve times. Unbelievable! How have I survived this horrid journey this long? And yet I have.

But this time is so different. With David went all our hopes and dreams. He was our youngest, our miracle baby, our hope for having a future after Erin, Heather, and Scott left for heaven. That was it! Yes, we are surviving. Berry has stopped taking his antidepressant meds because he said he wants to "feel" the sorrow in his heart. And he is. He is not talking much, not interacting as much. But this is what he wishes. We had a visit today from David's lifelong friend Josh Davidson. It was a good visit as we chatted about all our lives, saw Josh's new car, and heard of his adventures. It went well until he gave me a big hug. I lost it. I cried as I knew so well that he misses David too. He hurts for his friend. I felt and associated with that pain. So I wept openly for my boy. Tomorrow I will lay a dozen red roses and two white ones on the grave. The red signifies the love (there should be a boatload of red!), and the white signifies the years he has spent in heaven. I will give each person who comes to join us a special pen I had made with the children's names engraved. Then we will go to Krispy Kreme to get a doughnut milkshake. This is a sign this year. David told one of the doctors, when asked if he could get David anything, that he wanted a doughnut milkshake. Of course, it was in jest. But it was odd that the week before the second anniversary, KK came out with a doughnut milkshake. That would be David! He could make me laugh out loud. So laughter, tears, hugs, memories flood my soul as this day approaches. I will make it! I will live on until my day comes. And I will keep my David's memory alive and strong.

DAY-739

·········•••●•••·····

February 28, 2018
Shelving Grief

As I have mourned so deeply my beloved son the last two years and, prior to that, poured my heart and soul into his care during his illness, I often wondered where the grief for my Erin had gone. There were guilty feelings as her special days passed with little recognition as in the prior years since her passing. For the first time in four years, though, this week the mask fell off and the grief returned, uninhibited. How can a mom tuck grief away somewhere in the recesses of her mind as if she could just "deal with it later"? And yet I know now that I did just that. It may be the soul protecting me from overload. But this week it all unfolded, and every time I looked at a picture of my beautiful girl, the pain was great, just as in all the years since she first passed.

When asked how I deal with the passing of all my children, I simply say, "I don't know." One thing I am sure of is that God, in His mercy, has held me. I know that that poem "Footprints in the Sand" is the story of my life. In it, Mary Stevenson writes that when you only see one set of footprints is when He (God) carries you.

That is where I am this week.

Grief has been called selfish. But is it? I remember about seven years after my Erin left for heaven, I was praying, asking God, "Do you want people to just ride by my house, shaking their head as

298

they think how pitiful I am? Is this how you want people to think of your children?" It was after that that He decided to take our David home. And then... I sank into the depths of despair this week. I was told to just write, and that is what I am doing. Yesterday I wailed, I screamed, I grieved all my children. I grieved the future, the past, the loss of joy, the loss of purpose, the loss of the ones who made my life worth living. I woke up this morning crying again, crying out to God. The feeling overwhelmed me that God, like others over the years, was hurting me just to watch me hurt. (What lies the enemy of our soul will plant in our minds when we are low!)

Just last week, I had an epiphany on Thanksgiving. The thought came to me that I was thankful for the few years I had with my children. They grew up under my care, and I was allowed to see them mature into adults. This was surely a turning point in my grief journey.

Well, the turning point turned me all the way around, and here I am again, wallowing in the bottom of the pit of grief. It's hard to breathe down here, hard to think, hard to rationalize the swirling thoughts of continuing a life that is fraught with pain and sorrow.

I watched a TV show recently, and there was a man who was a chief of a fire station. Apparently, he had lost all his children and family. He had a blood test that revealed something amiss. Thinking he had some deadly disease, he went to the doctor for the results. Amazingly, the results showed he had a rare type of blood that could save people from a rare illness. He said, "This is God punishing me by letting me live." He thought he would soon be reunited with his dead children.

I have had a few bouts with physical ailments that sent me to the doctor/hospital the last six months. Amazingly, they have found no cancer, no heart disease, and given me a clean bill of health at seventy-one. So I live. I keep living, hoping tomorrow a miracle will happen and my children will be back. There is the tiny flicker of a flame of hope that somehow it will get easier to bear. So I keep breathing. With every breath, I cry inside. The tears wash over my soul as I remember Easters (like the one about to come) with new Sunday clothes, Easter baskets I made lovingly, searching all over town for just the right goodies to fill them with as the Easter Bunny comes to visit the children on Sunday morning before church. All the years gone by, filled with fun, laughter, color, sunshine, and fluffy clouds, float through my mind. And then I am pulled back to the reality of my black-and-white world now, struggling to find some sort of purpose for living each day.

Such is the face of grief. It's not pretty or smooth. It is wrinkled, washed daily with tears, bearing the marks of a soul torn between heaven and earth.

DAY-769

. . . . ● . . . .

March 31, 2018
Little Victories / Big Wins

Grief is a journey. Along the path there are rocks, treacherous drops, uphill climbs, and green meadows with cool water that washes over the troubled soul. There are baby steps, the occasional giant leap, and backslides that take you in the other direction. Some days hold little victories that warm your soul. Others hold big wins. And still others may defeat all your efforts to breathe.

Today is the day before Easter Sunday. I find myself reflecting on the cross and the suffering of my Savior as He, undeservedly, faced many of the same things that we face in life—false accusations, rejections, harsh words, the loneliness of being separated from His Father, agony.

This week, as I anticipated this event, I hoped desperately that the miracle of His resurrection would yield some small victory in my own desperation for peace. I found such a time just a few days ago. Someone who had hurt me with harsh words often in my life did so again. Rather than wallowing in self-pity, I decided to listen to some of my favorite music, which reminded me that God is for me and is a shield for me. As I listened to the song, the hurt seemed to just melt away into a little victory for me in my spirit. I yielded to the words as a reminder that no matter how hard life may be or what happens to us or our loved ones, God is still our shield. Just as we shield our children from whatever life throws their way, so does our heavenly Father shield us. In my case, I haven't felt that in a while as I struggled, and still do, with the whys of my children leaving this earth before I felt their short lives were finished.

Today I will just let the warmth of the love of God shine on my face. I will embrace this event for what it meant to me, to the whole world. Small victories for a sorrowing heart and yield big rewards.

I had a dream once that I was climbing a mountain. I would climb up a bit and then slide back a few feet. It seemed I would never reach the top where there was shelter and safety. But I dug in! I kept up the pace. And eventually I made it to the top and enjoyed the comforts of a shelter over my head and warmth for my body. Little victories for a grieving heart can feel like climbing. When I was a member of a grieving forum, we would praise the newer members by telling them sometimes that we were so proud of the 'baby steps' or 'giant leaps' referencing the little of big victories they had accomplished during their grief journey.

Faith is reaching out for God even when you don't understand His plan. I found out that He is still my shield. And I truly believe, even though I don't understand or see the whole picture, that He was my children's shield too.

This thought is a big win for my soul.

DAY-780

· · · · · · ●●●●●●●●●● · · · · ·

April 11, 2018
My Anchor Holds

As I write about each of my beloved children, there is a different emotion that comes. Today is my Heather Lynn's thirty-third birthday. It is also the day she entered heaven's gates after a very brief twenty-four weeks in my womb. She was very much alive, and I talked to her as I had my Erin. She kicked, moved, had hiccups, and all the wonderful little signs of a new life growing in my belly. Oh, the anticipation we had that Erin would have a little sister! Sadly, at twenty-four weeks, she was gone. Somehow, I think I knew, even as the horror unfolded in the next three days, that my baby was in heaven. When I woke up this morning, all those events seemed to re-enter my mind after all these years. A mother never forgets. There was a story of an eighty-four-year-old woman who was asked about her children. As she named each one, she included a little one who had been born still many, many years earlier. These babies are always a part of who we are, even if their feet never touch the earth.

As I have shared my story of great loss to many people over the last several years, and especially now since my youngest and last child has gone to heaven, the same question comes up every time: How do you stand it? My answer is the same: "I don't know. I just get up and breathe every day with no real purpose for living." But somewhere deep inside me, there is a small flame that has never, ever gone out.

It is called hope. That hope stems from a seed that was planted in me as a very young child. His other name is Jesus. I accepted Him of my own free will, although I was taught about Him from a very young age. When I accepted Him, I accepted His suffering and the chance that I would carry my own cross in life. Many are falsely led to believe that becoming a Christian believer means that life will be paradise on this earth. It is not. On the contrary, it might mean that you will be given multiple opportunities to be an overcomer. That very faith in Christ will be put to the test over and over in varying degrees. Mine was tested so tightly it was as if it were a very thin rope and I were suspended as if over the Grand Canyon. I really, at times, wondered if it would break, and it almost did. But that same flicker of hope in my heart stands strong still.

The reason I share this is to tell that God will carry you when you can't even stand. He will. I am a living, breathing example of His grace, which keeps me alive when I would rather be with Him in heaven. Our days are numbered, according to the psalmist. None of us know how long we will live, whether it's six months or one hundred years. But what we do know is that this short life is nothing compared to eternity. And why not be prepared for eternity than just for this short seventy to one hundred years?

In Christ, my hope, is where my children wait for me. That is how I stand. That is how I can visit Heather's grave today with her little baby roses representing the love of a life that is perfect. She waits for me in paradise.

• • • • • • ● • • • • • •

May 29, 2018:
Isolation or Inclusion

Isolation or Inclusion

After a while, a grieving parent may look for more than just answers. They begin to look for a way to "fix" their life. The loneliness, the longing for what was and will never be again on this earth, the endless sadness of an existence marred by pain begin to take a toll on the mind, soul, and body. Besides looking back for answers, the future looms large and uncertain. It seems essential to try to find a way to keep living while carrying their sorrow with them into the future.

I find myself in that state. Others have tried, fruitlessly, to get me to "get out of the house," try something new, go to the beach, go to the mountains, read this, watch this, and the list goes on and on.

Grief brings a sense of loneliness that is tough to assuage. There is a sense of not belonging to groups, even family, and the world that is broken suddenly when part of your world is snatched away. Finding that sense of belonging again can be daunting.

In my many years of grieving, I have met so many who handle things so differently, and yet there are still common threads. Many find it hard, especially that first year or two, to be part of family celebrations. Marriages, baby showers, birthday parties, and especially the holiday festivities emphasize who is missing. If it is your child, then there is this huge gaping hole that leaves almost the feeling that celebration is just wrong! So do you isolate yourself, bury your head in the sand, and hope for better days? Do you force yourself to go to the event yet have a quick exit plan? Do you make your polite excuse and just not show up?

For each it may be different. I have known a dear mom who finds greater peace in going places, traveling, keeping with a group she has joined just to avoid being home, where so many memories haunt her day and night. I know others who avoid people altogether, often sleeping during special days just to make it through the day. I have avoided graduations, weddings, family parties, and even outings for the same reason: the grief would be too great. My children wouldn't be celebrating anymore, getting married, graduating college, having babies, or being part of the greater family. It cuts to the core, and I can't stand it. On the other hand, I find it is easier to be in a group of relative strangers if it is not a large group or a party setting.

The bottom line is that each must do what is right for them, not what is expected, or even what etiquette dictates. Survival for a grieving parent may mean finding a new normal that is so different from the old it changes who they are. But survival means finding a way to keep living, keep breathing. And it is what it is!

If there were just a way to fix this, to put a Band-Aid on it, to medicate it, it might be simpler. But there is no way. When dealing with this life versus the life beyond the veil, only God has the answers we so desperately seek. Only He can fix our lives, or at least patch us up so we can keep breathing with this gaping hole in our existence. That's my conclusion to this endless searching for a way to keep going, keep living. It doesn't mean I will not reach out. It doesn't mean I won't try new things or keep searching. But it does mean I will "be still and know that He is God" (Ps. 46:10 KJV). It is true, as I taught my children in memorizing the one hundredth Psalm: "It is He that hath made us and not we ourselves" (Ps. 100:3 KJV).

· · · · · · ● ● ● ● ● ● ● · · · · ·

June 25, 2018
Pressure Produces the Sweetness

There is a little poem that I carry in my Bible. It is very old, and the page is yellowed. But it packs a powerful message. When researching this poem, I found that it is actually a song with lyrics written by Annie Johnson Flint (1866–1932). As I read her story, I was amazed. She lived forty years with crippling arthritis, not being able to teach after it progressed. But out of her suffering she wrote some powerful songs. I found she had written another of my favorites, "He Giveth More Grace." But the one below is truly applicable to my life and has been a constant reminder of God's help:

Pressed out of measure, pressed beyond all length;
Pressed so intensely, seeming beyond strength;
Pressed in the body, pressed within the soul,
Pressed in the mind till darksome surges roll.
God is my hope and God is my joy;
He is the resurrection life I enjoy.
Pressure by foes, and pressure from our friends;
Pressure on pressure, till life nearly ends;
Pressed into knowing none to help but God,
Pressed into loving both the staff and rod.
Pressed into liberty where nothing clings,

Pressed into faith for hard and hopeless things;
Pressed into life, a life in Christ the Lord,
Pressed into life, the life of Christ outpoured.

I love that poem (song). It has been a source of encouragement to me in my life countless times.

Nothing can prepare us for the trials in life, especially when they come suddenly or with such force they take our breath away. But if we are anchored in something, especially our faith, then we are like the palm trees that might bend completely over with the hurricane-force winds but won't break. It all depends on our anchor.

As I was harvesting my blueberry crop this morning, I popped one in my mouth. It was bitter. It was dark blue and big enough to be very ripe. But it was almost tasteless.

I have noticed that my berries, during seasons of extreme drought, produce the sweetest of berries. But during summers of lots of rain, good humidity, and favorable weather, they are almost tasteless. They just get very fat and good-looking. But they aren't as luscious and sweet as when we have extreme weather.

That seems to be a good lesson in looking at life's trials. While I don't believe that God took my children to produce sweetness in me, I do believe that verse in the Bible that says God sends trials our way to "harden us" to difficulty (Isa. 41:10 AMP). If you have ever known a person or a family who had been through extreme trouble in life to the point their life was threatened, or they faced insurmountable odds, often those very people just exude a sweetness or gentleness that others do not. Could it be that with those trials we change our perception of life itself? Could it be that the crushing produces the sweet aroma of Christ Himself?

The sweetness of the blueberry might indicate it has been through extreme weather. Our "sweetness" might indicate we have faced extreme trouble. That's a thought to ponder.

DAY-871

· · · · · · ●●●●●●●●● · · · · · · ·

July 10, 2018
Weeping May Endure
for a Night

Recently, I read that people who don't have a purpose or a dream in life do not prosper. This thought gave me pause. For thirty-three years, my "purpose" was to be a mother. With that job comes a plethora of challenges, joys, anxieties, tasks, love, love, and love. When that job is brought to a screeching halt, it is almost as if a mom has been thrown overboard into a dark sea, drowning. Suddenly, a colorful, fruitful life becomes colorless, barren, and lonely. Without a child to carry on the family name, traditions, or heritage, what is there left to live for, to hope for, to dream? This is a great challenge for a grieving mom.

I have found that, like the five stages of grief, there are questions that keep revisiting my mind. What is my purpose? is one of the most challenging. For it is in purpose that we live, that we can get up each day and put one foot forward.

After our Erin went to heaven, people told me that eventually I would be able to refocus my energies on my surviving child. Some people do, and others do not. But I did. Over time, I turned my attention to David and his needs, challenges, education, and well-being. But since he has now joined his sister in heaven, there is nothing to refocus my attention on. My husband is struggling just as I am. It's not that we don't love each other and focus on each other; it was just that we found great joy in our children. It brought sunshine to our marriage and home. There was laughter, struggles, and well, just life! Now we both feel empty.

This morning, I didn't want to get up and start another day. I lay in bed reflecting, as I usually do. I felt the Lord's presence very strongly. I always look at the wall at the foot of my bed, hoping to see David's face, as I felt I saw Erin shortly after she left us. But I haven't. I squinted and strained to see glimpses of light in the corner of my bedroom. But I did feel I saw the face of Jesus. People may call me crazy, but they have called the most intelligent people in the world crazy. So there! I did feel Jesus was trying to comfort me. I think I may be like the verse in the Bible that says about the Jewish people, who have lost so many children over the generations, "Rachel refused to be comforted for her children." The verse is found in Matthew 2:18 (KJV). The voice of weeping was so strong in the land. I am there now. The weeping for my children never ceases, even though there is often no outward display.

After Erin left us, I remembered the calls. Those voices still linger in my mind. One lady who is very dear to me said, "Joy is coming back into your house." I clung to that as the years wore on, and Erin was still gone as the three of us struggled with each of our own issues. When David was diagnosed and we were in and out of the house, staying with him in Atlanta for treatment, I clung to hope again. I prayed all the verses about our children being protected. I clung to that verse that says, "Weeping may endure for the night. But joy comes in the morning" (Ps. 30:5 KJV). There were little fluorescent-colored sticky notes all around my house, in my purse and car, where I had written, "Joy is coming." It was in my face all the time. And now…when we came home from the hospital that fateful day David left for heaven, I went around the house the next week pulling down those sticky notes, throwing them in the trash. One clung to the back of the kitchen trash can, refusing to come off. How can joy come back? How can a man and woman who gave their lives to raising beautiful children bury all of them and ever know joy again on this earth? It's a mystery to me. I'm stuck in this pain. Will I ever get back up?

We find ourselves focusing on preparing for an uncertain future by securing our assets, working on our house, and cleaning out unnecessary clutter. But in doing so, we are sifting through those thirty-three years of a wonderful life with our children. That brings joy and pain at the same time.

Finding purpose is just one more thing that is constantly before a grieving parent. Some find a new purpose. Some do not. I hope I can.

DAY-882

••••••••●•••••••

July 21, 2018
A Light in a Dark Place

I awoke early, 5:56 a.m., and after devotionals and a few house-hold chores, I stood alone in my living room, opening the blind to a still-darkened day because of a thunderstorm. My solar lights flickered as they do when the day breaks, but some were still shining brightly in the darkness. Grief is a very dark place. I could see myself, as I pedaled my stationary bike and continued to watch the darkness and solar lights, as a broken pot, its shards sharp and unshapely. But also, the thought of having a small light still within me began to emerge. Often, I think my life is basically over. I'm seventy years old, retired from a successful career, had raised two children to adult-hood, and owned my own home. But with my children gone to heaven, much of my husband's and my time is spent doing mundane chores, watching TV, and trying to stay healthy. I ask myself, To what end? Who inherits our seventy years of experiential knowledge? Who inherits all this stuff we have accumulated, much holding value to us but may not to anyone but our children? The questions are probably asked by any grieving parent. The my mind goes back to the light. The light shines on no matter how dark the night.

I think I made a momentous decision this morning, early, while my husband slept. A goal came into my heart. Finally! A goal! So, so many grieving, troubled loved ones have crossed my path over the past years since I buried my most precious treasures on earth, my children. Even when David was fighting the battle of his life at Emory Hospital in Atlanta, I talked with so many on the elevator, sitting in the hallways, at the vending machines, at the valet parking deck, in waiting rooms, or the cafeteria. Often, we would exchange the names of our loved ones with a promise to pray for each other. Sometimes I would listen as I saw the tears flowing. I made friends with people from all walks of life, from near and far. One dear lady still calls me frequently. Somehow, I was able to reach out through the darkness and be a light. When our Erin went to heaven, I was so distraught I began just searching the internet for any help. That was when I first connected with the MISS Foundation, Mothers in Sympathy and Support. It changed my life as I began to connect with other mothers, fathers, siblings, and grandparents who were grieving. We all shared the little bit of "light" that was left in us with one another, holding one another closely as we navigated the dark, troubled waters of grief together. So I decided my goal will be, for whatever time is left on this earth, to be the light. Jesus said, "I am the light of the world." He encouraged us not to "hide our light under a bushel." Even though I am a broken vessel, just crushed to powder, out of that brokenness, if you look hard enough, you can find the light. The light of God that He put within us when we first believed cannot be crushed, broken, or snuffed out. As a matter of fact, when I see the light in a broken person, it seems to shine brighter. That light guided them in the darkest night of the soul. And it still will guide if given a chance.

So if I never achieve another major goal in this life, may my light shine bright enough to help another grieving mother, father, sibling, grandparent, grandchild, aunt, uncle, cousin, or friend when they face the crushing darkness of grief until they can find that their light is still in there.

· · · · · · · · · ●●●●●●●●● · · · · ·

August 2, 2018
Come What May,
Finish the Race

Books and articles, especially about NDEs and other life-changing events, have been my choice of reading since our Erin left for heaven. This morning, as part of my devotionals, I read an inspiring story of a young athlete, John Stephen Akhwari of Tanzania. He came from the Kilimanjaro area, where he plowed fields and ran in events that were held there. His country sent him to the 1968 Olympics in Mexico City. In his training he had mastered the course in two hours, twenty minutes. But when he began the race in Mexico with seventy-five others, eighteen of them had to drop out. The atmospheric pressure there was so different he began to experience severe leg cramps. But he kept running, despite the pain. He made it back to the leaders' position, amazingly. But jostling for position, the group had a pileup and he was caught in that and took a fall that dislocated his knee. Blood was gushing from the wound. He also bruised his shoulder and had other bruises. Medics bandaged his leg and treated his wound. But he pushed on, even with the pain that radiated all over his body. About an hour after the first runner had crossed the finish line to thunderous applause, in the darkness a limping Akhwari came across the finish line. He was the last runner. His time was three hours, twenty-five minutes, twenty-seven seconds, exactly an hour after the winner's time. The crowd cheered him on when they saw him limping heavily on the wounded leg across the finish line. When the journalists surrounded him and asked him why he didn't just quit when he was injured, he replied, "My country didn't send me five thousand miles to start the race. They sent me five thousand miles to finish the race."

This story really inspired me today. Even if we are wounded with what we think is a mortal wound (such as burying a child), we still must make it to the finish line. It would be so easy to give up and just quit living. But when I consider what a gift life is, especially since the gift of children, no matter the time they were here beside me, then I feel that I must finish the race that God has sent me here to finish.

Sure, the future is uncertain since all my children are in heaven. But if I am still here, then God has a purpose. And it's up to me to fulfill what He wants only me to do. So here I go, limping to the finish line!

DAY-1,013

· · · · · · · · ● · · · · · · · · ·

November 27, 2018
No Matter the Cause

Much has been written about the "layers" of grief, the causes of grief, and the effect of the grief on the mourner. As a member of an online grieving group, I would often see people comparing grief to grief. Is it harder to mourn a child who was murdered, even accidentally, than it is to mourn a child who died of a deadly disease or who died of SIDS? There are so many factors or "layers" to the way a person mourns. The depth of the love is a factor. After having lost four children, I can say that each was "different." I can't say that one was any "easier" to bear than another. But I can say, after our David went to heaven, that my grief is longer and tougher since he was our last surviving child. With him went our hope for the future, the light in our home that he brought, the ongoing purpose for surviving our daughter's passing. So I would make the case for parents who lose their only or all their children. Finding hope and purpose after loss is key to survival. And when you have no children left in the home to refocus, it brings another lifelong battle for survival.

Having said all that, I would never, ever minimize any parent's grief. Grief is hard work. It consumes your energy, your time, and your very survival. It's a horrible event in any parent's life, the kind of nightmare that every parent fears. So while I have experienced far too much grief and am too acquainted in four different types of child death, my heart still breaks when I hear of any parent losing a child. It is unnatural, untimely, unthinkable, and unbelievable. It is something that you never get past, no matter how hard you try. You go on living, but part of you is gone.

I could add another "stage" of grief. It would be called the "if only, maybes, and why didn'ts." This might fit in the guilt stage, but it's a little different. This morning, I was thinking that maybe I wronged my children in having them at my age. I was only thirty-five when Erin was born, thirty-seven with Heather, but forty-three with David. Did I doom them to sickness because my eggs were as old as me? Did my older age have anything to do with David dealing with so much sickness? Since I didn't marry until thirty-one, I had no choice in having them younger. And I was beyond happy when I found out we were having each of them. It was like a new start in life, new life coming into our family. But I will always wonder if my age had anything to do with David being so sick. And with Erin, I have always wondered, if I had taken half the tuna casserole by her house at six thirty that last fateful night, if just seeing her and being with her would have prolonged her life. Then I would have known she was so sick and maybe could have headed off her taking that last pain medicine. I would have taken her to the doctor again if I had only known. And with Heather, if only I had known I was pregnant, I would not have taken the sinus medication that November. (The doctors never could determine the cause of death.) If that could have saved her, I would have not taken it and just suffered through the infection. But maybe we cannot change the final outcome. Maybe David was right when he said, "Mom, when your time comes, it comes!" How wise was my son!

• • • • • • • • ● • • • • • • • • •

November 30, 2018
Comforting Memories

Here comes Christmas again, ready or not. I am not ready. I never will be, don't want to be, don't care to be. When a young couple becomes parents for the first time, everything changes. Christmas becomes a magical time of fun, lights, eyes growing larger at seeing gifts, lights, music, and glitter. As the years go by and other children come into the family, it becomes a package deal of celebration all year long. When all that comes to a sudden halt when that same couple suddenly finds themselves alone with their children in heaven, there is a fog that descends, changing your world from magical colors to black-and-white.

How can I best describe it, this life without my children here on earth? I am sitting in my recliner, and suddenly I am thrust back in time to wheeling David, on his bed, from the hospital to the rehab hospital as we go through the underground tunnel at Emory. My greatest treasure lying on a bed in a hospital room as I trek the underground passageways later, trying to find some food that will entice him to eat again. Or I look at the box of Christmas flowers I will put together to put on the graves and think, *Erin should be here to help me with this. She was the one who could make everything look so lovely. But alas, she can't be here beside me, for she is in a world that I can only imagine.* I put flowers on Scott's grave today, and as I looked at the somewhat-faded picture of his handsome young face, I thought, *Who is enjoying life today because they were the recipient of his precious organs? Why didn't he get to be here to live out his retirement years after all those years of travel abroad, keeping our country safe?* How can I describe it? Well, I can't. I can just take a deep breath as I watch other families enjoy opening their gifts as their children and grand-children laugh and play around their homes. I can rejoice and, at the same time, be sad when I hear of an engagement, a graduation, or an announcement of a friend's new grandchild. I can remember my own unfulfilled dreams as I see the colored lights on a tree that used to bring joy.

It's the middle of the night. Erin has been gone to heaven only a few days. I get up and start searching, rummaging through drawers and closets to find anything, anything she has written or made. It's a search for comfort. Fast-forward ten years. I am walking into the bedroom of my beloved David. Where is he? He is usually there since he can't even get out of bed. I reach up to the little hook beside his bed where I hung his clothes so that they would be within easy reach since he was so sick. I fumble through the front ones to the back, where the jacket that he wore all the time hangs now, unworn. I hold the soft jacket sleeve to my cheek in hopes of smelling his sweet scent once more. Tears run down my cheeks. Memories...how they flood my soul! They bring bittersweet comfort, if there is such a thing.

How can a grieving parent find comfort? Is it in a book? Is it in others remembering and mentioning their names? Is it in a familiar shirt or dress or item that their child has touched? Is it in meditation, prayer, or Bible reading? (Ultimately, I believe this is it!) Often, it is in memories, or at least it is for me.

Yesterday I pulled a few very old Christmas decorations out of a box. I can't do the whole nine yards of Christmas for the pain of seeing all the handmade ornaments my children made when they were little. (Yes, I saved everything!) But I do pull out just a few nonsentimental things just to have some semblance of Christmas in my home.

I pulled out these red paper honeycomb bells. My mind raced back to when I was a little girl in my mother's home. There I felt safe, warm, loved. And I wrapped those memories, like a blanket, around my cold, sad soul. These little bells were one of the very few store-bought decorations that Mama hung in the windows as Christmas neared. Daddy would go into the woods and bring back a few holly branches with their brilliant green leaves and bright-red berries. Mama loved to hang those around the house for decoration until Daddy would cut down the familiar cedar tree closer to the day. As I look at this simple decoration, it took me back to a simpler time, a wonderful life. I always tried to make Christmas as special to my children as my mom and dad did for me. With the children all in heaven now, it seems pointless to do the whole thing. But isn't it grand that we all have those memories to wrap around us?

So I would say that even though I put the comfort of God above all, the warm memories hold a very close second when it comes to comfort for the soul.

DAY-1,018

• • • • • • ••••• ● •••••• • • •

December 7, 2018
The Angry Me

Sitting in my recliner, looking at the tiny ten-inch Italian Stone Pine I allowed myself this year for Christmas (to plant later), I could suddenly feel intense anger well up inside. Once again, I wanted to just throw the tree through the window. My mind raced back to 2006 and that first Christmas without Erin. I had the big tree up then, and that same feeling came over me one night. The intense, out-of-control anger that I had rarely, if ever, felt inside seemed to overtake my soul. I was angry that David and Erin were not here. I was angry that they didn't make it. I was even angry at them for a nanosecond for not making it! Isn't that crazy?

Immediately, I feel guilt for even thinking such a thought. The anger at God, at life, at loneliness, at the utter desolation that engulfed me just seemed to overtake my soul to the point I needed to act out, to throw a fit, throw something, or destroy something! Of course, being me, the quiet, peace-loving, strictly disciplined soul that I have always been, I suppressed the anger to calm down.

Part of the anger comes from feeling so cheated. When you have poured out your life to raise your children to adulthood and they pass suddenly, you feel that you have lost your reward. That reward is seeing them have their own children, seeing them succeed in life, and knowing the joys and even the pain that family life can bring.

Part of that reward is grandchildren that preserves your legacy for generations to come. When that is suddenly snatched away, it feels as if you have lost it all! The unfairness of it baffles the mind. In those moments, there is no comfort as the anger begins to consume the soul.

How can God be so cruel to His child? How can my children not be here, living out the life God gave them, giving me grandchildren, standing by my side when I am too old to care for myself? How can it be?

All the questions that many grieving parents face endlessly as long as their time on earth lasts go through my mind and soul. It is so hard, especially in those first few months, to find a way to keep the emotions in check, to sooth a troubled soul. And yet, I've been told that if that anger is not dealt with, it can turn into bitterness of soul. Bitterness eats away at a life. All of us have probably known someone who have allowed bitterness to change them. A grieving parent is wounded to the core of their being. They don't need any more battles than the sorrow that they deal with daily. And yet, the longer they live, there will be these layers and stages of grief that emerge and reemerge.

But I take a deep breath, cry out to God to show me the path of life one more day and keep living. Such is the life of this grieving mom.

DAY-1019

· · · · · · · ● ● ● ● ● ● ● ● ● ● ● · · · · ·

December 8, 2018
Letters

There are many ways to "vent" as a grieving parent. One of the best I've found is writing letters. In my many journals after Erin's passing into heaven, entries are frequently letters, letters to Erin, letters to other family members, even letters to God. Since David's passing into heaven, I haven't journaled as much, unless these entries could be considered journaling. But today I want to write a letter to God.

Dear God,

I am sitting, looking at my screen saver with two pictures, one of me hugging my Erin, the other of me hugging David. You gave me these two precious gifts. And You took them back. They were both miracles from You, especially David, after You took Heather and loaned him to me, allowing me to give birth at forty-three years old. Both were the result of acts of faith. And what a reward they were!

Thank You for allowing me to be real with You, allowing me to be raw and open about my feelings. Sometimes I know You have only heard tears.

There were times when I was so angry with You I didn't even think I would pick up a Bible again or utter a prayer beyond a recited one. But You were very patient, long-suffering, and forbearing. You never chided me, although I quickly repented for some of the hard things I felt and even said to You, almighty God.

Thank You for loaning these blessings to me for those thirty-five years. They were the best years of my life. Each one was filled with joy as I realized the love of a child for her/his mom. It was a love like no other. My life was so full. There was fun, laughter, tears, joy, sadness, excitement, secrets, learning, hugs, and the most beautiful smiles in the world. Each day was a new adventure.

Yes, I know. I am speaking in the past. I do hear You chiding me a bit for that. They are still alive, I know. But, Lord, I can't touch them now, can I? I can't feel their arms around me. I can't kiss their beautiful faces. I miss them so terribly at times my heart nearly bursts!

How do I live out my remaining years, Father, without my children? How do I reconcile all the injustice I feel? I feel so cheated! See, I'm still full of questions for which You are silent.

But my hand is finally back in Your strong one. I won't let go, no matter how low I get.

For with You is my life.

Love,
Your child,
Brenda

A precious friend just lost her husband, who was only forty years old. I see the agony as she posts her grief on Facebook. My advice to her yesterday was to journal. It helps to get it out on paper.

When the sleepless nights came for me and nothing seemed to help, I'd keep my Bible and a journal on my nightstand. I'd either read or write. Writing out the grief helps some.

There are no easy answers to grief. It takes hard work, 24-7. But sharing things that may have helped us with others seems to give them some ways to cope.

When I look back at the things I wrote, I feel the intensity and utter rawness of grief. I also see the gradual softening of its jagged edges on my soul. It never goes away, and there are days when I get thrown back into the depth of the pit. But I will keep writing, keep extending my hand to others.

DAY-1,024

· · · · · · ●●●● ● ●●●● · · · · · ·

December 13, 2018
Sharing Other's Burden

A dear grieving mom recently made a comment that she was amazed at how I could withstand this storm of four losses and still hold true to my faith in God. My reaction was, if she only knew the times I have gone from feeling that God didn't really love me, to God really loves me, to how He can expect me to weather this storm. And I would include many mixed emotions filled with questions for God in between.

We see a grieving mom or dad at a family gathering or in the store and think, *Hmm, they seem to be doing fine.* But if we could look underneath the facade of "All is well," we might see a totally different picture. That picture might be one of utter devastation, loneliness, and a sadness so deep it could be felt. The world and our loved ones want us to be okay. But we know that that will never happen until we are with our children once again where they are. And it is with that hope that I keep breathing.

A precious young man named Keith recently made his entrance into heaven. His family was and are good friends with whom we share a spiritual bond. I called his mom last night, and we had a long chat. There is a comradery among grieving moms. To truly understand the depth of pain of child loss, it, sadly, must be experienced. As we talked, we found several areas of common ground. Our questions to God, our deep feelings of loss all seem to come together as we each shared.

A dear friend of mine just recently had to say an earthly good-bye to one of her two living children. She has a baby in heaven too. Her son had suffered a debilitating illness since his early twenties. He was only forty years old when he passed into eternity very unexpectedly, leaving his wife, two sons, brother, mom, and dad heartbroken. I called my friend last week. We shared our sorrow, and she began to share her amazing story. Like me, she was very angry with God. She is a deeply spiritual woman who had prayed for her children all their lives and fully expected them to be covered with grace and protection. She shared how she had said hurtful things to God, to which I could relate. It's so hard for a grieving parent to grasp how our great and loving Father, God, can take our children without an explanation at the very least. But none had come. She said one day she felt the Lord saying to her, "I love you." It seemed to break down all her defenses, and in that one moment, she knew that it was true, that boundless, limitless, unfettered love of God that comes in time of crisis to soothe the weary soul. She knew then that no matter how dark the path, no matter how much we say to God about our own grief and what we perceive to be His failure to change things, God's love is still there, waiting so patiently for us to quit talking and just breathe it in. Even though she still mourns her dear son, she knows now that God has not turned His back. He is still there, no matter how she feels.

Amazing love, boundless love.

Yesterday, I had a chance meeting with a classmate from years ago. He and his wife stood and talked with me. I had never met his wife, but as he walked away after I had shared my story, she said, "I, too, lost a son. He was killed in an accident years ago. It was Mother's Day weekend. The memories run through my mind all the time. And Mother's Day is the hardest day of all now." Oh, how my heart ached for her pain. It had been years before, and the grief was still so real.

It has been my privilege to get to know moms from all over the world in the past twelve years since our Erin went to heaven.

And no matter the race, religion, economic standing, education, or background, we have connected on a level that I would call simply common ground. While each story is different, there are connecting points and a reason to share our great sorrow with one another. Don't we learn from others who walk the path ahead? Doesn't the Bible say that we receive "comfort so that we can comfort those in any trouble with the comfort we ourselves receive from God" (2 Cor. 1:4 KJV)?

Early on in my grief walk, I learned that one way to find a small measure of healing is to share with others. In that sharing, you almost give a "hand up" to another soul who is lost on life's sea of trouble.

There is a wonderful little story that truly tells the tale. It's called "The Pit" (author unknown), and it paints a picture of how a grieving parent may be perceived by different people. Some people are willing to climb down there with you, while others just stand around the top, expecting you to emerge the same person you were before. It is so true. I have determined to be one who will climb down there with you, if you are grieving. As you take those small steps, my desire is to be the one who helps you find your new normal and keep breathing.

• • • • • • • • ● • • • • • • • • •

December 16, 2018
Hope

Brooklyn Tabernacle Choir sings a powerful song called "I Never Lost My Hope." As I listen to the words to the song, my mind takes me back to the beginning of each grief journey. I remember the utter hopelessness I felt inside. With our David, I remember falling to my knees beside my bed and begging God, "Please, let's have a do-over." I wanted Him to undo David's passing. I couldn't bear the thoughts that I would live out the rest of my day without him here. Hope seemed to have vanished completely. As the days and long nights continued, I began to realize that David was in paradise. He wasn't suffering anymore. And I knew that one day I would see him again when I joined him there. I realized that, because of my Christian faith and my belief in the life beyond this earthly one, I did have hope. That hope had been almost vanquished as I struggled with the anguish that grief brings.

Yesterday I read about the apostle Paul as he was brought before King Agrippa, his last stop before being tried before Caesar. Paul was telling the king his story, and he said in Acts 26:6–7 (KJV), "And now I stand and am judged *for the hope* of the promise made of God unto our fathers: Unto which promise our twelve tribes, instantly serving God day and night, hope to come. *For which hope's sake, King Agrippa, I am accused of the Jews.*" As I read those verses, I realized that it is our hope that is put on trial every day. Even science has found that when people are very ill, if their hope is gone, it is very hard for them to recover. Hebrews 6:18–20,(KJV) says, "That by two immutable things, in which it was impossible for God to lie, we might have a strong consolation, who have *fled for refuge to lay hold upon the hope* set before us: Which *hope we have as an anchor of the soul*, both sure and steadfast, and which entereth into that within the veil; Whither the forerunner is for us entered, even Jesus, made a high priest forever after the order of Melchisedec."

1 Corinthians 15:19 (KJV) reads, "If in this life only we have hope in Christ, we are of all men most miserable." If my entire hope rested in the things around me and in my children being my legacy on this earth, what would I have left to hope for now? But knowing Christ, I have hope that my children will meet me on the other side of this earthly life. The things of this life are truly temporal. But eternity ahead holds my future.

Hope is an anchor of the soul! How great is that? Even when we face the direst of circumstances, the lowest hell we know on earth, the depths of the pits of depression, we still have that anchor, that hope in Christ! Yes, we will see our loved ones again. For this hope today, I am most thankful!

December 23, 2018
Validation

Last night, I began thinking of the one thing that I would really want if someone asked how they could help. The word *validation* came to mind. Grieving parents struggle to keep the memory of their child alive. Why do they struggle? It seems that many (including me before) seem to think when the funeral or memorial service is past that a person should just "move on." But how can a parent who has invested all they are into the child who became their heartbeat possibly move on? To move on is to leave behind the very reason for their existence. It is human nature to want to feel comfortable. It seems to make them feel uncomfortable to be around a grieving parent. So to make their life easier, they decide that person should just bury the past and move on. It really bothers me when I hear sermons and writings on how we should just "let go" and forget the past. Well, maybe for some who have lived a life of sin and have repented, that is great. But for a grieving parent, it just doesn't work. Our children became part of our identity. To say "Start over" or "Forget what was behind because they are in a better place" just doesn't cut it! The greatest gift a friend or family member could give a grieving parent is to remember their child with them. To remember them is not to idolize them or "build a shrine" for them (as someone told me when I posted pictures of Erin on social media on her birthday). But it is validating that their lives existed, their lives mattered, they made an impact on that person. It is joining the parent in keeping their memory alive. Then the parent doesn't have the struggle of fighting so hard to preserve their memory. I wish I could say how greatly I value it when I read a little post online of someone who remembered Erin, David, or Scott. When someone who loved them shares a funny story or says how great a person they were or how they influenced their lives or (and this is best) how very much they miss them, I feel a little relieved. It validates their lives and my feeling that they will be remembered long after I am in heaven.

I must tell you about my friend Sharon Fiedler. I didn't know her that well until Erin's memorial service. After the service, she began calling me. And it seems God has brought me comfort in her friendship. Our families began frequent gatherings. She and I began traveling to various church meetings and formed a wonderful friendship. Often, she would call just to check on me when I was really struggling just to "breathe." I made trips to the cemetery to Erin's grave at least two or three times a week and especially on birthdays and special days. Sharon always wanted to join Berry and me there at the cemetery, bringing a little garden ornament of something she had learned Erin enjoyed. Even when it was icy out and we thought we'd be alone, she would come and stand in the freezing weather with us. When David was so sick in Atlanta, she came to the hotel to bring a cake for Erin's birthday and to help celebrate him making the one-hundred-day mark past transplant, which was a big deal. She drove all the way to Atlanta to visit, sometimes bringing her husband, John, along with one of his specialty recipes, wonderful Italian soup to warm us on the chilly days. She loved our David as much as her own children. She called him Gentle Giant or King David and encouraged him to be all that God had for him. And she still doesn't miss any of the special days when we visit the cemetery. That's a friend who validates!

So when people ask how they can help a parent who has lost a child, I say, "Just be there for them. Let them talk about their child. Mention their child's name often." If I could write a new song, I think I'd title it "Just Be There." Isn't that what Jesus said before he left the earth? "I will never leave you nor forsake you" (Heb. 13:5 KJV). He's always there, whether we know it or not.

That is the greatest comfort and gift a friend can give.

DAY-1,036

•••••••••●•••••••••

December 24–25, 2018
To Celebrate or Not

I just shed a few tears as I said to God, "I miss hearing Your voice. Please let me hear it again today." (Oops, do I hear skepticism from my readers? Oh, well. I do believe that the Almighty still has a voice, and for those who listen, He can speak. It may not be audible, or it may be. But speak He can. And to those who have listening ears, He promises to speak.) But I digress. So after I prayed, I found myself writing once again. I had plans in the mind for today. Today is Christmas Eve, the eve of one of the most difficult days for us since all our children are in heaven now. So how do we assuage the grief? How do we spend these days? Do we sit in sorrow for what was and isn't here now, the big Christmas family celebrations of days gone by? I thought I might visit a couple of people who might be lonely now. Get out of this house, Brenda and Berry! Go, go, go. Escape. Run away, far, far away. I have known some who handle their grief by just going, staying away from a house filled with memories. And I am not judging them for doing that, because there are no rules to grief. You must deal with your own grief however you can. But do you know that you can't outrun grief? Just as you can't outrun problems. You turn around and run into the roar, as someone so aptly put it. The Bible says, "Be sober, be vigilant; because your adversary the devil, as a roaring lion, walketh about, seeking whom he may devour" (1 Pet. 5:8 KJV). Grief can devour you! It almost did me and still tries to at times. But I turn and run into the roar. And I become the roar. I become the voice of the child of God I am. And do you know who is standing behind me? The Spirit of God, who never, ever leaves me. When I was leaning over the caskets of my David, Scott, and Erin, kissing them all that last earthly goodbye, He was standing right beside me. He was the one who gently pulled me upright again and whispered, "Breathe, Brenda, just breathe." So I did. And do you know what? I am still breathing. I am seventy-one years old, mourning all my children and still breathing! It's because He is right beside me. I will always mourn my children until they are in my arms again. But He holds true to His promise that He will never leave us or forsake us.

On this Christmas Eve of 2018, my six huge bins of Christmas decorations and five-foot tree are still packed in my basement, where they have been since the Christmas of 2015, our last Christmas here with our David, our beloved son. Just a few minutes ago, I did hear the whisper, "Why are you celebrating Christmas anyway? Are you celebrating family? Or are you celebrating the birth of your Savior, My Son?" I began considering that. As I look at all the social media, I am inundated with pictures of big family Christmases, the kind I am missing so much. It just makes me sadder. And this year I notice each family is posting pictures of their family. But if only family is why we celebrate, I am a living witness that that can change in one moment of time. If we celebrate Jesus's birth and His Lordship over our lives, that is eternal. I wonder if they have celebrations in heaven while the whole earth celebrates this birth. He is not a baby anymore. He is King of Kings and Lord of Lords! That's more reason for us to celebrate. So my Christmases may look very different in the future than they have in the past. They might be visiting the sick, the imprisoned, or the lonely. They might be volunteering to play keyboard for a nursing home, or simply writing. They might be fulfilling the great commandment to "go into all the world and proclaim the gospel of Jesus Christ." After all, His birth brought salvation to all the earth. Every person ever born has that opportunity to be free. His name is called Emmanuel, God with us.

Another Christmas day has dawned. My first words upon opening my eyes were, "Happy birthday, Jesus." I do celebrate His birth. Immediately following were the familiar daily words "Show me the path of life" (Ps. 16:11 KJV). I knew today would be tough. I try to steel myself to face the days that were once filled with the laughter and joy of children. I remember the big Christmas brunch we would have to allow the children time with their new toys that "Santa" brought them. My hubby would sit in his chair and enjoy the fun of watching them run into the living room to find their new treasures. There are pictures of them still in their nightclothes, sleepy eyes filled with wonder. Then we would make the trip to the grandparents' house for the Christmas Day dinner, again filled with gifts and fellowship. We would have already gone to the other grandparents' house the eve before for a night of gifts and play and fellowship. And now…the day is strangely silent. It's a silence that can be felt deep within our hearts, one that longs for the sounds of our children. But we keep breathing, celebrating the birth of our Lord. We will go to my sister's home, where my parents once lived, and eat a Christmas dinner with them and their family. It will be a small gathering, unlike the ones of days past. But it will fill some of the loneliness with which we have become accustomed. We are so thankful for my sister Judy and her husband, Terry, for taking care of us, making sure we are not alone.

I will get the live tree off the grave to plant in my yard in remembrance of the lives of my children. The one I planted last year is doing well.

The day will soon be over. Another twenty-four hours that we had to endure will be behind us. Friends once told me that no matter how we dread the "special" days, we must remember it's only twenty-four hours. We can survive. And we can.

I wish I had an upbeat, inspiring message to include today. If I have one, it is this: Jesus Christ was born into this world to give us the greatest gift, hope! It is because of His life and sacrifice that we have hope to see our children again and to have the strength to endure the greatest of life's trials. He is our peace. He is our hope. That is the best message I could leave with you.

DAY-1,038

• • • • • • • • ● • • • • • • •

December 26, 2018
Endings and Beginnings

This is the last week of 2018. It has been an interesting year of survival for me and my husband. But we made it to the end. I have a little dry-erase board beside my desk that I use for appointments. It has been there through some of Erin's, David's, Berry's, and mine. After Erin passed, I was careful to outline a date she had written with permanent ink so that it would be there always. It has held our many Emory, rehab, wound care, and counseling appointments for David. It held Berry's appointments with his heart doctor after his heart attack in 1992. It has smudges of marker that can't be cleaned from so much use. Each day I erase the date and appointments for the day and write the new day next week. I have changed from wanting the days to pass slower to thinking, *I'm one day closer to being with my children again.* So now it is with joy that I rub the eraser over the days. I am not wishing the days away; I just have a new perspective. I look forward to new beginnings now. For each new beginning signals a way into the future, one that I cherish.

So I can bid this year goodbye with no regrets. I have given to others, helped in any way I could, and grieved my children. The long talks with my husband have helped, along with the calls from friends and visits with loved ones. I get up each morning and plan the one big thing I will do that day. When I have finished it, I feel I have accomplished something in a life that is broken. That was the advice of David's oncologist when he told her he was so depressed after the first few rounds of chemo didn't get rid of the leukemia. And I have shared that advice with many who expressed their own battle with depression. Just plan one thing each day. When you have accomplished that, there is no need to look too far into the future. You have accomplished that day's goal.

I don't know what 2019 holds. It doesn't really matter. For I will continue to breathe, to grieve, to even laugh when I can. But it is a new year, filled with promise of whatever God wills for me.

As each new year begins, it comes with uncertainty, as well as new hope, new challenges, and new days. Mine has begun with a challenge to my health. But I embark on this new year with confidence that there is grace appointed for each season in our lives. I have never believed, even with all the chaos in my life, that our lives are determined by the flip of a coin. We each have purpose and a destiny. To fulfill that purpose might mean we walk down a few "dirt roads," we cross a few rivers, we climb a few mountains. But thank God, there are lush green valleys interspersed throughout our journey. In those times of rest, we drink from the streams, and we eat of the pleasant fruit. And that gives us strength for the next challenge.

When I heard the words last week "There is a mass in your uterus," I could have buckled. But I just looked up at the ceiling in that ER room and said, "My life is in Your hands. God is my Father. He is responsible for me, and He will take care of me." Even though I may have some anxious moments, my underlying strength comes from that peace of knowing He is with me. And He loves me unconditionally.

Therefore, I push forward into this new year with hope.

· · · · · · · · · ● ● ● · · · · · · · · ·

December 27, 2018
Random Acts of Kindness

There was a dear friend whose son was in college. He went to the president of the college and asked, "How can I cope with the depression?" The answer was very simply "to help yourself, do something for others." The expression "Sharing is healing" rings true.

Over the past twelve years, I have met some moms who were so deeply grieving that I really didn't think they would survive the first year. And I'm sure there are some who don't. I didn't know if I would survive the first month! But as I observed these women, very slowly I would see them begin to share with others. They would reach out of their own great sorrow to either give advice, send a card or gift, or go to visit another grieving family. Then I would see them slowly transform from barely breathing to taking deeper breaths until they could cope with the pain of their loss a bit easier.

Random acts of kindness is an idea I learned first from the MISS foundation. Once a year on the founder's child, Cheyenne's, birthday, we were encouraged to perform a RAOK. It brought me joy to pay for the meal of someone who was just behind me in line, send a book that had helped me to another grieving parent, give out nice pens or gifts with my children's names on them, or send flowers and gifts to other grieving moms. There is a group in our area that gives money to cancer patients to help defray costs of care. My husband and I enjoy going to their annual car show and contributing in David's name, that others might be helped. Some moms have made little gift bags for new moms in hospitals. Some have begun scholarship funds in their child's name. After a time, I began to see this RAOK in different places, on the news, on special occasions in social media, or even experienced it myself as a gift from others.

Sharing truly does bring a measure of healing. When we reach out of our own great loss and sorrow, we find that we are reaching into that "pit" that held us bound so long to "sit with" or give a hand up to others who find themselves there now. It's very hard to take that first step outside our comfort zone of grief. It may take weeks or even months to actually feel that we are strong enough. But when we do, then we truly share the comfort for which our own soul longed for so recently.

Even though we will always mourn and hurt for the child(ren) we have lost, giving to others seems to bring a kind of relief. For me, it feels that I am honoring my children and keeping their memory alive.

• • • • • • • • • ● • • • • • • • • •

January 6, 2019
Faith Resurrected

This book named itself. I was called Job by many who heard my story of grief. I haven't encountered all that Job suffered, although I would put all your children leaving for heaven right there among the most important. But people are astounded that I am still standing after suffering such loss.

The subtitle *Faith Resurrected* came from a deep belief that no matter how angry I was at God, no matter how dark the pit of grief, my faith would stand the test and surface once again. And it did.

This might be sermonizing a bit, but I feel if a person is deeply rooted in faith, no matter how bad the storm, no matter how hard the wind blows, that faith will stand. I can only speak from Christian faith. There may be other religions in which people are grounded deeply in what they believe and cling to that when storms of life come.

Where does faith come from? The Bible says that each man is given a measure of faith. Perhaps it is just enough to enable him to connect to his Creator. We are exhorted in the New Testament to exercise our faith, thereby making it stronger. But how do you exercise something you can't even see? It is a fact that a body exercised is a stronger body. So, too, is faith. Over the course of a lifetime, we face a plethora of trials, tests, and temptations. Some try the body, the mind, the soul, or the spirit. Jesus said that we could expect these tribulations. But He also said, "Greater is He that is in you than he that is in the world" (1 John 4:4 KJV). Even though we are subjected to these things, we can be assured that He is with us and in us.

Personally, the tests I've faced have been insurmountable at times. In Atlanta, when David was so gravely ill in 2015, on a ventilator, dialysis, and ultimately ECMO (lung bypass machine), my husband and I slept on the floor of the waiting room. We anxiously waited for David to awaken from the deep, induced sleep and hoped he could breathe on his own. When I went back to the hotel on occasion to bathe, I would just fall beside the bed and cry out "Help!" to God, hoping He would answer. It was all I had left in this great battle for my son's life. I'd sometimes call my praying friends just to have their support. It was in those dire moments that I really believe God's faith had to bolster my own. Once, our pastor quoted a verse that says, "Have faith in God" (Mark 11:22 KJV). He said some translations of this verse say that in the original Greek it means "Have the faith of God." It doesn't say you can depend just on your faith, but sometimes we must rely on the ultimate faith of God. God spoke, and the worlds were created. He hung the sun in its immenseness in the heavens. He didn't worry it would fall. His faith never failed. Once Jesus prayed that Peter's faith would not fail. I wonder how often He has prayed that for me, since He is still interceding at the Father's right hand in heaven.

No matter how hard the trial that we face in life, God's faith in us makes us more than a conqueror.

Oh, what a joyous day it was for us and David's nurse when he gave David the simple command to squeeze his hand. The young nurse couldn't contain his own joy at David responding. Faith rewarded us all!

"Faith…is the evidence of things not seen!" (Heb. 11:1 KJV).

If faith does not stand the test of trials, is it there? If it is never given the opportunity to grow in extreme circumstances, does it lie dormant in an infant state in the soul? These are questions that, at some point, every Christian must encounter. For into "every life some rain will fall." Will you stand? I am not asking if you *can*. For I know that in Christ you can do all things. But I do ask, *Will* you?

· · · · · · · · ● · · · · · · · · ·

January 8, 2019
Walking It Out

Each day in life brings its own challenges. That's why Jesus said, "Therefore I say unto you, take no thought for your life, what ye shall eat, or what ye shall drink; nor yet for your body, what ye shall put on. Is not the life more than meat, and the body than raiment?" (Matt. 6:25 KJV). Basically, He was saying not to worry. Worry is fear. "For God has not given us the spirit of fear but of power, and of love, and of a sound mind" (2 Tim. 1:7 KJV).

I admit this has been a bit of a battle for me as I have waited the whole week for the report on the biopsy. Today I got a call that the sample taken was not enough to produce results. So now I go into the hospital as an outpatient to have the biopsy again under anesthesia.

A grieving parent knows that we have as many loved ones on the other side as we do on this side. But we fight to stay here, if we are permitted, for those who really express the need for us to remain. And I've had several friends and family who have urged me on this path. So without knowing the future, I plow forward with hope, hope that I can be here for those who still need me, hope that it is not malignant, hope that whatever it is can be resolved quickly.

I do have to say that the anxiety is not what it would be if my children were still here. I would know that I had to fight with every-thing in me to beat this. And I surely will try even with my babies in heaven waiting for me. My husband still needs me. He says I am his "world" now. And I would expect the same from him.

So I battle onward and upward

One of the things I count among my greatest blessings is that I was schooled in the Bible. Verses I memorized as a child and read over and over as an adult come back into my spirit when life goes sour. Countless times I have recalled a verse that speaks to me in my hour of crisis. The Bible says, "Finally, brethren, whatsoever things are true, whatsoever things *are* honest, whatsoever things *are* just, whatsoever things *are* pure, whatsoever things *are* lovely, whatsoever things *are* of good report; if *there be* any virtue, and if *there be* any praise, think on these things" (Phil. 4:8 KJV). Even though my mind might be encompassed around a current problem of life, in my inner man there is a word of life that rises to each occasion. This morning, when I woke up, the verse "He knoweth the way that I take. When He hath tried me, I shall come forth as gold" (Job 23:1 KJV) came to mind. I wrote it down.

DAY-1,051

· · · · · · · · ● · · · · · ·

January 16, 2019
It's All About Me

Never have I wanted the focus on me. And yet it seems I haven't been able to avoid the things that made my life "stand out" before others. Whether this is God's way of making me His ambassador in this earth or just the trials of life, it is what it is.

Now, like it or not, I'm being forced to focus on my health. The diagnosis that came in yesterday was that it was stage one endometrial cancer. Oddly enough, there is a peace and a calm that I walk in daily. Do I want to go under the knife? No! But my peace rests in Christ alone. I have faced the worst pain a parent can endure four different times. There have been many obstacles I have been forced to endure or overcome. But burying the precious earthly body of a child makes every other trial pale in comparison.

So I face this new challenge as I meet with the surgeon tomorrow with the peace of God that reigns in my spirit.

I keep telling everyone the words of Paul the apostle: "For me to live is Christ; and to die is gain" (Phil. 1:21 KJV). I do not fear death. But I felt very strongly when I was first diagnosed with a mass in my uterus that the Lord said, "You are willing to die. Are you willing to live?" It's as if He was giving me a choice. I will live and not die. I will declare the glory of the Lord in the land of the living as long as He allows me to breathe.

Fear Has No Place

The Bible says that "God has not given us the spirit of fear, but of power and a sound mind" (2 Tim. 1:7 KJV). Yet many people live in fear their whole lives.

I learned something years ago. After I had a breakup with a boyfriend, I fell into a depression. I went for counseling with my very wise pastor, who told me that depression is a spiritual thing and must be rejected. At first, I thought that sounded very complicated and was reticent to try it. But it worked! Every time I would feel the depression descend on me as a dark cloud covers the earth, I would say, "Depression, you must leave now." And do you know what? It left. It was as if, literally, the darkness left. From then on, I had a new weapon to use against the depression I had lived with much of my life. As a Christian, many think we have no real power. But we are loaded! And most never tap into the resources that the risen Christ has given us.

I am not saying that I have arrived. Just this morning, I woke up to fear trying to grip my soul as I face this surgery to remove all my reproductive organs. But when I am reminded that fear is not of God, I know that I can reject it and have a better day.

With every trial and test in life, there comes a reward. We might not even realize it at that time, but it is there nonetheless. Even with the horrible loss on earth of my children, as I felt so robbed, now I know that they were my reward. I can thank God for the six months in utero and the twenty-three, twenty-four, and forty-one years that each of them gave me. I can thank God that I was and still am their mother. I can thank God that not even death can take them away from me, as a believer. For I know that I will see them again, never to part anymore.

As I anticipate this surgery in just a few weeks, I mourn the loss of my reproductive system. It's been part of me for seventy-one years. But I know that it produced the most beautiful babies in the world. It served me well. And if God has allowed this loss, there will be a reward at the end of it. Maybe there is a pot of gold at the end of the rainbow. We are so skeptical that we think nothing good can come out of hard times. But God has instituted a law of rewards, a law of rewarding being an overcomer, a law of giving and receiving, a law of replacing seven times what was taken from us.

As hard as the trial, so great will be the reward. I look for it. I anticipate it.

DAY-1,054

• • • • • ● ● ● ● • • • • • •

January 19, 2019
Be Still

I love the early mornings, watching the sunrise as I sip my cup of hot coffee. It is as if nature itself is giving the earth a fresh start. As I think on this, I am reminded of a verse in the Bible that says, "Be still and know that I am God" (Ps. 46:10 KJV). When I first went to the ER with unusual bleeding and got the words "There is a mass in your uterus," I lay on that bed and just looked up and said, "My life is in Your hands. God is my Father, and He is responsible for me." And even when the doctor called and said it was grade 1 endometrial cancer, I don't even know why, given my history of nervous, jittery fear over so many things in my life, I had such a peace. Perhaps it is because I have faced the most horrible fear a person can know, the death of a child. And in my case, it is the death of all my children. But more likely, it is that I know that even with Job, God gave Satan permission to try Job severely, even afflict his body. But God would not allow him to take Job's life. If this affliction in my body has been allowed by the Almighty, then I have nothing to fear. And I do believe strongly that any affliction that comes to a child of God had to "pass His desk" before it hits that child.

I will be completely honest. There is no fear of death in me. Like Paul the apostle, I can honestly say, "For me to live is Christ, and to die is gain" (Phil. 1:21 KJV). My children are waiting for me

349

on heaven's shore. I am not welcoming death. I will do everything I can to preserve this earthly temple of God that He has gifted to me.

The questions I had for God, the utter devastation of loss, seemed to melt away as I got the diagnosis. There was no "Why me?" left anymore. I knew where my help came from. I had no choice but to "collapse into His arms." That is where I am today. When I was getting ready to leave my dear friend J. Marie's house last year after a wonderful visit, she and I went to the beach very early to watch the sunrise over the ocean one last time. As we got up to leave, I told her, "The only way I will be comforted is by God. He has been silent. But I will only receive comfort when He decides to give it." And that was true, and still is. Even though the questions are still in the back of my mind, "Why me? What if? Why my children when my faith for them was strong?" those questions can wait until I see Him face-to-face. Right now, I must trust Him for whatever is next.

Last night, my niece Amanda visited with us. She shared about her son's science project, creating a model solar system. My husband shared how very big the sun is in the grand scheme of things. As I meditated on this, I thought, *How big is God that He not only created this universe but also a great number of other universes spread through the skies?* If God can not only create but also control these unfathomable, vast systems, then I know of a certainty that He is mindful of me. My brother-in-law Terry told me Saturday night that his Sunday-morning sermon was going to be on Psalm 8, where it reads, "What is man that thou art mindful of him? and the son of man, that thou visitest him?" (Ps. 8:4 KJV). When we really begin to think on how big our God is, it should always bring a peace to our heart about the events of our lives. He who is mindful of dates, systems, and divine order is surely mindful of each one of us, His cherished creation.

I feel almost compelled by God to write this story. Some days nothing really comes to mind. But if I can share my own life's joys and struggles, then maybe I can help another soul.

It is just a few days until my surgery. A hysterectomy. It's almost ironic to think that after my children, who were and are such a blessing to me, have left this earth for that heavenly realm, I will now lose the organs that bore them. People say, "What else can happen to her?" But at this point in life, I don't even question anymore. I know beyond a shadow of a doubt that since my Savior died for me, He will surely be with me no matter what life throws at me. Since this is allowed by God, then who am I to question the working of the Father in my life. I want to bless others. And if this is the means, then so be it. I will keep praising the one who died for me.

I chose to add a subtitle to this book, and it still stands *Faith Resurrected*. Do you see it happening? Faith is really a mystery to the Christian. Is faith strong enough to endure the most horrible pain imaginable and still stand? It depends on where that faith is anchored. Mine was anchored in the rock, Christ Jesus. And He is still as strong as ever. We falter. We fail to trust. But He never, ever turns His back on us. He's my Father, and He is responsible for me. In the deepest, darkest night He is there. Be still!

· · · · · · · · ● · · · · · · · ·

January 27, 2019
Perspective

Our perspective on life, the future, ourselves, others, and even our spirituality changes as the "seasons" of life come and go. When the doctor looked at the ultrasound of our precious Heather and said, "She is gone!" our world changed in a moment. Nothing in my previous life prepared me for the shock of loss. When we got the horrid, proverbial "knock on the door" at 1:00 a.m. and Erin's father-in-law said, "Erin's dead," the horror of it all was almost more than I could bear. To say it changed me and my family would be an understatement. When we got the news that Scott had shot himself and was in ICU, the overwhelming unbelief and shock was so unreal we hardly spoke a word on the four-hour drive to Savannah. As we stood in the ICU and watched David's life slowly ebb away as they tried so desperately to restart his heart repeatedly, I felt my life was ebbing away with him. All the time he was battling leukemia and we were in and out of the huge hospital in Atlanta, I somehow pushed all my grief over Heather, Erin, and Scott somewhere to the back of my soul. I could not allow it to surface, or it would be the end of me, and David wouldn't have my help. Looking back, I don't even know how I managed. But I did. My perspective had changed. His survival became the uppermost goal in life and everything else had to take a back seat. When Erin passed into heaven, for months even my family took a back seat. I cried every day, visited the grave two or three times a week, walked around in a daze, and did what I did robotically. David pulled me back in when he said he couldn't take the crying. It is said that your surviving children and spouse feel the need to help. But they may feel they can't help in the case of grief. So I had to change. I took my grief cries "on the road" when I felt the need to cry it out. I'd tell David and Berry I was going to the cemetery or grocery store and just ride and cry. Eventually, my perspective changed to my surviving child, David. I knew I had to be here for him. It gave me the strength to survive my daughter's not being here. But when David passed, my husband and I both felt we had no real reason for being here. It has been much harder to find that purpose. But God has given each of us a prompting and purpose, so we are here, surviving once again. I have found that each event in life changes our perspective. Often it broadens our horizons. But sometimes it narrows them. It changes relationships, jobs, health, and even daily living.

Everything we do, see, feel, or touch on earth affects the outcome. It changes our perspective. That is an ongoing challenge in everyone's life. I have seen the world turned upside down, inside out too many times. But I go back to the thing that has remained solid, my faith in Christ. That is the one thing that hasn't changed. I may have wandered in my quest for answers to my trials. But God never changed. He remains the same, no matter what. He is the anchor for my soul.

As the old song goes, "On Christ, the solid rock, I stand. All other ground is sinking sand."

Perhaps the greatest change in perspective for me was my reliance/understanding of the Holy Scriptures. One of the struggles I have faced since all my children went to heaven was reconciling myself to certain verses in the Bible. I was constantly writing down the "promises" in hope that God would grant the fulfillment (or at least as I viewed them). As a Bible scholar for many years, I knew how to pray the verses over my children. If you have visited my home, you know I had them "plastered" all over my house, on the fridge, beside my desk, even in the bathrooms. When David left for heaven, one of the first things I did upon arriving home was to rip most of them down. I was angry. I didn't understand. Before you judge me too harshly, please read on. Even though most of my life I read the Bible morning and night and studied it with passion, I found myself not even picking it up. When I did flip through my Bible one day, I immediately saw marked passages that referenced all the promises for the children of the righteous. And there were so, so many! But I refused to even read them. They hadn't come true for my children. How would I reconcile this great thing in my life? Over time I did begin reading again every morning (only). One very important thing I learned from studying the book of Job repeatedly was that, in the end, after all Job's friends had given him their opinions about why he had to suffer, Job said, "But He knoweth the way that I take: When He hath tried me, I shall come forth as gold" (Job 23:10 KJV). Job didn't have the answers. But he never turned his back on God. As I prepare to face this new health challenge in my own life, I again remember the promises. One passage that I refused to read after David passed was Psalm 23 (KJV), the beloved Psalm, because it begins, "The Lord is my Shepherd, I shall not want." I knew *want* because it means "lack," and my children were all gone into eternity. But as I read further this morning, it reads, "Though I walk through the valley of the shadow of death, I will fear no evil" (Ps. 23:4 KJV). I realized that the several times I have walked through that very, very dark valley, I never feared any evil. And I don't now. Do you know why? It is because the Lord is with me. That's the reason. My perspective on the Bible has changed. But even in my questioning, my struggle to find truth, He was there all the time. And He still is! God is faithful.

DAY-1,074

· · · · · · · ● · · · · · · ·

February 7, 2019
Post-Op

It's good to see the words *post-op*, for you know the operation is over. Our pastor used to remind us when we were going through tough times that "this, too, shall pass." When we are amid life's troubles, it seems they will never pass. But they usually do. We are left with scars, emotional trauma, a laugh, a song, a tear...but they do pass. And it's "on to the races," on to whatever is next. I hear people saying life is good when everything is rosy—there's a new grandchild or a new car or a celebration of a life event. But how often do we hear "Life is not good" when there are trials thrown into the mix? Not often, I can assure you. Sometimes, even as Christians, we think we must put on a happy face and pretend to be some super spiritual, above-the-fray kind of person. But I have found, especially in this troubled world, that many now want to see real, true, raw life. People search for truth. And it is up to us to show them the truth, the life, the way through our own broken lives. It is through the brokenness that so often the light of God shines the brightest.

I must tell you that when they wheeled me into the operating room, I was still awake. That's a first and can bring a little terror into an otherwise calm. But as I stated earlier, I knew that God was with me. When the nurse said, "It's twelve noon," I had this overwhelming peace that Jesus was walking into that operating room with me. I had felt Erin and David's presence earlier. But now He was near. Oh, what calm filled my soul before "lights-out"!

Research has shown that 95 percent of what we worry over doesn't come to pass. Yet many of us live in that 5 percent. The future is unclear for all of us. We have today. We have the present moment. No one can adequately predict their future, no matter how mundane and routine their life seems. David's oncology doctor so wisely told him, when he was faced with depression over not successfully beating back the leukemia after two rounds of chemo, that he should focus on one day at a time, accomplishing what he could that day. She said to set a goal, however small, and seek to complete that one thing. When we look at the big picture, we may feel failure, depression, and discontent. But when we set our focus on achievable goals, we set ourselves up for success. Fear is a liar. Fear can paralyze, distort, and handicap. The Bible says that man was not given the spirit of fear. So I believe fear is a dark spirit and one to be conquered. Often it takes everything within us to do that when faced with overwhelming odds of life.

Life's events can change radically in a moment's notice. I am a living example. As I have faced this current health challenge, the "big picture" has changed. Burying a child, or all of them (as I have), changes the perspective wholly. My husband and I agreed that nothing, *nothing*, can compare to what we have faced already. Facing a diagnosis of cancer would once have so devastated me that I would not have been able to function. But now it is a bump in the road. A grieving parent feels at times that their life is over. I have felt that. But God still has a purpose for me. There are still goals to be met for a few more days, weeks, months, years to come. As His child, I am obligated to fulfill those days that He has given as a gift.

None of us knows what tomorrow holds. And we really don't need to. But we do need to look at this day and savor it as a gift from God. So whether you are going through pre-op or post-op in your life right now, be the light in someone else's night.

DAY-1,076

· · · · · · · · ●●● ● ●●● · · · · · ·

February 9, 2019
Limitless Infinity

What happens when we are not limited by our natural man? I read that humans only use 5 percent of the brain. So what happens with the other 95 percent? There must be so much untapped potential. Along this thought I must share an experience I had this morning. When you read this, you either will think I have lost it or you will tap into the supernatural, the (maybe) 95 percent? I woke up early and thanked God for waking me up once more. I battled the last few days with this huge bruise that seemed to be spreading across and down my entire hip area into the groin and down the leg. Of course, the old spirit of fear tried desperately to get a stronghold. I called the doctor's office Thursday and talked to the nurse, who tried to assuage my fears. Then finally, last night, after talking to my niece, who is a nurse, I called my doctor's call line, only to get cut off before leaving the message. I decided, "Oh, well" either it will heal or not. But when I went in the bathroom, I heard the "whisper," the "still small voice" of the Lord, who told me that by morning the bleeding will stop in the bruised area. There was a peace and calm that came over me, and I slept like a baby. Of course, I looked this morning first thing, and it did look like it had stopped spreading. So I believe! Yes, I believe that that was God, my Father, who is the ultimate in stopping fear in its tracks.

There was another incident this morning as I was in the bathroom (what is it about being in the bathroom?). I was thinking back on holding my husband's strong hands as we sat outside of ICU when David was struggling during those last hours. We held hands and prayed together for our precious son. As I thought on this, I thought of holding David's hand so often. He'd reach out for me as I slept on the sofa beside his hospital bed in the middle of the night, take my hand, and say, "Mama, let's pray." So many times, I held that precious hand. I so, so longed to hold it now. Then I could just "hear" David saying, "But, Mom, I'm with you all the time now, closer than ever. I was in that operating room with you. Erin was there too. Don't you know that if anything had gone wrong, we'd have been all over it?" As I thought on this, at first, I thought, *They didn't have this kind of medical knowledge to be all over it!* But it seemed so true. When we are not limited by this physical body and brain, what's to hinder us from knowing all things? Doesn't the Bible say, "Now we see through a glass darkly, but then face to face" (1 Cor. 13:12 KJV)? Adam had no limitations at first. He named every tree and animal. How could he even do that unless he had limitless knowledge? But then that first sin separated him from God. And with that separation came limitations in every area. Oh, the boundless, limitless love of God that caused Him to redeem mankind back to Himself. Now we know that one day we will see face-to-face and there will be no more darkness or limitations. Freedom will be ours at its greatest for all eternity—infinite freedom!

DAY-1,086

· · · · · · · · ● · · · · · ·

February 19, 2019
God Won't Give You More Than You Can Handle and Other Clichés

The daffodils are blooming. Erin loved daffodils. She'd always picked the first ones, even if I just had three, to make a little bouquet for our kitchen table. The first few days after she passed, the birds were singing, the daffodils blooming. So now each spring, a season I loved, it's almost like a stab in the heart as I see and hear the "beauty" of spring. That's where I am now. Let's see…hmmm… David went to heaven February 12. Erin's birthday is February 26. Erin went to heaven March 2. Scott's birthday is April 10. Heather's birth/death date is April 11. Mom's birthday is April 20. My dad went to heaven April 26. David's birthday is May 6, and Mother's Day is the second Sunday in May. Do you understand why spring might not be so beautiful for me anymore?

Let's get back to the clichés. God never promised in the Bible that He wouldn't give us more than we could handle. It does say those who "mourn will be comforted" (Matt. 5:4 KJV). "He is near the brokenhearted" (Ps. 34:18 KJV). "In this world you will have tribulation, but be of good cheer, I have overcome the world" (John

16:33 KJV). "My strength is made perfect in weakness" (2 Cor. 12:9). I could go on and on. But I have never read a passage that says He won't give us more than we can handle. If we could handle it all, why would we even need God? And sadly, there are those who believe that we don't. Some believe we have all we need within ourselves.

When we confront another person who is facing a trial in their lives, why do we feel it is necessary to offer advice based on inexperience or ignorance? Unless we have walked through a similar trial, we are clueless. And even then, each person's perspective of their own trial is different. I speak from my own experience that no one on this earth has comforted me as have other grieving moms and dads. Grieving mom friends have called ourselves sisters in grief, members of the club no one wants to join. I even had one person tell me that grief was a spirit that would attach us to other grievers in an unhealthy way. I find that hard to believe since the Bible clearly says that "He, Jesus, was acquainted with grief." He was sinless perfection. No evil spirit had any hold on Him.

Based on my life experiences, I can tell you that God will give you more than you can handle. That is something no one wants to read. But you can also pick up a copy of *Foxe's Book of Martyrs* and read the stories of many God-fearing people who gave their lives because of the gospel. Even Jesus's own disciples died very horrible deaths. And He had handpicked each one. So how should we, who are His own children, escape the things that life brings our way? I heard something last night that is very appropriate. It was "look at this as your battle scars." I said that to David when he came out of ICU with an open wound on his back that we had to carefully nurse back to health. He had open wounds from where they laid him face down in a "mask" to recover his lungs. There was a huge scar on his nose, shin, and neck when they made the huge incision to put the tube in for lung bypass. There was a scar on the other side of his neck where they put the dialysis tube in. These scars didn't fade even as the skin began to heal. Battle scars. Some of our battle scars are not visible to the naked eye. They are scars of the soul and spirit. But they are just as real as David's visible scars.

Lest this chapter discourage you, I must say that in each of these circumstances we face in life, we have a choice. We can be overcomers or victims. There are so many references to the rewards of the "overcomer" in the book of Revelation in the Bible. An overcomer often rises "out of the ashes" of grief, divorce, or losing every material thing to help others who face similar loss. An overcomer gets up again. David's tae kwon do instructor told him once, when he had not passed a test for the next belt, that it is always the student who keeps going, keeps reaching for his goal that gets to the finish line, the black belt. David kept going and did get to that line. Life is not easy. I read so often the line "Life is good." But I just think…well, not so much. It is filled with challenges. It is interesting to read the stories of many of the greatest hymns and songs ever written. Many of them are born out of great tragedy or trial. There is joy spread along the path, though. There is laughter and song. But it is in the trials that character is built, that strength of faith is built, that hope is put to the ultimate test.

God never promised us an easy life. But He did promise a soft landing. Keep reaching for that goal!

•••••••••●•••••••••

February 24, 2019
Surviving Your Children

The good news today is, my doctor said the cancer was stage 1A, the lowest stage of cancer. It was all removed with the hysterectomy, so he feels there is no other course of treatment needed. Thank God for that! I am grateful that I will live another day.

This new problem has made me feel that each day is a gift from God. I plan to savor each day I have left, whether many or few. I want to make each day count and help others in some way.

Surviving your children is the upside down to life. It is unnatural. It is unfair. It is not supposed to be how we live out our days. No one holds that precious newborn miracle in their arms and even begins to think, *I will outlive him or her.* They only think of a bright future for this blessed little one. They see husbands, wives, children, and for them, grandchildren. Never does it enter the mind that that child may not be here when old age creeps in for those parents. But such is my story.

Erin once told me, when we were having a rather-difficult time with my mom after Daddy died, that I wouldn't act like my mom because she wouldn't let me. Mom was being a little stubborn, which would be natural, since as she aged, she had to give up some independence. But I was blessed to be able to help care for my mom. David also, upon visiting a nursing home to sing with his school chorus, told me that I would never be in a nursing home. He'd see to that! But alas, they are both in heaven and my husband and I are left to age as gracefully and strongly as we can. It's not just being taken care of when we are old that matters; it's all the tomorrows, seeing grandchildren grow up, participating in celebrations of life's important events, sharing joys and sorrows, happy times and bad times with your child. It's all gone in a heartbeat.

How does a parent survive when there are no children left? Do we hunker down in our house, never to see sunlight again? I have tried that, and it is no fun. But some have made that their way of life. It adds another layer to grief to feel abandoned and alone. I keep doing the things I love, gardening, shopping, reading, finding funny shows to watch on TV, going places with my hubby, short vacations with my sister's family, visits to friends' homes, or long walks in the sunshine. I have plans for a future bucket list of things to accomplish in my remaining days. Or am I just looking for things to lift my broken spirit? Hope must have a plan. It must have a future. If you see no future, just plan one thing for each day and try to accomplish that. Then plan something for next week. Keep adding to that length of time until you have something, anything to look forward to with anticipation of joy.

After this health challenge, my thoughts have turned to helping others. I will savor each day! I am now a survivor in more ways than one.

DAY-1,093

• • • • • • • • ● • • • • • • •

February 26, 2019
Erin's Birthday: Challenge
of Never Forgetting

Thirteen long years have passed since we last celebrated Erin's birthday with her on that fateful last Sunday before her birthday. It seems an eternity since I have held my precious daughter in my arms. Erin made a pact early in life that we would never leave each other without a big hug and an "I love you." I think every grief-stricken mom wants to fight to preserve and protect the memory of her child. I probably went overboard when my children were small, but I saved every toy, every school creation, every bit. I cherished my children. Did I cherish them too much? Can you do that? Even God, in His great wisdom, tells us through Isaiah, the prophet, that He has "graven us on the palms of His hands" (Isa. 49:16 KJV). If He loves us that much, why shouldn't we cherish our own children, who are loaned to us for a very short time? I have been criticized for putting so many pictures of Erin on Facebook during her birthday and angelversary, which are only three days apart. There was even an accusation of me creating a "shrine" for her. It was only on her birthday or angelversary. Why should I not remember my child in pictures when I constantly am reminded of my loss by seeing others all around me posting pictures of every event of their child(ren). I will never, ever forget! I hope my friends and family won't forget either. I will remind them. Yes! I will do that every chance I get. My children lived! They enjoyed their brief life here. It was filled with happy moments too. And it will never be forgotten.

It's March 1, 2019. Today is the day again. There is no stopping the passing of years. It has been thirteen long years since my beautiful Erin left so suddenly for heaven's shore. Every day has been a day of survival. There have been smiles that returned and joys. There have been multiplied sorrows as we said earthly goodbyes to our Scott and our David. But Erin has never been far from our hearts or our thoughts.

Tonight, marks the thirteenth year since we got the proverbial horror of the knock on the door at 1:00 one a.m. and the words "Erin is dead." It still rings loudly in my broken soul! Every year on this night, at 1:10 a.m., I can almost hear it again as I recount every single detail of seeing my precious firstborn, the light of my life, lying on that bedroom floor, her hair spread around her head as the paramedics had surrounded her to try to and get her breathing again. Those details will never leave my memory nor will the depth of grief that engulfed me in the weeks and months following. At that time, it felt like a fog. There seemed to be no light and no air. The very life seemed to ebb and flow out of me.

Now I keep breathing, trying to still make sense of something that yields no answers, no reasons.

Erin was a beautiful soul, who loved with all she had, who gave everything she had to give to those she loved. She wasn't perfect. But she was my daughter and greatest confidant. She was part of the reason my heart kept beating when life got tough. She was sunshine in my days. She is missed beyond the telling, beyond the tears.

My greatest peace comes from knowing that she is in the arms of God. He loved her far more than I did, and that is saying a lot! I will see her again one sweet day!

• • • • • • • • • •●• • • • • • • • • •

February 27, 2019
Reconciling Scriptures

By now you realize how very important my Christian faith is to me. I clung to it during the darkest hours and recited Bible verses over and over. I even posted them in David's hospital room. I prayed them over and for him and Erin so often. When David went to heaven after battling so hard to beat the leukemia, scripture reading was not part of my life for months. I found no understanding for the horror that was suddenly my life. I felt clinging to the promises found in the Bible hadn't "worked" for me. Now, in hindsight, I see a little more clearly. Now I know that no matter what we do, how hard we fight, how much we pray, ultimately God will have the last word. The Bible clearly says that our days are all numbered. When Jesus was in the garden of Gethsemane that last fateful night, he laid down His own will for the will of the Father. He didn't want to die. He didn't want to leave his earthly family and friends. I believe those drops of sweat as great drops of blood as he agonized and said, "Father, if it is possible, let this cup pass from me: nevertheless, not as I will but as Thou wilt" (Matt. 26:39 KJV). This was a testament to his giving up his own will for that of the Father. He wasn't afraid. He wasn't backing out of the greatest sacrifice ever. He just probably felt that God might have come up with another plan. But alas, it wasn't to be. He had to be the conqueror that He was destined to be before the foundation of the earth was formed. In those fleeting moments, He laid down His will. That had to be a great struggle! For all of us humans have strong wills. That is my struggle even now. To lay down or surrender our own will means that we believe in a power that is greater, wiser, stronger than our own. It would mean giving up all my questions and struggle to understand why God, who is all merciful, could take my children back to Himself before I felt they had lived out their days. Daily I battle this very thing. I don't want to hold unforgiveness in my heart toward the God who created me. I want to lay that down too. Maybe I am not there yet. Maybe I am close. Maybe I didn't even understand the implication of all those scriptures. Several months back, I decided to write down all the scriptures I had clung to in my darkest night. I have a long list of them in my journal. I hope one day God will reveal their meaning as it relates to my own children. For each of them mentions *children* and is a promise to the children of a believer. But for now, I will keep writing, keep hoping, keep praying, keep reading.

I would be remiss if I didn't tell you, quite frankly, that I did have a problem with some of the verses when my children went to heaven. With Erin and David, my brother who brought the eulogy at the memorial service asked for my favorite scripture to read. It has been Psalm 103 and Psalm 91 for several years. But the end of Psalm 91 reads, "With long life I will satisfy him and show him my salvation" (KJV). I couldn't have him read that because my Erin was only twenty-three, and my David only twenty-four. That's not a long life. So even though I may have verses that I feel didn't come true in my life, I won't throw out the book. I just file that in the back of my mind under "things I will ask God about when I see Him face-to-face."

DAY-1,098

• • • • • • • ● • • • • • • •

March 3, 2019
Do the Questions Never End?

A parent's endless warfare never ends. They seek to protect and defend their child until their dying day. It is just something instilled into a mom or dad. When a child dies for whatever reason, the parent is left with this defense mechanism that has no object. I believe that is where the endless questions come from. Why wasn't I there? If only I had done this! Why didn't the doctor try this? Where was the one caring for her/him? Why my child? What if I had been the one driving? Did I love him/her too much? Was I overprotective? Did God think I idolized my child? What did I do to make God mad at me? Did they hurt at the end? Did they know I was there? And on and on, endless questions that flood the mind and soul. Do they ever end? I think not.

I vividly remember when our baby Heather was born still at twenty-four weeks. One of the very first things that came to mind was, *What did I do to displease God that He would take my child?* When our Erin, our joy, went to heaven at a moment's notice, that same question was foremost in my mind. With our Scott, the question was prevalent. And with our David, the questioning was profound and even could be called a lashing-out at God. How could God do this? I asked him, "Can we please have a do-over and undo this horrible thing?"

Early this morning, as I lay awake, I thought on this very thing. I remembered Job stating that he couldn't question God. And yet he did. As the Almighty who hung the stars, the sun, the planets, and now we know, even universes beyond this one, who can question His ways, His wisdom, His plan? David, in the Psalms, said God had frustrated his plans. I have said that over and over the past years. And now, even though the grief has softened a bit, I still don't have any answers to the endless questions. But I do know that I never rejected the God of the universe, the one true God, who sent His own Son to become a sacrifice to redeem mankind back to Himself, the one true God who has all power, all pre-eminence. He is so much a part of who I am, who my children were, that I think we are connected on a cellular level that goes beyond what science has even discovered. How can I reject Him? How can I question the Almighty? I am thankful for His mercy in allowing my questions, although only He knows the answers. His ways are higher than mine. Didn't the great prophets of old say this? So for now, I will table the questions. I might come back to them, maybe over and over. But ultimately, I should just trust the God of all creation with my most precious children, who were my life. And since He is my life, I am one with Him and with my children.

While over time, the raw edges of grief soften, the soul-searching endless questions remain with a parent. There is sometimes an abject feeling of failure, even if they have been an excellent parent. There is a feeling that they failed their child in those last moments, even if they tried everything, had the best doctors, counseled with their child, protected them until the last breath! The role of parent doesn't cease just because they have left this earth.

There is that innate protection mode that parents keep deep within. Often it turns to protecting their memory. Say anything negative to a grieving parent and see if they will not rush to the defense of their child. They struggle to keep their child's memory alive. You may enter their house and find there are pictures of the child everywhere. I vividly remember after our Erin went to heaven, David told me once not to buy another frame. He had counted the pictures I had hung of Erin. He said there were forty of her and eighteen of him! It had not really entered my mind that I was obsessing over keeping her memory alive with pictures. Now, alas, there are pictures of him everywhere. I haven't counted, but I'm sure his are near forty now too. Some parents create a memorial space in their home where they put pictures, candles, and tokens in remembrance of their child. Some must move, but they are careful to preserve the contents of their child's room so they can create a memorial space in their new home. Grieving parents face accusations from friends and family. If those accusations come at a time of struggle—i.e., special dates or remembrances—it can cause added pain. I would say to those who put forth those things that they must allow a parent to grieve however they must. There are no rules to grief. For each parent it is different, with some commonalities. Until their dying day, a parent will remember and mourn the child who is not on earth with them.

There was a story of an eighty-five-year-old woman who, when asked how many children she had, told them she had four, three on earth and a baby in heaven. She never forgot or minimized the memory of that baby although it had been many years past.

• • • • • • ● • • • • • • •

March 4, 2019
Stages of Grief

The stages of grief have been listed as denial, anger, bargaining, depression, and acceptance. A person very close to me, upon losing her dad, told me just a few months after that she had been through all the stages of grief and come to peace. Oh, that it was that easy! Grief work is hard work. It's easy to think there are just five stages and when you complete each one you are near the end. But not so! If one thinks they can just get through all five stages in a short time and be done with grief, then I think they are in denial. In my years of grief, I have observed many others managing grief. While it is an individual thing, the stages of grief can be observed. But the odd thing is that we go in and out of these stages, often repeating a stage out of order with no observable triggers. Factors may include the relationship with the deceased, the cause of death, the age of the deceased, and the age of the bereaved, which all play a role. No research can be cited, but this has been my observation. This is not comparing grief to grief. I detest that! Grief is grief, no matter the circumstances. This is about observable management of grief.

David told me just prior to his passing that he felt he was dealing better with Erin's passing finally after ten years. He had a very tough time with it. But he was at peace. That was such a comfort to my heart. Would that I could say the same! I felt I had. But I have realized with Erin's recent birthday and angelversary that while I was caring for David during the traumatic illness and his passing, I must have put my grief on hold. The last few days have brought unchecked avalanches of grief and tears. When I am in the shower, when I sit and remember, when I walk in David's room and the finality of it all slams into my being, the tears flow in buckets. My girl! My boy! It's all too much to bear. I excuse some of it as part of my recovering from major surgery, the diagnosis of cancer, the drugs they plied me with during the surgery, and the aftereffects. But it probably is grief suppressed, grief over my sunshine girl, my sweet and gentle boy, my strong and energetic stepson, and the baby girl I never held.

One thing I know is that we must all face the grief. We must face it down. We must cry. We must go through the stages no matter how often and out of order they appear. We must work hard. We must mourn until the last tear is shed, until the last breath is taken. I call it warfare. I call it facing down the grief. I call it survival. I call it love.

"And now abideth faith, hope, charity, these three; but the greatest of these *is* charity" (2 Cor. 13:13 KJV).

DAY-1,109

• • • • • • • ● • • • • • • •

March 14, 2019
Looking for Perfection

All our lives we seek perfection—the perfect dress, the perfect career, the perfect mate, the perfect child, the perfect house, the perfect look. We see others who we think have the perfect life. Often, we measure ourselves based on our perception of others. If only we had this, that, or what they have. Oh, if my family was perfect like theirs is! But we only see the surface. That dress might not look good on me as it does on them. That career that they have chosen might not be a match for me. Their husband might seem more imperfect if I were married to him. Their "perfect" child might be very naughty at home. Their house may be steeped in mortgage so they can't pay their other bills. We see only the surface. We can't see what lies behind that door or beyond that wall. Many today paint a picture of perfection when their lives are a living nightmare. I have found since being in the throes of grief that people want to see the real you. They want to see the truth. The youth of today are tired of fake. It seems they seek the truth more than adults.

When I was in the early days of my grief, I began to share my true feelings on social media. There were times I felt guilty for sharing the raw and unfiltered grief with my friends. When I attempted to apologize, they wouldn't have it! They insisted that it was okay. Showing others that life is sometimes hard is a good thing. We face obstacles in life to "harden" us. When a child first attempts to walk, they fall and fall often. Sometimes there may be a bruise or two. But in staying the course, they learn to walk unsupported.

As I read my Bible, I see that the word *perfection* is mentioned only a few times. The first one that comes to mind is "Perfect love casteth out fear" (1 John 4:18 KJV). Since we know our earthly love is fragmentary at best, it must be referring to the love of God. That is where perfection dwells. That is where truth dwells. That is where, after all our earthly searching, we will find perfection.

As a grieving parent, we are bombarded by the if-onlys, the what-ifs. If only we could go back and make this or that change, our child would be here. It seems to haunt our path of life as we race into an unknown future. Often the fear of the future tries to hinder our breathing. But it is in those times we must trust in that perfect love that casts out all fear. It is only in trusting in someone bigger than ourselves that peace drives away the fear.

DAY-1,111

• • • • • • •• ● •• • • • • • •

March 16, 2019
My Funny David

Looking through David's childhood photo albums lets others know that he was a happy child. And it's true! Nearly every picture shows a huge smile or laugh. He loved comedy, often asking for joke books when the school would host book fairs. I was thinking of him this morning when I got my little plastic tool that helps open five-gallon buckets to try to open a can of pineapple. It didn't fit, and I was thinking I should order a small one that would open cans. David would have said something funny, like, "Why don't we get me another PlayStation game? That would fix it!" He was so funny and fun. Oh, how I miss you, my David!

Even when he was so sick, he could just surprise the nurses with his humor. When he was admitted to the hospital, his blood sugar spiked after the first chemo and the drugs that accompanied it. Every morning he was given massive doses of steroids, I think about twenty small pills. In response, he had everyone in the room laughing as he sang thus, to the tune of the old Folgers coffee song:

The worst part of waking up
Are steroids in your cup!

We were all laughing.

Another thing that happened that would depress anyone else was that he had C. diff, a fungal infection that affects the whole digestive tract. (I've learned that this is common in hospitals, but one they fight fiercely). Because of the uncontrollable diarrhea, he had to wear disposable briefs. Once, he said when putting them on, "Ten most embarrassing things about having leukemia: Number 1, wearing these briefs!"

He would say things just unexpectedly and have us and the medical staff in stitches, laughing. Some that I wrote down were these:

- "That was the best-tasting vomit, pure Boost flavor, sugar and all!"

- On coming off IV lines to go to the bathroom, he did a little dance and sang, "I am Free!"
- "Can I go home? I'll make tally marks on the wall with red magic marker to make them think its blood!"
- He passed some gas and said, "Mama, are you going to write down, 'He farted,' in your notes?" (He said this because I took notes on every single thing that happened!)
- Responding to the doctor saying, "Can I get you anything?" he said, "Can you stuff the doughnut with insulin?" and once, "Yes, I'd like a doughnut milkshake!" Sometimes he'd substitute *pizza* for the *doughnut*, knowing that because his stomach was so upset all the time he couldn't eat pizza. (The day he was dismissed and sent to the rehab hospital after nearly passing in ICU, his favorite nurse showed up with, you guessed it, pizza! He was overjoyed!)

My funny boy! He always loved a good laugh and had a gift of making others laugh, even while enduring great suffering!

DAY-1,116

· · · · · · ●●●●●● ● ●●●●● · · · ·

March 21, 2019
Forgiveness

Many years ago, I read a book about forgiveness. After much research, the author believed that many diseases than mankind contract are related to unforgiveness. He cited one person who had cancer. They had held unforgiveness in their heart toward their mom for many years relating to their childhood. When that person was able to forgive their mom, the cancer disappeared. The author felt strongly that forgiveness was a key to healing.

Forgiveness is easier said than done. When we are wounded or betrayed, it is easier to hold that unforgiveness in our hearts than to turn it loose. It's been said that unforgiveness does not hurt the person being forgiven, but it keeps its hold on the person who was wounded.

From a biblical point of view, unforgiveness leads to bitterness. And the "root of bitterness" can cause all sorts of trouble. Jesus said something that no one had heard before when he said to "love your enemies" (Luke 6:35 KJV). It's easy to love those who love you. But He said there is a new commandment, "Love one another even as I have loved you" (John 13:34 KJV). While that seems like a logical thing, it is harder to do than just reading the words. When we are offended or hurt by someone or, God forbid, someone kills our child, the forgiveness seems like a far, foreign country that we will never reach. How would you react if someone killed your child? That is the question we must ask before we are quick to judge others. I have known some who have been able to forgive this very thing. It probably took every ounce of courage and help from the Almighty to be able to forgive.

It might seem strange that often grieving people come to a point where they blame the person who died for leaving them. They have this unforgiveness of the person they loved most. There have been fleeting moments when I have done that very thing. I quickly repented and felt a weight of guilt for even having those thoughts.

The hardest of all for me was blaming God. Yes, I said that. I knew that God held the ultimate power over life and death. So I knew that my children would not have passed from this life without the "approval" of the Almighty. I did blame Him. I remember falling beside my bed to my knees that first night home from Emory when my precious David was lying in a morgue ten miles from here. I cried out, "God, can we have a do-over? Can you fix this? Can you take us back to when David was here and give us a different outcome?" I was angry and was bargaining all at the same time. But I keep going back to David's own words, words I had taught him on our first transatlantic flight, flying through a thunderstorm and the huge Boeing 777 ditching. He was a bit afraid. I told him that it wouldn't matter where we were, whether we were driving down the road in our car or sitting at home or shopping; when our time came, it would come. I assured him we were as safe in the plane as anywhere. With that thought, he calmed down. There in the Emory Winship Cancer Clinic, when he first got the news that the cancer was back, he said, "Mom, I'm going to fight this for you and Daddy. But you know, when your time comes, it comes." He never forgot! But I knew that God was the responsible one. The Bible said our days are numbered. And it is only God who knows the number. So while I did blame God for a while, I know that I cannot question His final decision. It is His alone. I feel I have begun to forgive Him. I know I must!

· · · · · · · · ●● ● ●· · · · · · ·

April 10, 2019
Scott

Today is Scott's forty-eighth birthday. We will lay flowers on his grave as we remember his life and the love we shared. His dad grieves quietly, as he does for all his children gone too soon. But I can tell the grief is great.

Scott was only nine when I married his dad. He would come for weekend visits, but often he chose to stay with Berry's mom and dad since his cousins were there and he could play with them. Many times he would come stay with us. He was always a delight. He was a quiet little guy and very respectful. His mom had moved back in with her parents after the divorce. So their income was limited even though my husband did pay child support. The town they lived in was small, but Scott had friends there. As he became a teen, he chose to spend more time with them. We did attend his football games and saw him working on his bodybuilding skills in high school. I was delighted one night when Scott called me from a teen retreat in Myrtle Beach, South Carolina, to tell me he had received Christ as his Savior that night. It was truly a moment of joy to him and to us. After high school, he decided to join the Army. This would be a life-changing event for him. Coming from a small rural community into a bigger worldview changed him. We drove up for his graduation from basic training in Fort Knox, Kentucky, and were so proud of the stronger, more outgoing young man who stood before us. He decided to take extra training there to be a tank mechanic. While in Kentucky, he met a woman and we thought he would get married, but it didn't work out. Then he was deployed to Korea for a year. He seemed to like Korea and called often, telling us of the cold weather and the crowded streets. He was sent back to Fort Hood, Texas, for a while. The visits got fewer as he traveled the world and made lifelong friends in the Army. But he would always call often and we'd talk for hours. He was then sent to Fort Stewart, where he was in training again. He called one night and said he had been sick and was having trouble with his nerves. He had moved off base into a mobile home and would ride a bicycle to work each day. He was intent on keeping his body in shape, which I'm sure saved his life many times. He met a woman there in a gym and began a relationship that would lead to marriage when he got back from the war. In 2001, he deployed from Fort Stewart in Savannah, Georgia, to Kuwait when the war began. When he called, I could tell he was a bit anxious as they waited in the temporary base set up there until they got the call to deploy to Iraq.

During the war, my husband and I would get up in the middle of the night sometimes to turn on the news and see what was happening. Many times, I would just lie on the floor on my face and pray for Scott's safety as we'd hear of the fighting and bombing. I know that God was with him, because he returned safely a year later. He married his wife shortly after. But they had not been married long when he had to deploy again. He deployed three times to Iraq and once to Afghanistan. He didn't seem to mind Iraq, because they were well established there. But he didn't like Afghanistan. He got very sick there as a flu spread through the ranks. I was so glad when his feet hit American soil once again and we could hug him and know he was safe. He wasn't sent back to Savannah, but to Fort Riley, Kansas. His wife had to stay in Savannah since they had just bought a house there, which she didn't want to leave unattended. So he was alone in Fort Riley, dealing with the aftermath of being in a war zone. He went for counseling once, I think. But sadly, the military at that time did not seem to be doing enough to deal with the PTSD that afflicted many soldiers. Scott made the very long drive on weekends to Savannah often to see his wife. On one of these visits, as he was making the long drive, he called and talked at length with me and his dad. He even called his mom to tell her he was stopping by on his way back to Kansas. He had been calling his dad every night for about a month. We could tell he was fretting over someone there at his base who was implying he might have to go back to Afghanistan again. He didn't want to go back. He had re-enlisted before coming home because they had convinced him that this would be a quicker way to get out. He was only a few weeks away from retirement. Sadly, after driving so far to get home, getting a few hours' sleep that Saturday night just a week from Christmas, he got up Sunday morning and pulled the trigger. Our world was shattered when his stepdaughter called at 5:00 p.m. that day to tell us he was in the hospital and was not expected to survive. When we arrived, he was on life support in ICU but had no visible signs of injury. Our beautiful son lay there unable to speak or even know we were there. I kept praying as we kept vigil with his wife and stepchildren the next few days. My husband never left his side except for a few breaks. David and I went back to a hotel to get some sleep but came back quickly. On Tuesday, the neurologist said there was no brain activity so he should be taken off life support. He was an organ donor, so there was a small ceremony where we were each given a little keepsake heart as we said our last goodbyes on this earth. He was kept on life support until the organs were taken, and then our Scott was laid to rest. Our hearts were crushed once again as we said an earthly goodbye to a son who grew up a shy little boy but became a successful man who saw the world and was so near retirement. He could have enjoyed a wonderful life by the beach with his wife. He had earned it! It seems so unfair.

My desire is to keep his story alive. I told the Tragedy Assistance Team officer who visited if they could do anything in Scott's memory, to please give more counseling, more assistance to our servicemen and servicewomen when they arrive home from a war zone. I have heard that there are an average of twenty-two per day who take their own lives. It is so tragic that we lose these young men and women who have already given so much to our country.

Scott's wife decided to bury him here near his grandparents because he loved them so. That is where we will lay fresh roses today for all the love we still have for our Scott.

DAY-1,132

• • • • • • • • ● • • • • • • • •

April 11, 2019
Heather

Heather Lynn Fitzpatrick was born April 11, 2019, three months before she was due. Sadly, she went straight to heaven without me or her dad getting to hold her or kiss her goodbye. In 1985, parents of a stillborn were not encouraged to hold their baby as they are now. I am so glad that moms and dads can see and hold them now to say that last earthly goodbye. Having kissed and held my others, I know the peace that comes with that final goodbye, although it is so very painful. Heather was our most anticipated second child. The pregnancy was a good one up until when she had to go to heaven. No tests revealed the cause of death, so all those questions I had tucked in that envelope for thirty-four years are still there. Some things God chooses to keep secret. But as I visited her grave every year, often with Erin and David on either side of me, I kept those questions in mind.

I had a dream of her once shortly after she passed. I saw a little girl standing in a beautiful meadow with little flowers growing among the grass. She was standing in front of a beautiful shady oak, holding a little lamb in her arms. Her hair was curly and reddish brown as it flowed down onto her tiny shoulders. The long white robe she was wearing was almost transparent, as was her skin. She was beautiful and at peace. I have held that vision close to my heart over these many years, in hopes that when at last I reach her, that will be what I see. Every year that day grows closer. Oh, what joy that will be!

My mom wanted so to hold our baby. But the doctors and nurses discouraged us from even seeing her. Mom also wanted to buy her a little dress for burial. But, sadly, she was wrapped in a little pink blanket, they told us. I'm so glad things are different now and parents are allowed to hold their babies. Below is a letter my mom wrote to the granddaughter she never held.

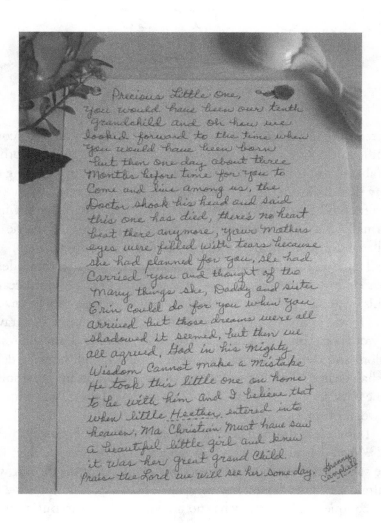

......••••●•••••••••

April 15, 2019
Overcomer

Overcoming obstacles or trials in life is to be expected. Trials come in different degrees. Some people might seem stronger than others and able to navigate through the worst of things. But overcoming the many downswings of grief can be daunting. It may mean alienating from friends or even family members. It may be changing your whole "normal" to a new "normal" just to survive. There may be health challenges or psychological trauma that must be addressed.

I take great solace in God. I realize that He overcame death when He rose from the dead and stepped sout of the tomb. Because of this great day, I will see my children again, because they embraced who He was and is when they were alive. On Erin's stone I engraved the words of John 11:25 (KJV), "Jesus said unto her, I am the resurrection, and the life: he that believeth in me, though he were dead, yet shall he live." This hope of seeing them again gives me great solace in the dark seasons of grief. This is my anchor. This stabilizes me in the worst of times.

I don't fear death. There is a Bible verse in Hebrews 2:15 that reads, "And deliver them who through fear of death were all their lifetime subject to bondage." Most people are afraid of death. But why be afraid when death has "lost its sting" because of what Jesus did for us in conquering it? It really has no hold over a believer. But we must put that thought "under our feet" and conquer that fear by believing in the finished work of Jesus Christ.

This morning, as usual, I began listening to some of my favorite songs by the Brooklyn Tabernacle Choir as I played my solitaire games on the computer. I was thinking back to a time of my life that was very difficult. Someone said to me, "Just praise God." Do we praise God just to get us out of difficult situations? If we are praising Him in that way, we are almost trying to buy His favor with praise. It doesn't work that way. When we praise the Almighty, it forms a connection to Him. The Bible says that God "inhabits the praise of Israel" (Ps. 22:3 KJV). It does a work in us to bring us to a higher plane that this earth can afford. We are letting Him know that we know, despite the trial we may be in, that He is still God. He is still in charge of our lives. He is our God. Should we only praise Him during storms, during trials of life? Isn't that using God? He won't be used. Praise begins when things are all right. It begins when we have seasons on the mountaintops. If we praise Him, then it will not be so hard to praise Him in the storms.

· · · · · · · · · ●●● ● ●● · · · · · ·

April 20, 2019
Survivor's Guilt

Shortly after our Erin left for heaven, David began saying things that shocked me. He said that he should have been the one who died because Erin was so much more social and knew so much more about handling things than he. Later, I found there is something called survivor's guilt that many experience. Often, this is found in siblings. I couldn't understand why David felt this way. It seemed maybe we had fallen short of letting him know how very much we loved and valued him too. But seeing the focus on all of Erin's achievements right after her passing must have made him feel inferior.

Since that time, I have witnessed this many times in others. I even experienced it myself when my own dear sister Kathryn passed. Kathryn always was so outgoing and very artistic. Her home was filled with her craftsmanship, and often gifts she gave to us were handcrafted with her loving touch. She seemed able to reach out to others with the gospel of Jesus Christ so easily. My eldest brother and I admired Kathryn as a child and often depended on her to initiate the ideas for our playtime. So when she passed so suddenly, I, too, couldn't understand why I was left and she was gone.

Now that I understand a little more about survivor's guilt, it helps me to help others, especially parents, when they witness this in their surviving children. It's very tough to see your other children suffering. When they face this, it is very frightening because a parent's great fear is losing another child. But to understand this is a normal feeling gives a bit of peace in a troubling time.

It may be because I just had two surgeries in two months, but there are days when I feel I am in pea soup fog. No past. No future. The nothingness seems to engulf me. But I look around and begin to count my blessings. When I feel that I should have been the one who died instead of any of my children and my sister Kathryn, who left for heaven in 2013, something happens to remind me that I am loved, valued, and still contribute in this life. During my recovery, my nieces, nephews, sister, brothers, and friends have all rallied around me, making me feel the love and the value I have in their lives. My husband has been a protective force around me, making sure I follow doctors' orders and doing so much to ensure I have a good recovery. It's during these times that the fog lifts and the sun shines again. Even if it is of short duration, it gives me strength to go on.

I would be remiss if I didn't mention the grace of God. Yesterday I awoke and it was 5:05 a.m. Today it was five o'clock sharp. And 5 in the Bible is a number associated with grace. Whenever I see a 5, I know that grace is nearby. I am a big believer in numerology. I believe that God orchestrates much, much more than we know, and numerology is important. If you look at dates and the number of things in the Bible, they are so exact! So I'll take the number 5 as a special one for me. Grace, grace, God's grace that sustains the life flow, the very essence of who I am.

DAY-1,143

•••••••••●•••••••••

A Glorious Hope

Today is Easter Sunday, the day that changed the world. With the resurrection of Jesus Christ, hope was born. It is a hope that has not diminished, and neither has the Christian religion. Christians have suffered at the hands of the world for two thousand years and yet have overcome. Rulers have tried to annihilate this religion with stoning, feeding Christians to hungry lions, imprisonments, killing children in front of parents, and even burning churches and homes of known Christians. But they have failed. Even to this present day, whole groups of Christians are being persecuted and killed all over the world. Even a nonbeliever must ask what it is about Christians that make them overcomers, even when facing death. It is hope! It is not a hope born by a world full of chaos, but it is a hope that goes beyond this worldly existence.

When Jesus was about to be crucified at the hands of an angry mob of the religious leaders of that day, He told His disciples something profound. He said, because of His own death, the Spirit of God (Christ) would be released into the whole world. It is this Holy Spirit that enables Christians to stand when all around them fails.

People have asked me how I can stand or even still be alive after burying all my most precious children. They have told me they would have died. When my children were growing up, I always encouraged them to make their own peace with God through the cross. I constantly told them that we live on this earth around seventy years, maybe longer if grace allows. But that is a very short time in relation to all of eternity. That time will be spent with God if we have honored the sacrifice of His own Son. Jesus said in John 14:6 (KJV), "I am the way, the truth, and the life: no man cometh unto the Father, but by me." There is no other way to God. My children embraced Christianity as their own decision. That is why I can still breathe today when it would be easier to go on to be with them. That is my greatest hope.

It is this hope that breathes life into me when I arise each day. There is no uncertain future ahead for me, whether I live or die. Even with all the questioning that has bombarded my mind about the passing of my children, there is a sure peace in my heart about where they are. It is a peace that is indescribable, unsearchable, and unending. It is a peace that transcends any peace this world can offer. My answer to the nurses and doctors when they saw my calmness as I sat by David's bedside day and night was that my faith in God gave me hope.

And it is all because of the resurrection of Jesus Christ. This is our glorious hope!

• • • • • • • • ● • • • • • • • •

April 25, 2019
Teach Us to Number Our Days

There is some controversy about whether God only assigns a certain number of days. Some believe that certain events or actions shorten or lengthen our days. Some believe that we only have a certain number and when our time is up, it is up! There are a few Bible verses on the subject. "My son forget not my law but let thine heart keep my commandments. For length of days, and long life, and peace, shall they add to thee" (Prov. 3:1–2 KJV). And another, Psalm 90:10 (AMP), "The days of our years are threescore years and ten (seventy years)— or even, if by reason of strength, fourscore years (eighty years); yet is their pride [in additional years] only labor and sorrow, for it is soon gone, and we fly away." There are many verses as well. So how does a parent who has lost a child accept this, and does it change their belief? I had a real problem with it all. I remembered one of the commandments that has a promise attached. It says, "Honor thy father and thy mother, as the LORD thy God hath commanded thee; that thy days may be prolonged, and that it may go well with thee, in the land which the LORD thy God giveth thee" (Deut. 5:16 KJV). I kept going back to that and remembering the depth of love and respect between our own children and us. David said, repeatedly, that he was so weak and it was so hard to fight the disease but he would do it for us. That is surely honoring parents. And Erin would have laid down her own life for us. Yet she is not here on earth now. So was the promise wrong? Was I wrong? Why? It's another one of those questions I put in my "book" of questions, which grows steadily day by day.

I do believe that we have a certain number of days, a certain number of heartbeats allotted to us. David felt the same way when he said to me upon learning the horrible news that the disease was back, "Mom, I'm going to fight this. But you know, when your time comes, it comes." He was willing to fight to the end.

Yesterday, I went to the cemetery to treat some weeds that were growing inside the granite coping around the graves. As I drove away, I noticed a very small nicely decorated grave. I stopped the car and got out to look. It was a baby, whose picture just melted my heart. She was born in October and died in February the next year. Such a beautiful little girl! What happens to a child who lives only six months, or one who is born still? Was their time limited to this short an existence? When I think on these things, they are too much for this finite mind. But I must wonder, how does God, who is the ultimate, all-powerful God, decide on the time we live? Is there a magic formula He uses? What are the reasons He could have for ripping a child away from a parent? Is it wrong for me to think these things?

I always go back to the statement I made to myself after months of questioning why David did not survive after such a fight. Finally, I thought, *God is God, and I am not! His knowledge far surpasses any earthly knowledge, and His wisdom is truth.* That is the only comfort I can find in the constant barrage of questions that fill my days and nights.

There is no doubt whatever that God could have healed David. So (and here it comes again) why not? I was just listening to a song, "God Who Moves the Mountains." It provoked the thought that maybe it was that I didn't believe God strong enough that was why David was not healed, not here today. But immediately I assured myself that I *did* believe that God was able to heal David. There is no doubt that He is able.

A verse in Luke 4:25–27 (KJV) explains something very important. "But I tell you of a truth, many widows were in Israel in the days of Elias, when the heaven was shut up three years and six months, when great famine was throughout all the land; But unto none of them was Elias sent, save unto Sarepta, *a city* of Sidon, unto a woman *that was* a widow. And many lepers were in Israel in the time of Eliseus the prophet; and none of them was cleansed, saving Naaman the Syrian."

This raises yet another question: How does God select those who are healed and those who are not? Is it because they have more faith than any around them? Is it just a random pick? I think not. Jesus addressed this very issue in John 9:1–24 (KJV). "And as *Jesus* passed by, he saw a man which was blind from *his* birth. His disciples asked him: 'Rabbi, who sinned, this man or his parents, that he was born blind?' Jesus answered, neither hath this man sinned, nor his parents: but that the works of God should be made manifest in him." This leads me to believe that whatever happens in life is to exemplify the works and glory of God. But a grieving parent will not want to hear this. There would not be any reason enough for them to have to give up a child. It doesn't even feel just to me.

Again, I must conclude by saying that I now believe that God is God and I am not. We cannot see the whole picture. But God can. I cannot rationalize what the Almighty does or does not do. All I know is that I trust Him. I have faith in Him while I still mourn my children.

DAY-1,150

● ● ● ● ● ● ● ● ● ● ● ● ● ● ● ● ● ●

April 28, 2019
The Importance of Remembering

Remembering is a key to comfort for a grieving parent. Our great fear is that our child will be forgotten especially after we are gone.

With that in mind, I want to share some precious memories here of each of our children. Yesterday my husband stood outside, talking to a deliveryman for quite some time. Later, he told me that when he tipped the man, the opportunity came for him to share about David's generosity. David, Erin, and Scott all had tender hearts when it came to others.

When Erin was in school, one Christmas she wanted to get all her friends gifts. And she didn't want to get cheap gifts. I tried to tell her a small token would be enough. But she really wanted to express her love for her friends with a nice gift. So she did. The gifts she got in return, if she got any, were the smaller ones that I suggested she give. But she loved *big*! After she was married, there was a friend who had left his parents to move out on his own. When she and Adam visited him, he had no money and no food. She came here and asked if she could take him some groceries. Well, she about cleaned out my pantry, which was okay, and took him plenty. Once she sent a dear friend flowers when the friend was sick. She got no thank-you later, but I was proud of her kindness. She always made sure that her family was celebrated on every birthday or special day. Her delight was giving to others, even if she didn't have the money to buy something for herself. When my mom was hospitalized, Erin was right there. If I was sick or just feeling down, she'd show up with flowers or a balloon. We came to depend on her sweet spirit to lift our own so often. Her dad was at a friend's house and she called, as she did frequently to all of us. She said she was bringing him a milkshake. When I was taking care of my mom after Daddy died, she would often just show up there and bring me a Reese's peanut butter cup and a Dr. Pepper, my favorites. She adored her little brother. I remember he told me how proud he was once when she picked him up from school when I couldn't. He said all his friends were saying how pretty she was in her white Mustang. One of David's grieving points was that Erin had called him the morning of her last birthday, just three days before she passed. She wanted him to sing "Happy Birthday" to her, and he didn't. He never forgot that. She always pushed all three of us to be as happy as she was.

Some people thought David was shy because he was very selective about friends and people he allowed into his inner circle. But I never saw shyness in him. When we'd go on vacation, it wasn't long before he met a friend in the pool or in the hotel where we stayed. He loved being with his friends, often spending a week with one or even just a few days. Unlike Erin, when he would be with them, he wouldn't call unless the mom of the friend reminded him to call me to let me know he was okay. He worried about his friends if they were in what he considered a bad relationship. If they drank of smoked too much, he worried. He just wanted them all to be okay. He had had several girlfriends. He told me he didn't go looking for them; they would find him and begin calling him. Two of those relationships ended badly. The last one was very difficult. I think it was because he was dealing with suppressed grief over Erin's passing when he was only fourteen. His counselor told me that she felt the bad relationship had had an impact on his health. But he loved this girl and gave 100 percent of himself to her and to making it work. He used to be upset when they would have trouble and I blamed her immaturity or some unusual behavior for it. He said, "Mom, it's not all her. I'm to blame too." His counselor said he had abandonment issues with Erin's passing and us being older parents. This last girl would disappear suddenly for hours or days at a time. And he began having panic attacks as a result. So it did affect his health. But he just loved people, even to his own hurt. He believed in being kind to people. When he'd go out with me and my mom to her doctor's appointments, he'd always open the door for her and others. If he thought something was too heavy, he'd carry it for us. He never wanted his friends' birthdays to go without a card and a gift. He could never stand for injustice in any form. I remember once we shopped at Best Buy, and when we got to the car, I realized the clerk had omitted one item. We got in the car and I was about to drive away, and he said, "Mom, you need to take that back. Even if they don't know it, we do." I was not even thinking about it. But he didn't let that slip. He was at a friend's house, and when the friend and his grandmother drove him home, his grandmother said, "You have to be proud of David. We were going to watch a movie and he said he couldn't because you would not approve of it. There aren't many children who would obey their moms like that." When David and his friends would go out to eat, he said he'd give the waiter/waitress a big tip, often using the allotted money in his allowance just to see they were tipped well. He said he knew they probably didn't make much money. Even when David was so sick just before he passed, he found out another young man, Glenn Savage, in his uncle's church was very sick and his heart had even stopped once. David said, "Mom, we have to pray for him." And we did. He also was very worried about a dear grieving mom friend of mine, Laura Harris, who was having open-heart surgery. He wanted to text and see how she was recovering. His heart just reached out to others. And the ultimate was his sacrificial surviving. He knew how very weak he was when he went in for that last big round of chemo. He really felt that he was not strong enough. But he told us he wanted to fight to stay alive for me and his daddy. And he tried with all that was in him. Oh, my son, how I miss you!

Scott was also considered a shy one when he was young. He came from a small hometown. But after high school, he joined the

Army and traveled the world. He was the sweetest kid, though. When he would spend weekends with his dad and me, he loved going shopping with me. And he always expressed appreciation for everything I'd buy him. Erin was very young but got to spend more time with him than David did, since he was in the Army, when David was very small. He loved Erin and David and always spent as much time as he could with them. When Scott passed, we realized how many friends he had. There were quite a few at the visitation in Savannah, and they shared such great stories with us about Scott when they were all overseas in Iraq and Afghanistan. One story was that Scott would give his MREs to some of the Iraqis that were in his work detail. They said these men would save the MREs to take to their families since they only made about $3 a week. One story was that once Scott drove to the mess hall and asked for five meals. He brought them back and gave them to some dogs they had been taking care of. He felt sorry for the dogs because they were hungry. There were many others, some funny, some just kindness. When I see the comments on Scott's social media page, I know how many friends he made during his many travels in the Army. And they all miss him and respected him. Scott loved his new family, caring for his wife's two daughters as his own and really loving his little granddaughter on the rare occasion when he could be home for a short while. During the few years he was married, he was only to spend months with his new wife since he was deployed four times. But he'd make the long drive from where he was stationed after he got home to Savannah to spend as much time as he could with them.

So if you are faced with a friend or family member who loses a child, please, please let them tell you about their precious child. You could give no greater gift. Remember them with them!

DAY-1,151

• • • • • • • • ● • • • • • • • •

April 29, 2019
Remembrance

David's twenty-eighth birthday will be here in a few days. The anticipation of a birthday can be overwhelming as the sadness creeps in to try to take our breath away. But God sends comfort in many ways.

I found this little poem that my aunt Francis Childs wrote and sent to me just a few days after David made his heavenly journey. My aunt Francis is the only surviving sibling of my dad and is a published author as well. This brought me such great comfort.

Remembrance
by Mary Frances Childs, 2016

Remember me when spring's
First essence fills the air.
I can be found where every
Flower grows.
Think of me at quiet twilight times.
Remember me in festive candle glow,
Where memorable music plays,
There I shall be also.
Remember me when silent snowflakes waft.
I'll see your smile when you look

Into a moonlit summer sky.
A soft touch on your shoulder,
When no one is there, means that
I'll be standing before the stones
In your pathway.
My Spirit will be near you always.
Cry for me a little while,
Because I know you cared.
Then, smile at remembrances of me.

DAY-1,152

· · · · · · · ● · · · · · · ·

May 1, 2019
The Anchor Still Holds

May has arrived, and with it David's twenty-eighth birthday, the third with him in heaven. How does a parent face the birthday of a child who is not here on earth? How do they deal with the sorrow of facing yet another day that was the best and now is the hardest? When their heart is breaking, how do they keep living? It is simple. They have an anchor that cannot be moved. The "ship" may be tossed around by the ferocious waves, but that anchor holds if it is an eternal anchor not affected by the tide of life.

I have had those who asked how I could keep breathing, keep living. They admitted they didn't know what they would do. But I read something that sparked the answer for me. It said the test of the anchor is in the storm. The fiercer the storm, the more valuable the anchor. I have such an anchor in Christ Jesus, my Lord. The hardest days I want to share so that if you, or a grieving parent reading this, must navigate days like this, you will know that you can survive.

Today is May 3. A mother's heart always holds the most precious memories. Twenty-eight years ago today, David was due. We were so incredibly excited about his coming to add one more to our little family of three. My doctor was scheduled to be out of town that weekend. It was on a Friday, just like today. But David decided to wait until Monday to make his grand entrance into the world. Since these days are falling on the exact weekday again this year, it all comes back to me, every moment, every precious memory.

As the warm memories come back, so do the drops of salty water dripping from my eyes. I know that with Monday's coming, I will mourn my sweet boy as I once again place red roses and a birthday balloon on his headstone. I wish I could apply the brakes and that day would not come now. It brings such pain and sorrow. It was the happiest of days in my life and now is one of the saddest.

But I take a deep breath and keep breathing. The way I have learned from other grieving moms to survive the day is to

- have a plan for the day, even if it is to do nothing;
- invite a friend or family member to visit the grave with us;
- remember it is only twenty-four hours, and anyone can get through twenty-four hours;
- do a random act of kindness on that day to reach out to someone else in need;
- allow myself to cry, to grieve however loud and long I need to get the grief out;
- let the warm memories flood my soul; and
- spend some time alone with God, asking questions, listening for His voice during my chaos.

A mother's heart never forgets. The child we bore is forever tied to us with heartstrings.

DAY-1,161

······●●●●●●●●●●····

May 10, 2019
Setting Goals

We survived another of David's precious birthdays without collapsing into agony, although the tears were falling continuously.

Every morning I play a few games on my computer as I sip my ginger tea and contemplate the day ahead. Several times I caught myself just playing without really thinking what I was doing. The game would seem endless as I tried to win. Then I would glance at the bottom color strip that contained the goal for winning that game. As I played it anew, I would win handily without much effort as I went for the goal.

My grieving mom friends and I have discussed at length the question of our purpose for still being here. I admit, there are some days that just feel it's not worth the effort to try to linger. But as a Christian, I know that I have a destiny that does not just affect me but others whose path I may cross as well. Setting goals does not just help us survive our grief journey, but it establishes groundwork for completing our destiny.

As I continue to recover and try to gain back the strength from two surgeries, I'm finding it frustrating that I can't just get out and dig in my gardens and go back to the "git 'er done" woman I have always been. There must be a goal of one day at a time, one task that might be the only task for that day, no matter how trivial. If I over-work, then I will pay the price the next day and in my overall health.

Such is our life with grief. At first, with the shock and numbness of our loss, just being able to breathe seems an overwhelming task for the day. Getting out of bed some days takes all the strength we have. Goal setting even then is a must for survival. It is by no means a goal to get over it or get past it. It is a goal for survival until our destiny on earth is fulfilled. When I think back to the two years our David struggled for his survival, I know it would have been much easier to just give up. But he wouldn't! When I get weary and almost beg for God to take me home to heaven and my children, I just think about David. Then I know I can't give up either. I must be here for my hus-band, my sister and brothers, nieces and nephews, who have told me they still need me. I must be here for my grieving friends who need me to help reach down and pull them up or sit with them in the pit as we cry together. I must be here for that random act of kindness that might change someone's life. There are reasons to still live after extreme loss. It is not a choice. It's a necessity. When I see that per-spective, I know that I can live. I can continue to look at the colored strip that contains the goal for each day. I can survive.

If you are grieving and you can't find the strength to go on, I challenge you to set a goal. It doesn't have to be a big one. It can be as simple as getting out of bed, taking a walk in the sunshine, doing a random act of kindness for a stranger, or just reaching out to another person struggling with grief. I promise you that it will give you another breath, another chance at surviving your sorrow.

DAY-1,162

•••••••••●•••••••

May 11, 2019
Erin

Tomorrow is Mother's Day. I am still a mother. But while others are gathering with families, going out to dine with moms, giving gifts to their mothers, I will sit alone, wishing, longing for my children.

Today my husband and I ran some errands and stopped at a restaurant to eat. Across the aisle from us sat a young woman chatting away with her grandmother. My mind raced back to the time Erin sat beside me in that very restaurant on the same seat I was sitting on today. I could almost see her and hear her sweet voice and envision her smile. When I came home, I tried to remember if I have shared Erin in this book. I know I wrote much about her in my grief journal in the days and months after she went to heaven. But let me share her now.

I was career oriented, and after a few failed relationships in my twenties, I finally met the man I was to spend my life with when I was thirty-one. It was a whirlwind courtship, and we married just four months after we met. We had gone to high school together. But I was away at college the first year after high school. He was in the National Guard and was married twice and had two sons. A dear friend set us up on a blind date. We quickly fell in love, and he was the answer to my prayers. Our first year was a bit rocky as we both brought the usual baggage of failed relationships, mistrust, and the merging of two worlds into our becoming one. Three years later, I was pregnant and beyond joyful to be having my first baby. She was a big baby, weighing nine pounds, five ounces, and was twenty-one and one-fourth inches long. Erin Leigh brought a love into my life that I had never known before. My husband used to say I kissed her too much. But I would rush home after work just to see her. I got my first and only speeding ticket rushing to my mom's to pick her up. She was a showstopper everywhere she went. When I was out shopping, strangers would stop and tell me what a beautiful child she was. Berry showed her picture to a lady whose appliance he was checking. She said she was a member of the Pilot Club and he should enter Erin in the beauty contest they hosted. But Erin would have none of it. She didn't want to parade in front of anyone unless I walked with her. She was a very strong-willed child and yet had an innocence about her that everyone loved. I vividly remember the day she came home from day care so upset. She had gone inside to use the restroom when the class was playing outside. But she saw something she had never seen before. She saw a little girl taking something out of someone else's cubby, where the children stored their personal belongings. Erin was appalled that anyone would steal! As she grew, she witnessed injustices time and again and each time was deeply affected. If she knew someone was lonely or in need, she would quickly step up to the plate and meet that need. She had a caring heart that was easily broken. Erin grew up tall and beautiful, tanning easily with the wonderful tan skin like her dad. When I would go shopping with her or just be out and about, I would notice people would treat her in a very special way because of her beauty.

School became a pleasant experience for her. She made many friends and loved going each day. She always was our little social butterfly, bringing friends home, hosting or going to parties far and near. She excelled in school, always making good grades, and got to skip to the next grade for her reading/language arts instruction. In middle school, she was in the classes for the gifted. Middle school became a challenge as it was a much bigger school than elementary and there were more discipline problems with some of the children. Again, she saw injustices but often couldn't do anything to change a situation, so she would become frustrated. When she went to high school, she became more independent, started driving, and wanted to get a part-time job in her junior year in a job training class. So we allowed her to work at the local grocer. She was quickly a hit with some of the customers, who would try to get in her checkout line just to talk to her. She broadened her work experience by working at a farm supply store, then an insurance agency, and finally a dress shop before she graduated. She scored a perfect score on the English final exam in high school along with just a few others.

During her early childhood years, we bonded on a level that I heard others say they wished they had with their daughters. We shared every secret (well, maybe she had a few she didn't share). She did go through a few rough patches but came through them with much prayer on our part and many long talks. She married her childhood sweetheart, whom she loved with her heart and soul. Even though she didn't go to college, just before she passed, she told me she wanted to go still and was about to try to take the college entrance exam. She always wanted to be a teacher.

She loved her family with a passion. I can still remember the tears rolling down her cheeks as she stood with her dad as David and I got on the transport vans with our church group to catch a flight to England. She couldn't bear to be far from us. As much as she wanted to go on the trip, she loved her husband more and needed to stay with him since he and her dad couldn't get free from work. She helped David with his homeschooling often, coming over to help with his physical education by playing ball, or coming by to help him study for upcoming tests. She would help her dad with projects or anything for which he needed her. Her husband could count on her to help manage their finances, do the paperwork for his business, or help him find new jobs welding. She worked, too, much of the time.

She was sunshine to our days. She helped me pick out more modern clothes, styling my hair when we went to England, and help-ing us stay abreast of the latest technical innovations. If we were sick, she was right there, bringing flowers or food or whatever we needed.

Erin wasn't perfect, as none of us are. Her temper would flare a bit when provoked, and she would stand up to anyone who tried to hurt someone she loved. But she loved with the same fierceness. Most of her friends would attest to that too.

Erin loved fast cars and trucks, name-brand clothes, good makeup and perfume, country music, cats, dogs, boating, swimming, good movies, and Subway Italian BMT sandwiches. She was in Girl Scouts, twirling, softball, cheerleading, swimming, piano lessons, and took cake-decorating classes. Her passion was interior design. She and Adam bought a house that she redecorated inside and out and modernized. Her yards were another passion, and she spent hours and hours landscaping it so beautifully. She was never afraid of a new challenge.

How does a mom put into a few words the depth of the love for her child? Erin was our world, as were David, Heather, and Scott. She made the sunshine brighter, the breezes blow cooler, the world a wonderful, fun place to be for all her loved ones.

When our Erin left so suddenly for heaven after an accidental overdose of her prescription medication for back pain and root canal pain, our whole world collapsed. Suddenly, our world, which was sunshine and rainbows, became black-and-white, with cold winds blowing and no sun in sight.

We miss our Erin with every breath we take. David missed her too. It changed all of us to lose her. But we know we will see her again on heaven's beautiful, bright, sunny shore, where she waits for us now.

· · · · · · · ● · · · · · · · ·

May 16, 2019 God Sees Our Tears God Sees Our Tears

This chapter is one that God had to "drag me kicking and scream-ing" to write. I didn't want to write it. So it must be written for someone special.

Last Sunday was Mother's Day, perhaps one of the most diffi-cult days on earth for a grieving mom. When I woke up, I knew it was not going to be a good day, one that I would struggle to keep breathing through. I didn't want to get out of bed, but I did. When my husband came in to wish me a happy Mother's Day, I wanted to just crawl in a hole and die. I didn't answer my phone when a friend called. I didn't want to talk to anyone. My husband drove me up into the mountains to just get away. The tears just wouldn't stop as the day wore on. We drove almost to the North Carolina line and ate at a nice country restaurant along with a few hundred others, many in parties of eight to fifteen since many were taking mothers out to eat. There were, surprisingly, quite a few older couples who were alone, though. So I didn't feel so isolated being alone with my husband when I knew there should be our children there. To further occupy my mind, my husband stopped at a favorite flea market, and I browsed the vendor's goods, making a few small purchases as it poured down rain outside the covered areas. We began the long ride home, and on the way my phone rang. It was my niece Amanda. As I reached back for the phone, it fell under the seat. But I thought of calling her when I got home. As we drove in our driveway, there was a car there, and it was Amanda, along with her three sons. She had stopped by to leave some beautiful flowers and visit. So we opened the gate, and all came in for a short time of hugs and fellowship. The flowers brightened my day, along with the peach chamomile tea that she knew I loved. The next day, a beautiful wooden plaque arrived from her. It read, "Be strong and courageous, for the Lord, your God, is with you wherever you go." Their acts of kindness lifted me out of the not-wanting-to-live-anymore stage, and I pressed forward. My aunt Carolyn also showed up just as they were leaving to bring a beautiful pot of flowers that brightened my day even more.

There are times in life when living seems pointless. We feel we have lost everything and there is no reason to smile, much less keep breathing. But it is in those moments that God sees our tears, even if there are no prayers attached. I believe He reads those tears as words from our innermost being, and He acts quickly to assuage our down-trodden souls. It may be a visit from a niece or aunt, a card in the mail, a phone call, or even a chance meeting in a store. But it is what some call a God wink. I believe He sees our great sorrow.

Just last week, as I thought on grief, I realized I didn't think God knew what it felt like to know this sorrow. But then the thought came that He had to witness His only Son being not only crucified but also beaten and treated so horribly beforehand. At that moment in time when His own Son had to bear the sins of the whole world, God had to turn His back, for He could not look upon sin. In that moment, eternity was changed forever. God became acquainted with grief. So yes, He does understand the deep sorrow that I and others feel. He knows! And that is even more reason for Him to see our tears as prayers. He will respond every time, even when we don't realize it.

DAY-1,176

· · · · · · ●●●●● ● ●●●● · · · · · ·

May 25, 2019
Who for the Joy Set Before Him

It is said that confession is good for the soul. So I will confess to you that there are more than a few days that I long to go be with my children. I am not suicidal. I still believe that each day we are given is a gift from God. But the sheer loneliness, longing, and impact of grief overwhelms the soul. As long as we had David, after Erin left for heaven, we did have a reason to keep living, keep strong. But after he left for heaven, it is getting harder to find meaning in each day and purpose for living. But God gifts me with new days and new grace for each day.

This morning, after I watered my little flower gardens, the phrase came to me, "Who, for the joy set before Him, endured the cross, despising the shame" (Heb. 12:2 KJV). I thought of what Jesus suffered at the hands of those who were the religious leaders of the day. They treated Him cruelly. Yet He didn't even open His mouth to justify Himself. He could "see" beyond the cross into the glorious resurrection life that awaited Him when He would be seated at last at the right hand of the Father, God. As I thought on what He endured, I took a deep breath and realized that I, too, could endure this life. And because of what He did, I knew that when I was failing in strength, His strength in me would help. Some years back, I was a praise leader in my church. I wrote a few songs based on scripture, and one came to mind this morning. It is based on Psalm 56 (KJV).

Every tear I shed is noted by the Lord.
He puts them in a bottle of remembrance.
When I call upon the Lord, He hears my prayer
and causes all my enemies to leave me.
For He is God!
I praise His name!
I will not fear what man can do unto me.
When I'm afraid, I will trust in Him.
In God I will praise His name.
In God I've put my trust.

When I am at my lowest, He is at His strongest. There is a verse that from my youth seemed to resonate with my soul as a life verse. It is in 2 Corinthians 12:9 (KJV). "My grace is sufficient for thee: for my strength is made perfect in weakness. Most gladly therefore will I rather glory in my infirmities, that the power of Christ may rest upon me." So to you, my audience, I would say that you can find a strength that is beyond your own. I have. I have the strength to live. It doesn't come from me, which is the most amazing part of it all. It is when we feel the weakest that His glory manifests through us.

DAY-1,182

· · · · · · · ● ● ● ●●● ● ● ● · · · · ·

May 31, 2019
Every Life Has Some Scars

It has been said that a little rain will fall into everyone's life. How true! Some will face horrendous thunderstorms, and some will simply have some heavy rainfall. If we look behind the doors of most lives, it won't be all rosy no matter how hard it is made to look perfect.

It is so easy to compare our lives to others'. But when we try to measure up to others' lives (or facade of lives), we may fall short and find ourselves in depression. So it's best to get up each day and live that day out whatever may come.

Often, when I am asked how I even keep breathing, I simply reply that each morning I ask God to show me the path of life today. Each day brings new mercies for whatever that day may hold.

Recently, I found myself tending to cats! Two cats showed up at my door a few months back. It seemed to be a cat and later her kitten. I named the kitten Velvet because its solid-black hair looked so velvety. I thought it was a boy. But lo and behold, it was pregnant, and the mom was too! So this week I have had to make some tough decisions. I knew that if I didn't do something, I would have twenty-something cats in no time flat. Well, the mama cat had four kittens, and Velvet had her kitten(s) last Sunday, but she has kept them well hidden in the woods behind our house. When I saw a big yellow tomcat lying on my carport one night, I decided to act quickly and take the mama cat and two of her four kittens to the animal shelter. I took her at her protest because her kittens had begun eating solid food. I told them I would have to bring two of the four kittens. My niece and a friend agreed to rehome two little yellow ones. But when I went to try to entice the other two into a carrier, they were gone! All gone! Velvet comes each morning and night for her meals. I wonder if they have followed her and are still nursing on her. That's my path of life right now, trying to care for and find all these kittens. Oh, well, it has breathed a little life back into our ho-hum existence. I will keep Velvet and have her spayed as soon as she weans her little one(s).

Even the bond to animals is one that I keep at a distance, however that may seem. When we lost our Ms. Priss, our little goat and last surviving farm animal, I determined I couldn't form any more bonds that would possibly end in death. But do we take that risk, even though we know it might come?

Forming bonds costs commitment. It might be harder for a grieving parent because of the protective shield we put around ourselves and our emotions. We think we can't take another bad thing in life. But are we hurting ourselves more by doing this? So many questions.

But for today, I will tend to the cats and kittens. Loving brings risks. But I'll think about tomorrow when it comes.

DAY-1,186

• • • • • • • • • • ● • • • • • • • • • • •

June 7, 2019
Beginning, Middle, and Ending

Every good novel has a beginning, middle, and ending. Life, no matter the years, has a beginning, middle, and ending. But time changes dramatically for a grieving parent. It gets all tangled up in the past, present, and future, which is sent scattering to the four winds. When a child dies, no matter what age, the past with them comes back into full view. Otherwise, it would have been the past, preserved with pictures and snippets of conversation with them. The present is a gaping hole filled with loneliness and finding purpose in life when your purpose was wrapped up in the child. The future is a bleak hole filled with nothingness and endless questions that roll through the mind to make sense of it all. For a Christian, there is a future beyond this life that will be filled with a grand reunion with that child and endless bliss for eternity. But it seems so far away when you live with the longing for what was and what could have been every day when you awaken.

There is an old song that comes to mind that describes this journey so well:

Life's Railway to Heaven
by M. E. Abbey, who was a Baptist minister in Georgia
Published 1890
(Copyright status is public domain)

Life is like a mountain railroad,
With an engineer that's brave.
We must make the run successful,
From the cradle to the grave.
Watch the curves, the fills, the tunnels.
Never falter, never quail.
Keep your hand upon the throttle,
And your eye upon the rail.

Refrain:
Blessed Savior, thou wilt guide us,
Till we reach the blissful shore,
Where the angels wait to join us
In Thy praise forevermore.

You will roll up grades of trial;
You will cross the bridge of strife;
See that Christ is your conductor
On this lightning train of life;
Always mindful of obstruction,
Do your duty, never fail;
Keep your hand upon the throttle,
And your eye upon the rail.

(Refrain)

You will often find obstructions,
Look for storms and wind and rain.
On a fill, or curve, or trestle
They will almost ditch your train.
Put your trust alone in Jesus,
Never falter, never fail.
Keep your hand upon the throttle,
And your eye upon the rail.

(Refrain)

As you roll across the trestle,
Spanning Jordan's swelling tide,
You behold the Union Depot
Into which your train will glide;
There you'll meet the Sup'rintendent,
God the Father, God the Son,
With the hearty, joyous plaudit,
"Weary pilgrim, welcome home."

(Refrain)

We never really know what is around the next bend or over the next mountain in life. But if we know the conductor, we are safe.

So no matter how tangled our timeline, we can have peace in the Creator of all things.

• • • • • • • • ● • • • • • • • •

June 10, 2019
Human Rationalization
of Divine Intentions

Grief has us searching for meaning, understanding, and reasoning. Many books have been written on this topic in a quest for answers. Sadly, most of them, if not all, come up short. Recently, I chose one off my shelf that was yellowed with age, written many years ago with a title that would catch the eye of any bereaved parent. It is titled *When Bad Things Happen to Good People*, by Harold Kushner. The author goes to great lengths to find some answers. Finally, he puts forth several theories about why bad things happen to good people based on his findings.

We try desperately to figure out God, His plan, His thinking, His logic in some people dying of disease, accidents, or tragic events. I guess we think we can outthink God Himself, not stopping to realize that, as the Bible says in Isaiah, "For *as* the heavens are higher than the earth, so are my ways higher than your ways, and my thoughts than your thoughts" (Isa. 55:9 KJV). How can we, as Job put it, dare to question the Almighty? And yet we do. You may say, "Oh, no, I would never do that!" But let something happen to your child(ren), a fire or storm destroy your home, or you lose your lifelong job and find yourself struggling. Then answer this: Look at the tragedy of

September 11, 2001. There were three thousand people whose lives were cut short. Some were young, just beginning promising careers; some were new dads or moms; and some were hardworking custodians who had families who depended on them. And yet a few were several minutes late. One was late because they couldn't find a child's shoelaces. One got stuck in traffic and was late. And their lives were spared. So why them? A plane crashed and no one survived. Some might have canceled their flight just before takeoff and were spared. Can we really figure out God's plan? Do we know more than He does about justice and fairness?

Many years ago, I remember hearing a sermon by a minister who is in heaven now. The title of the sermon is one I will never forget. I have quoted it more times than I can remember. It was "Our Lives Aren't Determined by the Flip of a Coin." So often, in my finite mind, thoughts of God's reasoning for determining who lives, who dies, who succeeds in life, who fails, who gets sick, or who lives many years, have raced through my mind. And when it is overwhelming, I quote this minister's sermon title. Even though my life has more than its shares of downs, I still believe that God is a God of order, a God of justice. I can almost hear you saying, "How can you say that after burying four children?" Well, no matter how angry I get at God, no matter how many questions I ply His Majesty with, the bottom line is that I believe He is a God of order. And unlike some authors I have read, I don't believe that chance or evil determines the number of days we live. There are some who would avidly disagree with me. I believe it is ordered of God. Doesn't it say in Psalms in the Bible that "our days are all numbered"? If God knows the number of stars in the sky, the number of hairs on our head, and each time a sparrow falls, why would He not know the number of our days?

All that we can do is as the Psalmist asked of God, "So teach *us* to number our days, that we may apply *our* hearts unto wisdom" (Ps. 90:12 KJV). Live each day to the fullest. Do the best you can and treasure each day as a gift. And then, whether your life is a long one full of days or a short one, you are treating it as a precious gift from God.

· · · · · · ● ● ● ● ● ● ● ● · · · · · · ·

June 12, 2019
David, Phone Home

When Erin was small, she wanted to spend the night at Grandma Fitzpatrick's home. But we, inevitably, always got that midnight call (or sooner) that she wanted us to come get her. She never really went far from home, even after she grew up. David, on the other hand, loved being at home. But when he went to a friend's house for the weekend or occasionally went to spend time with his lifelong friend Josh Davidson and stay a week, we would get no call. Josh's mom, Alicia, would prompt David to just give us a quick call to let us know he was okay. David would just enjoy whatever he was involved with at that time. Oh, he told everyone when they kidded him about me taking care of him that he was a mama's boy and proud of it. He never shied away from that. But when he went on a trip, he didn't let homesickness stop him from having fun. This morning, the thought came to me, like ET in that old movie: "David, could you please phone home?"

This book seems to be turning into a mishmash, a tangled mass, like Christmas lights. But such is the story of a grieving mom. I won't sugarcoat it. I won't pretend that it is an all-conquering, victorious, overcoming-all-the-time life. It is a tangled mishmash of chaos. It is a returning to those moments of pain, those moments of joy over and over without any warning. It is thinking these great philosophical thoughts of moments of how far you've come and how good you are doing. And then, in the next breath, you become this blubbering mass of tears, pain, and hopelessness. It is, as some friends aptly put it, an emotional roller coaster. So if my book seems unordered, such is my life. When your world is suddenly changed beyond recognition with the passing of a child, disorder follows, no matter how hard you try to maintain. There are memory lapses and flashbacks. There are days of sunshine and many days of rain. There are good times with friends and family and days when loneliness seems to engulf your very soul. Such is the life of a grieving parent.

I know David can't phone home. But I know that one day I will have him in my arms again. The one constant in all this chaos that is my life is my anchor, Jesus Christ. And it is that same anchor that David, Scott, and Erin all embraced early on in life, which is why I will see them again. Asleep in Christ for now. Alive forevermore! Thank God for my anchor!

DAY-1,192

....·····●●●●●●●....

June 13, 2019
Life Without You

Browsing through Erin's journal, I found this poem I wrote about her on October 20, 2006, just a few months after she made her heavenly journey.

Life without You

The days are long,
The nights are too.
This life we live
Now without you.
The sun went out,
The stars don't shine,
The birds don't sing
In this world of mine.

Where is the spring?
Where is the warmth
Of your pretty smile
And your loving touch,
The beauty that was you
As it graced the earth,

The fun, the joy, the life
That was with us?

I still look for you
When I see someone
With long blond hair,
Who is tall and young.
But they turn to face me,
And it is not you.
My Erin, my doll, my lovely
Daughter,
Where are you?

David says it's surreal
To think that you are gone.
We cannot grasp it.
It just can't be!
Our loving family,
So close, so warm,
Has been broken apart
By your departure from earth.

We know you're in heaven,
Near the Father's great throne.
But how can we see you?
How can we hear your sweet voice?
That was comfort to our ears.
You held us up when we were down.
Now, who will do that,
My dear, sweet girl?
Who'll beg for a pan of
Corn bread dressing for herself and Adam?
Or smother it with mopping and come back
For more?

Who'll hang the lights and help decorate the house?
The seasons will be so long and lonely
Now that you're gone.

Every day without you is so barren for
All of us.
For daddy, me, and David,
And of course, our sweet Adam.
He is a lost young man
Without your love and care.
Trying to grope in the dark, cold world for the
Love he has no more.

If we could go back in time,
We'd do a little more.
We'd shower you with love
And show you that we adore
Your sweetness, your kindness,
Your loving ways.
You'd never, ever doubt the impact you
Made on our lives.

But we can't go back.
We must move with time,
For although it should have stopped,
It keeps ticking endlessly.
But one sweet day, when the Lord says, "Enough,"
We'll be reunited, dear Erin,
And be apart no more!

• • • • • • • • ● • • • • • • •

June 15, 2019
How to Help Others Grieving

Often, I have the question, "[Someone] just lost a child. How can I help them?" Usually I just say, "Be there for them. You don't have to say anything or do anything. Be there and allow them to talk about their child. Say the child's name often."

Galatians 6:2 (KJV) in the Bible says, "Bear ye one another's burdens and so fulfill the law of Christ." Jesus gave one new commandment, and that was "Love one another; as I have loved you, that ye also love one another" (John 13:34 KJV). Love packs a powerful punch! Love can change a person, bring healing and hope during despair. Love never fails!

Recently, a cousin buried his last surviving child, a son. His firstborn son was a policeman who someone brutally shot while he was in the line of duty. When I heard that they had lost their only other child, Jason, my heart broke for them. I thought of them all day into the night as I knew the horror of loss and grief. I felt the pain even though I wasn't physically with them. And I knew the weeks and months ahead would bring more pain and sorrow as the loneliness set in. I plan to go and sit with them in a few weeks and try to listen, be there for them in their great sorrow. Months later, I did see them at an antique car show sponsored by a cancer support group who had helped David. We go every year to contribute in David's memory. They were there, proudly showing Jason's truck, which was so special to them. As we stood and talked and I saw the tears welling up in my cousin's eyes as he shared the very difficult feeling he had now, my heart broke for them both. Burying one child is overwhelming; burying your last child is truly heartbreaking.

When we face others who are beginning this journey of grief that we have walked for a time, it brings back our own sorrow as we empathize with them, as we know the path ahead will be long and tough. We don't want anyone to experience the grief that has been our portion in life. And yet we know that there is little we can do to ease the pain. It is a journey on which each must find their own path, their own peace in the times of trouble. But even though each must walk their own path, there is comfort in knowing others have gone before you on this road.

A very wise person said that sharing is healing. At first, I didn't comprehend that statement. It seemed I would never be able to accomplish that task. But having lived it, I can attest to its eternal truth. I have heard many things from many people who try desperately to comfort. A grieving parent must find it in them to forgive the platitudes that often come from friends. There is another chapter in this book that addresses this problem. But I wanted to share something I read this morning that struck home with me. The book I am currently reading, as I shared before, is *When Bad Things Happen to Good People*, by Harold S. Kushner. One thought that stuck was that is difficult to know how to address someone's grief. But the hardest thing is knowing what to say. This is so true. My husband has said so often, when we are in conversation with friends, and they say, "I have no words, for I have never been where you are now," that that is the most appropriate thing to say.

The best thing is to be present, be mindful of what the mourner is saying. Stand there without condemnation if he/she weeps or talks nonstop about their child. That is so powerful!

· · · · · · · ·●●●●●●●· · · · · · · ·

June 26, 2019
Physical Effects on the Grieving

After having witnessed the physical effects of other grieving moms over the past thirteen years since our Erin left, I realize that there are manifestations in the physical body as a result of prolonged grief. One dear mom suffered a stroke shortly after her son passed. I witnessed one become an alcoholic because of her extreme grief over her twelve-year-old hit by a drunk driver. There is now scientific evidence that there is an ailment called broken heart syndrome that really does affect the heart muscle.

When grief first strikes, the body protects the mind from overload by numbing the emotions. I sat beside Erin's bed on the floor after kissing her precious face that last time and planned the entire funeral. Now I look back and wonder how I could even accomplish that! The first six months or so, a grieving parent is in a state of shock and numbness. But around the six- to nine-month mark, I have seen over and over that a parent just has a more difficult time physically and emotionally. I believe it is this time period when the reality of it all comes full force. The numbness has worn off. The raw details of death must be dealt head-on. It's a time of extreme pain and anguish. During this time, it is good to have a support group surrounding you.

Maybe a year or two after the death of a loved one, physical symptoms can manifest. Perhaps a grieving mom or dad has had to stay "strong" for other children or for each other. And in that coping with grief, they have let their own body suffer. It may not have even seemed necessary to care for their body because they felt it was hopeless at times. But then the body fights back, and even illness can occur. (I am no medical expert. I am just speaking of what I have witnessed.)

I just was released from the hospital for a stomach virus. It was a bad one that had been circulating our area. But for me it became life-threatening. I felt at times I wouldn't make it. But God saw fit in His mercy to keep me here a while longer. I don't know if my bouts with these common illnesses are made worse because of my grief. But I tend to think that they do.

Recently, I talked with two people very dear to me. One had lost her twelve-year-old son many years ago. She has struggled with her extreme grief and has had many health problems too. When she came to comfort us with a warm pound cake one night after our David left for heaven, I told her one of my grieving points was that I would never have grandchildren. She took my hands in hers, looked me square in the eye, and said, "Brenda, I have a daughter and two precious grandchildren. But if I went to heaven today, it would be all right!" That let me know that the grief was still real after so many years. Another dear friend, Laura, grieving the death of her beautiful nineteen-year-old Katie, has had heart issues since her teen years. When David was last hospitalized, she had to have heart surgery once again. David would check on her, and I talked with her too. She told me that sometimes she felt it didn't matter if she made it through the surgery or not. She has a husband and a living child, but it would have been okay with her if she had gone to heaven then. Again, I see that grief takes away fear of death in a mom.

Physical manifestations of the grief within will come in different forms to different people. But they do come. How we deal with them is up to us. We could easily succumb to the smallest symptom. Or we might screw up our courage and live on to fight another day.

DAY-1,210

· · · · · · ●●● ● ●●● · · · · · ·

June 30, 2019:
Everything You Never Wanted
to Know about Grief

My plan was to name this book *A Woman Called Job*. The reason was, so many who came to me early in this grief said I was like Job since I had buried all my children.

While that is true except for losing every possession I owned, as Job did, when I read back over the pages, it seems to be becoming a book I could call *Everything You Never Wanted to Know about Grief*. Often, I search my memories for others who have lost all their children, and I come up with very few names. But I haven't searched the world over. I am sure in war-torn countries around the globe and in military families, there would be many...too many. It seems to be a way for me to reach out to others who walk this nightmare of a journey. If I can only be the "salt and light," as the Bible says, then I will have accomplished something far more valuable than simply selling a book.

So if this has become a book of instruction on grieving based on my own long, tedious journey, then so be it! If we draw into ourselves, which is the case more times than not, then our child's memories become like faded pages on a book put in the back of the shelf that no one ever reads again. But reaching out and sharing, however tough, we reach down into that pit where others sit and offer a hand up. And our children are honored as we do. We don't quit!

I live, not for the acclaim of selling a book about a woman called Job or for any financial gain or fame. I live for the Christ, the light within me to shine out and light the way in the darkness for some other mom, dad, or sibling who is walking this very dark path.

"For me to live is Christ and to die is gain" (Phil. 1:21 KJV). That's what the apostle Paul said about the troubles of his journey. And I say a hearty "Amen!"

DAY-1,211

•••••••••●•••••••••

July 1, 2019
The Difference Christ Makes

Today I completed reading the book *When Bad Things Happen to Good People* by Harold Kushner. I realized as I read that this was one man's perspective. We come from different backgrounds and that affects the difference in perspective. There are differences in the way people perceive and handle grief. But there are commonalities as well. It has been my privilege to meet men and women from all over the globe since our Erin left for heaven. Most I have not met face-to-face but through the advanced social media we now enjoy. Seeing different people from all different cultures shows me that even though we differ, we all eventually seem to find our "grounding," our anchor, that keeps us alive. It is wrong for any of us to judge another and what may bring comfort. We each have our own unique place to occupy on this globe. So I embrace and respect people from all religions and cultures.

Having said that, I do have to say that knowing Jesus Christ and the life He brought to me through His sacrifice on the cross of Calvary has brought me a unique kind of peace that has sustained my very life's flow. I feel, because of the unique relationship that Christ has brought me into with the Father, I can present my questions and requests to Him without fear of reprisal. Also, the author of the book I was reading said several times that God did not cause the deaths or tragedies. I have read in Scripture that God created the evil and the good. And I feel certain that death cannot come to a believer in Christ without God's approval. Of course, then that opens the question, Is God to blame? But like Job, I cannot blame God. How can I, finite and human, dare to bring a charge against the almighty God? If He chooses to number the days of those I love, who am I to reprimand Him? Like Job said to his wife, "Shall we receive good at the hand of God, and shall we not receive evil? In all this did not Job sin with his lips" (Job 2:10 KJV). Doesn't it say the rain falls on the just and the unjust? In war-torn countries, are not the good sometimes taken along with the bad? Again, I fold the page neatly and tuck it in my book of questions that may not receive an answer while I am here on earth.

When I completed reading this book, my first inclination was to text my friend who suggested it and ask if she had another recommendation. For this book did not answer for me the question that was the title. Then I began to think that a grieving parent keeps reading, keeps searching for an answer that will quench the burning longing to know why their child died. It more than likely is a life-long, fruitless pursuit.

So for now, I will trust that the Christ, the comforter sent by God, will comfort my aching soul.

Solomon, the wisest king who ever lived, offers much advice in the Proverbs, Song of Solomon, and Ecclesiastes in the Bible. When we look for answers, we often seek the advice of those with experience, those who have walked a path like our own. Solomon, when given the chance to ask one thing of God, asked for wisdom. The wisdom given to him, along with great riches for making this simpler request, was touted by kings and rulers the world over. They came to visit him and behold the greatness of his wisdom and treasure. I would like to share a few things he said, particularly about children and grief.

A good name is better than precious ointment;
and the day of death than the day of one's birth.
(Eccles. 7:1 KJV)

It is better to go to the house of mourning, than to go to the house of feasting: for that is the end of all men; and the living will lay it to his heart. Sorrow is better than laughter: for by the sadness of the countenance the heart is made better. (Eccles. 7:2–3 KJV)

Vanity of vanities, saith the Preacher, vanity of vanities; all is vanity. What profit hath a man of all his labor which he taketh under the sun? (Eccles. 1:2–3 KJV)

To everything there is a season, and a time for every purpose under heaven: A time to be born, and a time to die; a time to plant, and a time to pluck up that which is planted; A time to kill, and a time to heal; a time to break down, and a time to build up; A time to weep, and a time to laugh; a time to mourn, and a time to dance. (Eccles. 3:2–4 KJV)

My husband and I were discussing this last night. Having no living children on earth now, we naturally think about who will inherit all that we have accumulated over our lifetime. We both inherited things from parents, and it is only natural to want them to stay with family. But we both have sentimental attachments to the things belonging to our children and ponder just who would try to keep their memory alive and cherish their memory. In the end, we both agreed with Solomon that all the things we have in this life are vanity. They are simply things that will perish with time.

In the end, it is all about eternity. That's where all of mankind is headed, ready or not.

July 3, 2019
Does It Ever End?

The question has often been asked, When will I get better? I hesitate to tell any grieving parent that they won't get better. *Better* is a relative term and indicates almost a healing. But for a grieving parent missing part of their heart, there is no *better*. I tell them that they will smile again, even laugh again. There will be days that are not as hard. The raw, jagged edges of grief will soften over time. It has been said that over time the scar of grief heals over. But it is easily reopened.

It would be easy to lie and say that a wounded parent would get over it. But they themselves would not want to get over it. That's because getting over it is to say the child never existed, that they weren't a vital, integral part of their identity. Therefore, so many, like me, fight hard to preserve and protect the memory. We want our child's name mentioned often. We set up scholarships, do random acts of kindness, establish trust funds and other types of memorials in their names.

"You'll get through this." How often have I heard those words! But when you bury your child and someone says this, it almost takes your breath away. How does a parent get through the loss of a child? Every single day you get up to face it once again. When you begin to age, you are constantly reminded that they are not here. There are no grandchildren, no celebrations of events, no one to even take care of you as you get older. But most importantly, there is no child to wrap your arms around to give and receive the affection that only a parent and child knows Every day you wake up to an empty chair at the table, an empty hole in your very existence. Nothing, not money, not another relative, not another child, not another house, vacation, or anything, can fill the void that is left in your life. When someone says, "You'll get through this," I almost think they are equating my grief with an injury, lost job, any of life's troubles. But there is absolutely no comparison.

No, you won't get "through it." Someone aptly said once that it is like a wound. It scabs over, but it doesn't take much to pull that scab off and it's open again. We learn to live with the pain of loss. It does soften over time. But it never, ever goes away. And it only takes a remembrance, a sound, a song, a smell, a sight, to bring it fully open once again. If we say there is an end to our grief in this life, we bury our child all over again, and that would complete our demise. Grief is a never-ending, strong force in the life of a parent who has buried a child. To see them, you might think that they are doing okay. They may seem to have gotten back to a normal existence. But if you could see inside, you would see a gaping hole, a chasm that draws them back to days of pain, days of love, and fun of earlier years. They seek out comfort in friends, family, projects, books, and even counselors. But even with all the comforts, they still have a missing piece that cannot be filled with any other thing. Time changes nothing.

I would say to a parent who asks me if this will ever get better, "It doesn't get better. It gets different." You learn to cope. You learn to live with the pain in your heart. You learn a new normal that will help you exist in a world that is lonelier, sadder than the one you knew before. You survive.

DAY-1,213

• • • • • • • • • • ● • • • • • • • • • •

July 4, 2019
Speckled Glasses

Memories come back frequently of my children's childhood. But occasionally my mind races back to my own childhood, a time that had few worries and much joy.

I haven't spoken much of my mom, probably because I was a daddy's girl and followed him wherever he went. But to fully know this author, it's important to know her mom. My dad used to say when my sisters and I were dating that we should look at the dad because an "acorn doesn't fall far from the tree." Such is the case also of a girl and her mom.

My nephew brought me some fresh corn yesterday. As I shucked and desilked and blanched it, I was taken back to my mom's kitchen. The kitchen was always a buzz of activity, from laying out our dress patterns on the huge table Daddy had built because there were so many of us, to harvest time with a big number 10 tub of butter beans soaking in water and our chairs all around it as we all helped shell the beans. I could see Mama blanching the corn, laying it on a layer of towels spread on the counter, taking her sharp knife and cutting only halfway through the kernels so she could scrape the rest and get the milk out to make creamed corn to freeze. She was very careful in all her canning and freezing of the vegetables Daddy brought in from the garden. She believed everything should be as bacteria-free

436

as possible. As I packed up the two little pints of creamed corn last night, I thought of the big pot of soup corn and fresh biscuits along with juicy sliced tomatoes that we would have each summer during harvesttime. Mama worked hard, long hours in a hot kitchen (we didn't have AC then), putting up a whole plethora of yummy jars of vegetable soup, green beans, beet pickles (I'd sneak and drink some of the purple juice), okra, peaches, apples, and more. What a harvesttime we had!

Mama's kitchen was the center of our home. She always fixed delicious meals, and whoever came to visit was invited in to eat. When we were young, the pastor and his family were frequent guests, along with our friends from church. Often after that big old Sunday dinner, we'd sit in the living room with piano, guitars, and whatever new instrument my brother Rabun brought in that he had swapped for at school, and we'd sing for a few hours. The memories of Mama and our childhood still bring warmth to my troubled soul. She loved the five of us with everything in her.

As I thought of Mama last night, I could see her cutting that corn off and the speckles of corn going everywhere on her glasses and on the table. Those speckled glasses saw a lot of hard work. Through those glasses she saw five children grow up and prosper. She never stopped worrying about each of us even after we had families of our own. She loved her family, which was truly her career. She insisted we have clean, freshly ironed clothes, bathed before bedtime, and that we went to church every time there was a service. Her greatest pride was her children and grandchildren. She enjoyed participating as a viewer in all our activities. She, truly, was a Proverbs 31 woman, full of grace and love. How blessed I was to have a mama like her, even with those speckled glasses (which she washed immediately, I might add)!

Memories do race through the mind like "sand through an hourglass," as the old song goes.

DAY-1,219

· · · · · · · ● · · · · · · ·

July 9, 2019
Pressing Toward the Mark

One of the greatest and most quoted followers of Christ in the Bible was the apostle Paul. He faced many challenges during his years of ministry, often beaten, stoned, imprisoned, shunned, and rejected. He felt very inadequate for his calling, saying that he was not an eloquent speaker and yet speaking some profound truths upon which many Christians hold sacred in their own lives today. As he shared his story, he was always quick to say that he was "pressing toward the mark of his calling in Christ Jesus." He pressed on despite the obstacles in his path. He wrote the little book of Philippians while in a very small prison cell, with only a hole in the floor for a bathroom and just a little light shining through a small opening in the top. It was in this little book that he wrote in chapter 3, verse 13–14 (KJV) "Brethren, I count not myself to have apprehended: but this one thing I do, forgetting those things which are behind and reaching forth unto those things which are before. I press toward the mark for the prize of the high calling of God in Christ Jesus."

I could dwell on the losses in my own life and the downside of life. But I, like Paul, want to press toward the mark for the prize of the high calling of God in Christ Jesus. When I am at my lowest, and we all know there will be more days of that in life, then He is strongest. This is because He is greater than any trouble or trial in this life.

As the Bible says in 1 John 4:4 (KJV), "Greater is He that is in you than he that is in the world." David sent me this verse on my phone for a screen saver, which I still have today. He knew!

We often think that people we love who have battled cancer, tough battles, accidents, or trouble in life have lost in the end if they don't make it. But did they? If they fought until the end, they were conquerors. I think some of my heroes of the faith are people who weathered the storms of life, like Mary Rose McCurry, our pastor's wife, who battled liver cancer after suffering the loss of two of her own children. She, while suffering her own battle, always kept encouraging me and others to step out and be our best self and do what we felt God called us to do. I saw her courage in the face of a very ruthless disease. She never gave up until her last breath. Also, I think of my aunt Sara Christian, a true woman of God who not only prayed and encouraged others but also gave of herself to them. She sat with her uncle as he was dying of cancer to give assistance to his wife. She also pushed me gently to receive all I could of God and prayed for me and her other nieces, nephews, and children. After losing her own dear husband at fifty-two and living alone for several years, she was diagnosed with pancreatic cancer and lived only four months after the diagnosis. But I truly believe that she won that battle, for she is where she longed to be, with her Lord. There are so many other examples of courage in the face of daunting odds in this life. But true believers never give up, for they see what's ahead.

My encouragement for me and for you, my reader today, is to press toward the mark. What is ahead of us is far greater than anything behind!

• • • • • • • • • ● • • • • • • • • •

July 10, 2019
Links to Our Loved Ones

I know that in the course of this book, I have touched on this topic before. All the things our child owned, touched, wore, or had contact with become treasures to our broken hearts. For me, when our Erin left us, I found myself sitting in her house that first Christmas, on the floor in her closet, crying as I packed up her shoes. I don't know what it was about the shoes. But it might have brought me back to the hospital in 1985 when our little Heather was born still. The nun at St. Mary's sat on the bed as I cried when I saw the little card with Heather's tiny footprints. I said, "These little feet will never touch the earth." That little card was the only thing I was able to take home with me as my husband and family had the burial, which I was not allowed to attend because I was still in the hospital. As I sat on Erin's floor, it must have been in my mind that here was my only other daughter, one I had cherished so, who would never set foot on this earth again. I held those shoes close to my heart as I lovingly packed each one away to bring home. All her clothes and shoes and special things that Adam allowed us to bring home are still in plastic bins in our basement. I wore a few of the clothes and the jewelry, but all else is tucked away safely. David's things are still where he left them. I have given just a few things that he liked to friends. But his room is still as he left it.

Today we had to get my husband a new phone. As I walked in that store, I remembered the last time I went in. David had dropped his phone on the floor of the hospital, so we had to get him a new one. He was too weak to go in, so he asked me to just choose one for him, which was unlike him. That let me know how he felt. So here I was again, entering this store. I have kept David's phone with mine in my purse, so afraid I would lose it or for something to happen to it. I asked the lady if I could merge the data on mine and David's and keep his. She said I would lose his number, so I opted to just keep it as is for now. His phone was always with him, as it was his only means of communicating with friends when he was neutropenic after chemo. He spent hours on it conversing with friends, which helped him cope on so many occasions. So I treasure it probably above anything else. His two guitars sit in their stands, unused, but they are also treasures since he spent many hours playing and teaching himself new songs.

How does a grieving parent part with clothes and treasured items that were such a part of a child's life? This was discussed much in the grief forum I was part of for many years. Some pack up everything. Some give the clothes to relatives or friends. Some, like me, leave everything where it was. Some create a memorial corner in a house if they must move. Since there is no time limit to grief, there is no reason to get rid of anything. My own mom couldn't part with Daddy's clothes. She finally washed and neatly pressed as few shirts for me to try to sell at a garage sale. But I could tell it was difficult for her. My husband's grandmother lost two young sons, aged nine and fourteen. One of his aunts told me that she kept their clothes. And she had thirteen children, so to keep those packed away was probably hard. But they buried those clothes when they buried her.

There are many layers to grief. This is just one. Each person must learn to deal and cope with each layer in their own unique way. There really shouldn't be any condemnation of how they learn to cope.

In my heart and mind, I know these are just material things. My children are in eternity and will never need them again. But to me they are links to my babies.

DAY-1,221

• • • • • • • • ● • • • • • • • •

July 12, 2019
Peace

"Into every life some rain will fall." The adage is so true. But it is how we handle the rain that makes or breaks us. My very wise pastor once said that it is not the trial or trouble that affects us as much as how we act or react to it. I have seen it go both ways. Some have succumbed to the heartache, and the rest of their lives were lived out in utter devastation. Some have gone through the shock and disbelief of trouble and risen out of the ashes into a life filled with purpose, even if it was a totally different direction from their life before the trouble.

Personally, I have been a "crier" for much of my seventy-one years. I cry when I'm sad, when I'm glad, when I laugh, and when I see injustice. I felt guilty for crying so over my sorrow. But I read that crying gets the grief out. So crying can be a good thing at times. Finding a way to vent our frustration, anger, downtrodden souls when trouble strikes is one of the most important actions to take. Some criers like me learn to garden or get involved in a hobby that becomes a solace. Others may volunteer in different ways in their community. There are so many ways to vent and to find purpose in each day. That is key to be an overcomer, in my opinion. In reaching outward, we find strength to overcome in life.

Everyone seeks peace. Great men of old have written great speeches on peace and how to obtain it. The word *peace* comes in speeches from Miss America to the president of these United States or from world leaders. And yet peace is difficult to obtain. Peace is sought in much-needed vacations. It is sought in medication and meditation. The rich seek it along with the poor. Great volumes have been written by very wise men and women in search of peace. Often people travel great distances to hear speakers who preach peace. There are divorces because of the lack of peace in the home. Some even choose to live alone in a search for peace. But even with being alone, peace can be hard to find at times. All these may bring a temporary peace, and each probably has its merit.

The greatest man who ever lived, Jesus Christ, the righteous one, said, upon departing earth, "Peace I leave with you; My peace I give to you" (John 14:27 KJV). He spoke of a supernatural peace that man cannot obtain in all his worldly searches. He spoke of a peace that is without understanding, beyond the scope of human intellect. It was a peace that He "left with us" when He released unto man the Holy Spirit of God. It was a lasting peace that never leaves us, although at times trials of this life may cause us to lose sight of it. This peace will sustain you in the darkest hour, in the most dreaded day you face, on the highest mountain, or in the lowest valley. It will keep you when your child cries all night with sickness, when you look into the face of a beloved one in a casket, when you see your parents slowly fading away, when you lose a cherished job or home, when a storm tears up everything you have worked for, or when the person you loved best walks away.

When people ask me how I can have peace in the face of the home-going of all my children, descriptive words seem to evade me. How can I explain a peace that is indescribable? How can I tell others how I can lie down at night and sleep in the face of such tragedy? I can't. The best explanation I can give is that I am intimately acquainted with the Prince of Peace, Jesus Christ. He is my peace.

• • • • • • • • • ● • • • • • • • •

July 18, 2019
He Bore Our Grief and Carried Our Sorrows

How can God possibly know our grief? In Isaiah in the Old Testament of the Bible, it reads, "He hath borne our griefs and carried our sorrows" (Isa. 53:4 KJV). As I thought on that this morning after a particularly rough day of mourning yesterday, I wondered how God, who knows all, sees all, and is perfect in every way, could possibly know how I, a mere mortal, feel. Then I remembered Jesus. He was God in man form, the second person in the Trinity of God the Father, the Son, and the Holy Spirit.

When Adam disobeyed God, he caused a separation from God. It would take a miracle, a divine intervention, to bring man back to the place that Adam held before the fall from grace. I believe that God missed those cool walks of communion with Adam in the early part of each day. I believe that God wanted to bring His own creation back to Him. So part of Him had to be born as a man and experience all that man experienced to bring that back.

When Jesus came and lived a relatively short life of thirty-three years, He was man and God. The man in Him experienced every emotion known to man, including grief and sorrow. He must have grieved greatly when His dear friend Lazarus died, even though He

444

knew, as God, that Lazarus would be resurrected and live a full life. It must have brought Him sorrow as He saw Mary and Martha openly grieving their brother. When His own disciples all fled as He was led away to be crucified, He had to have felt the sorrow of rejection of those who knew Him best, His friends who had never left His side before. As He witnessed the sickness, the sin, the careless living of some, the lust for money and greed of power-hungry politicians and religious leaders, it must have brought sorrow of heart.

As God Almighty, who sits on the throne of the heavens and wields all power and might, He was insulated from the human feelings of an earthly tabernacle. But as Jesus Christ, the Son of God and Son of Man, He knew firsthand the feelings of grief, sorrow, pain, shame, rejection, and temptation. The Bible says He was tempted in all points as man, yet without sin.

I guess I have felt that God couldn't really know what grief felt like since He is almighty. And yet as I thought on His Son, the Savior of the world, I realized that God Himself now knows exactly what grief feels like, for He has experienced it. And don't you know that God must have felt the pain of loss when, for that moment in time, He was separated from His own Son that moment when Jesus took on Himself the sins of the whole world on the cross? He couldn't even look on His own Son because God cannot look on sin. That had to be the moment the earth became as black as night at three in the afternoon and a great earthquake shook the ground! That had to be the moment that God Himself knew the depths of the pain of separation.

While I mourn my children, I am so thankful that God knows! Yes, He knows how I feel. He is "touched with the feelings of my infirmities," as the Bible says in Hebrews 4:15 (KJV). And since He knows, He will comfort me in His own way, in His own time. Of this I am certain!

DAY-1,239

• • • • • • • • • ● • • • • • • • • • •

July 30, 2019
How Long Has It Been?

Exactly 1,130 days ago, a portal was opened into heaven. My son, my last living child who I gave birth to, ascended through that portal into paradise. The earth on which I live became a little darker, a little lonelier, a little more isolated, and much more distressing.

This week there have been several times that an echo from the past came to fill my mind with memories, usually of David's hospital stay. Each time I am just filled to overflowing with tears as I remember the pain that my son endured and there was nothing I could do to ease it. Here I am, seventy-one years old, received a cancer diagnosis last January, had the operation, and it is completely gone with no additional treatments necessary. I am very thankful and don't mean to belittle God's mercy in allowing it to be over so soon. But David was only twenty-three! He had so many years left! He had never been married, never really got a start on life. Why? Why? Why couldn't it have been me instead of him? I looked at a social media post of a friend of Erin's today. She was also a former student of mine. She was such a kind and lovely girl. As I saw the joy as she brought her third child into the world, a baby boy, I rejoiced with her. At the same time came a flood of tears as I thought of Erin and David. Neither of them experienced the magic of the moment of childbirth and holding that miracle in their arms. My fragile heart broke all over again as

I remembered all the wonderful events that they would never know on this earth.

I want to remember every detail of all their lives, the good, the happy, the sad, the painful, the joyous, the love. At the same time, I wonder how much more my heart can stand the pain of memories instead of real hugs, real celebrations, live births, live parties, joyful Christmases of long ago. The conflict continues for a grieving parent. I cherish the memories. But the hurt is raw and real. It hurts to remember. I look at the number of days that have passed since and wonder how I have survived. Can it be that my sheer willpower to stay alive, to keep breathing, has kept my feet on earth? Can it be that friends and family who surrounded me sustained my very life here? I say a hearty "No!" None of the above. I don't ever want to minimize the gift of friends and family who have helped me. I am thankful for each person who has wrapped me in the warm blanket of friendship, love, and comfort. But in my heart I know that God and God alone has sustained my very life through the most difficult of days and nights. When I try to explain this to others, words fail me. It is so obvious that many look at me and think, *How can she still love God, who has taken all her children? How can she still praise and honor the very one who has chosen to crush her heart to powder?* Again, no explanation comes to mind except that God truly does understand the grief and heartache since He, too, felt that very grief over his one and only Son.

Now I know that neither height nor depth, nor angels, nor principalities, nor life, nor death can ever separate a believer from the love of God. Now I know that no matter how far I stray, I am still His child. He still loves me with all my doubts, fears, questions, anger, questioning his ways and all my faults.

Time has not diminished my love for David or Erin or Scott or Heather. Their removal from earth has not diminished my love or my caring for them. The only connection, other than by the Spirit of God that we all share, is where their physical bodies now lie in the ground. I tend it as if it is a warm blanket over them. Having this purpose has helped. For some, it doesn't, and they cannot even go to the cemetery. But it is the only thing left physically that I can do for them here on earth. I still can honor each of them by reaching out, by giving of myself whenever the need is presented. I can wrap my arms around another mom, dad, or sibling who is grieving. I can text, send a card, or do a random act of kindness in each of my children's names.

Love never dies! It is eternal, just as the love that God has for each of us. Time shall be no more one day. There won't be any more countdowns or count-offs. Eternal bliss awaits us! And I wait for it with anticipation!

DAY-1,244

•••••••••●•••••••••

August 4, 2019
Healing

The amazing physical body has the ability to heal itself. We are truly fearfully and wonderfully made, as the Holy Scripture reads. The longer I live, the more and more I learn about the body, mind, soul, and spirit. There were decades where my entire educational focus was on the mind. Then the spiritual world became very important to me as I was trying to raise my children in the fear and admonition of the Lord God. I learned so much about spiritual things.

The mind is an awesome thing to study. Negative thoughts lead to much distress and even physical sickness. The researchers could have saved themselves much research if they had only read the Bible. It clearly states that we should think on "whatsoever things are true, whatsoever things *are* honest, whatsoever things *are* just, whatsoever things *are* pure, whatsoever things *are* lovely, whatsoever things *are* of good report" (Phil. 4:8 KJV) and that "a merry heart doeth good *like* a medicine: but a broken spirit drieth the bones" (Prov. 17:22 KJV). Recently, I also learned that all our memories, *all* of them, are stored in the brain. We have a cousin, Allene Barnett, who just passed into heaven last year who had Alzheimer's disease for the last years of her life. Her daughter Betty Ann took such loving care of her and made sure her every need was met. Betty Ann shared videos of her on social media where she was in a favorite restaurant and wouldn't even know who her daughter was. Betty Ann had a waitress friend watch her so she could go out and come back in. Then her mom would know her. Through Betty Ann's postings, I watched the steady decline in cognitive ability and, eventually, the physical decline. But even near the end of her one hundred years, she could sing! It was so amazing to watch as she sang a song from years ago in its entirety without a single mistake. Just this week, I read that it takes an amazing mental process for a person to sing. It is quite a complicated thing for the brain to help the body accomplish this task. Also, I found that singing brings joy to the singer. This lets us know that every memory is truly stored. But it's amazing how the memories can emerge in the most trying of times.

I saved the soul for last. It is in the soul that the emotions are stored, along with the personality that the person acquires over a lifetime. The soul is contained within the spirit, according to my former pastor, who was such a wise teacher. Since every memory is stored in the brain, all the joy, the happiness, the sorrow, the sadness, the love, and even the animosity is there. The body can heal, even the heart and liver have the amazing ability to heal, and the mind can heal. But the soul can bear horrible wounds and can only go so far into healing. What I am saying now is my opinion. While I have read much in my seventy-two years, including scientific and research articles, I am no expert. Here I share what I have lived. A grieving parent stores up all those wonderful memories of the childhood of the love of their life. Every laugh, every accomplishment, every tear, every goal met is burned into their memory. Then the circumstances surrounding the death of their child, with all the details, the emotions, the memories of the days and nights, the memorial service, if there was one, the people surrounding them, the doctors, nurses, EMTs, policemen, family members, and friends, are forever etched into the brain. There is no erasing it. There is no magic cure for healing. It is there. We can search for laughter by being with funny friends, watching funny movies, going to events that are lighthearted and fun. But we come home to our grief again. For me, there is no momentary lapse of memory of my children. They are with me wherever I go, whatever event, whatever movie I watch, whatever thing I try to do to help me cope with the hurt. I would have it no other way because they will forever be part of my identity. It aggravates me when I hear people say, "You will heal" or "You will get past this." A better phrase would be "You will survive or keep breathing." It is difficult for me to believe that the soul can be healed, at least on this side of eternity. I don't know if the soul dies, leaving only the spirit to move to heaven. But I don't believe those bad memories will be part of paradise.

I almost want to put a hashtag here, if I could, #paradiseawaits!

DAY-1,245

· · · · · · · · ●● ● ●● · · · · · · ·

August 5, 2019
Empathizing Other
Traumatic Events

After my morning devotional each day, I take a few minutes to read a bit in a book. I have finished several this way since it seems hard for me to be still long enough to read once my day begins. This morning I began a new one, which was about brokenness. I only found out as I began reading that the author had dealt with suicidal thoughts since childhood when her own dad had committed suicide. The book is about dealing with depression and suicidal thoughts. I found that it was too much. Maybe it was because of our Scott. Maybe it was because just dealing with grief times four is too much. Or maybe I just can't delve into other traumas right now. I had recently begun another book on dealing with husbands who are addicted to pornography. And I couldn't read it because of my own emotional overload.

When our Erin first left for heaven, my mind and memory were in such turmoil that I found it hard to read anything beyond short paragraphs. A dear friend sent me a comforting passage of help that was a page long and I found I couldn't even get through the page. In the first few weeks after the traumatic loss, short-term memory is affected greatly.

Is there a point in life when we have had our "cups running over" with trouble so much so that we just can't cope with anymore? This made me wonder, Am I still in recovery mode after two surgeries earlier this year and another hospitalization just recently? I have always been an overachiever, going above and beyond what is expected. I have a type-A personality syndrome, if I can label myself that way. Rest of body and mind is very difficult for me, and even more so now that I am trying to stay alive, and cope with the grief. I feel almost guilty that I cannot read these books. But maybe it is my own emotions that are protecting my fragility right now. So often I have counseled others to "take care of you." That is so important for a grieving mom or dad who may, at times, not care for themselves as they bear such a burden of guilt, sorrow, and pain.

DAY-1,247

$$\cdots\cdots\bullet\bullet\bullet\cdots\cdots$$

August 7, 2019
Collapsing into His Arms

I was watching a movie about a young woman who had lost her husband to a disease for which there was no cure. She was a doctor and felt helpless as she watched him die. Later, she worked with orphaned children because the townspeople rejected a woman doctor. As she shared her experience with the manager of the orphanage, she told her she had rejected God because He had allowed her husband to die. She said God didn't listen to her anyway, so what was the point of praying? The manager told her, as she observed the struggle for faith, to talk to God and then be silent. This stuck home to me as I have faced my own battles of faith. Another point made was that God may not say what we want to hear. And it's true. I have decided, as Job, that I can't really question the wisdom of God. He is so much bigger than me. But I will not turn away from Him anymore. I realize that I can't make it through the remainder of my life without Him. I may not hear another Word from Him, but I must keep the faith, although, at times, it seems so thin.

"If in this life only we have hope in Christ, we are of all men most miserable" (1 Cor. 15:19 KJV). That quote from the Bible is so true. There are days when, for a grieving parent, hope seems so far away, almost nonexistent. But for a Christian parent, there is always hope that we will see our children again. I may have shared this before, but it bears repeating. There is a verse in the Bible that reads, "Be still and know that I am God." A friend told me that "be still" in that verse means (in the original language of the Bible) "to collapse into His (God's) arms." So many days I have battled all day, seeking peace, seeking meaning for my life, seeking answers, only to be unable to find them. Often at the end of the day, in the shower, I begin to sing a praise chorus. It is at that time I become "still" enough to feel God's arms holding me, comforting me.

Sometimes we must still this aching heart and mind and just collapse into His arms.

Whether a person is religious or not, there is a war taking place in the mind during a lifetime. I hope, by now, my reader, you have seen a return to my faith, the faith that has sustained me for these seventy-one years. It has been a common thread, I have noticed in people of faith, to question their faith, to question God's motives when they have lost a child. It cuts to the core of our spirit, soul, and mind. As the weeks, months, and years pass slowly, there is an endless war in our minds. It is a battle fought against negative thoughts, the what-ifs, should-haves, whys, and if-onlys. It is facing an uncertain future that may seem a fog, a dense darkness with very little light ahead. Yet still there is a flicker of hope.

The only way I can address this battle is from a Christian perspective since it is all I know. I studied psychology in college and know a little of how depression, and even grief, is treated by psychologists. Even from a Christian standpoint, there is a battle. Just because I am a Christian, I still have to "cast down imaginations" and keep my mind focused on the positive Word of God. Fear is an enemy that is fought much by everyone, no matter how strong their beliefs. When fear tries to paralyze me, I turn to a verse in the Bible, 2 Timothy 1:7 (KJV), that reads, "For God hath not given us the spirit of fear; but of power, and of love, and of a sound mind." How often have I recited that over and over in my mind and even aloud to myself? I found that after burying the body of one's most precious on earth to me, death has no hold on me. I don't fear death. But there are other fears that try to grip the heart of a grieving parent. There are thoughts that I have heard recited by other grieving parents, "Does

God really love me?" "Did I do something wrong to bring this on my child?" "Could I have done more or done something differently and they would still be here now?" The string of questions seems endless and will probably last as long as we live. But peace only comes when we can "lay them down" at the feet of the one who does love us best. It takes a huge sacrifice. But it is something that I struggle to do almost daily.

As we sat in the hospital room, David sent me a screen saver for my phone. He thought I would like it, and it is still there today. It is simply a dark-blue background with the words in a lighter blue. It reads, "Greater is He that is in you than he that is in the world" (1 John 4:4 KJV). I cherish it, and that is what brings me peace, the knowing that no matter how the battle goes, He that is in me has already won! And that makes me a winner, too, just as I know that that made David a winner over his battle! That is my peace!

DAY-1,252

•••••••••●•••••••••

August 12, 2019
Do I Measure Up? Faith versus Reasoning

Something caught my eye as I read my morning devotional yesterday. It was that Job fell on his face and worshipped immediately upon learning the news that his house and children had been destroyed. My first thought was, *I can't be called Job after all!* It was because I didn't worship when my last and youngest child went to heaven, leaving me destitute beyond tears, beyond despair. Instead, I asked God to please have a do-over; let's fix this and get it right this time, implying that God might have made a mistake. I'd like to say that I had the faith of Job in that moment. But even Job, later in the book, said he wished he had never been born. So he, too, was destitute. I do have to say that I never completely turned my back on God. I never wanted to sever the relationship that I held so dear all my life. But I did wonder how God could allow this in my life. Job said it is not right to just expect good and never evil in our lives. Bad days will come. Some will be horrendous days if we live long enough. But God is God! Who are we to question the Almighty? Can we reason with God and get Him to change His mind? There are instances in the Holy Scriptures when men did just that. Abraham bartered with God to save Sodom and Gomorrah. But in the end, God destroyed the city! Moses told God he would not go on unless God went before him. He sought God time and again on behalf of the people of Israel. Sometimes God did spare them. Sometimes, He didn't spare all of them. But reasoning just doesn't work! Reasoning is depending on our human, frail, finite minds to calculate and logically reason out the workings of an omnipotent, all-powerful God. As the Bible states, "For my thoughts *are* not your thoughts, neither *are* your ways my ways, saith the Lord. For *as* the heavens are higher than the earth, so are my ways higher than your ways, and my thoughts than your thoughts" (Isa. 55:8–9 KJV).

Maybe I can't be called Job because I am not him. Each of us is unique in our creation. Each of us has human frailties. Each of us must develop our relationship with God by spending time in His holy presence. That is where I am like Job. I know that God is almighty, and I dare not try to reason away His plans. I just must trust Him. That's where faith takes over.

DAY-1,254

· · · · · · · ● ● ● ● ● ● ● ● ● · · · · · ·

August 14, 2019
Expect the Unexpected

As people go on with life day by day, same old, same old, it begins to fall into a pattern of expected events and surroundings. After a profound loss, especially child loss, life does not seem so secure. People even begin to expect the unexpected, always waiting for the next shoe to fall, the next earth-shattering, heartrending thing to occur.

I look at others, especially the young families who were friends of Erin and David. They are living the expected life, having children, buying homes, going to sporting events, school events, vacations, and church outings. It all has that familiar ring to it because it was what I lived. They walk on, blindly trusting that all will be the way it is supposed to be. The children will finish school, start a job, or go to college, get married, and then the grandkids will come, and they will grow old, watching wonderful sunsets together. Never does the thought enter their minds that everything could change in a moment, in an instant! But I and many others know that it can and does.

One thing I have learned in my life is that change is inevitable. We want to keep that trusty old car, but it will break down on the highway one day, leaving us stranded. Then we change. That job is our dream job until some coworkers begin to taunt and criticize us or the boss is tough on our evaluation and we begin to look for a different job. Some even find that the mate they have chosen is not the person they thought he/she would be, and their dream marriage ends in divorce. Parents die, and our world changes and seems less loving as we step up to become the older generation for our kids.

With change comes a shift in our mindfulness of a secure and happy world. Some changes make it brighter; some make it tougher. But change will come as we live and breathe.

For a grieving parent, there is a whole shift in the paradigm of living. They must find new normals, new ways of coping, surviving, being. They must find ways to integrate their grief and their child into a life that is a strange and different one. They must find an "anchor" for their soul, which is as if on a storm-tossed sea, with no land in sight. Books have been written about this. Psychologists have researched grief to find a magical soothing "balm" for these troubled souls. For me, I have an anchor in Christ Jesus. The Holy Spirit, one of the persons in the Holy Trinity that is God, was called the comforter by Jesus. Truly, I am a witness that He is. He is the soothing balm for my soul. I don't have all the answers. But I can attest to the soothing comfort of the Holy Spirit of God.

DAY-1,261

August 22, 2019
Replacing Bad Thoughts
with Faith

This week I have finally found the strength to get outside early and walk again. It felt so good to walk and sing praises to God along with the birds and crickets, who were making their morning music. There is such a freedom of soul and spirit when we are out of a building and the warm sun is shining on our face. It seems to have energized me once again after all the medical issues I've been dealing with for six months now.

It is good when we have the rare moments of revival in our soul. Even though things on the surface haven't changed, sometimes the change comes within our spirit. We take a deep breath and breathe in the good thoughts when they flutter by.

I find myself singing of God's greatness to Him along with eventually a crying out in pain of sorrow. Many mornings as I have ventured out for a walk, I find myself trying to focus on God and yet the sorrow comes bubbling up and the tears begin. But in life, I remember how compassionate my own father was when he saw my tears. My heavenly Father is perfect. So why should I not cry out to Him when I am hurting? There is no condemnation in God's eyes for tears. He is full of compassion and tender mercies in spite of whatever we have done or not done for Him. A friend told me once that it is like climbing up into your father's lap and resting your head on his chest. God wants us to do that! I may have tears. Yet I know that He bottles up my tears. "Put Thou my tears into thy bottle. Are they not in Thy book?" (Isa. 56:8 KJV). So it's okay to cry to my Father. He wants us to be open and real with Him.

As I walk, I think of the story of Esther in the Bible. She was a chosen bride to the king. But she could not enter his courts unless he summoned her. When a person entered uninvited, the king would hold his scepter out if he accepted their interruption. Otherwise it meant sure death. When I walk and talk to God, it is as if He is holding out that scepter and accepting me into His Presence. What a privilege we have to come freely to our Father, God.

Lately, I've been reading a book by R. T. Kendall called *40 Days with the Holy Spirit*. I believe it has changed my view of who the Holy Spirit really is. I now see Him as a person, a vital part of the Triune Godhead. I invite Him into my days and nights. He is called comforter by Jesus when He walked the earth. I need Him and find that He is so near all the time. My desire is to know more about God to further my relationship with Him.

DAY-1,262

· · · · · · · · • • • ● • • • • • • · · ·

August 23, 2019
Reflections on Grace

As I did my Friday chores, my mind raced back to my younger years and how grace has kept me. I was born, sandwiched between my blond-haired, blue-eyed, outgoing older sister and my life-of-the-party, outgoing, fun-loving, adored firstborn-son brother. Later, my younger brother, Tim, and, five years later, the baby and pet of the family, Judy, would be born. But I always felt like the proverbial middle child, never really feeling like I was even noticed. I felt I had to become an overachiever to accomplish that. But I was loved, with never a doubt about that. In school, I always made straight As but still felt shy and a bit isolated. When I was in fifth grade, the teacher was like a short Army sergeant and never smiled. So I rebelled by refusing to go to school, crying each morning for a couple of weeks, saying my stomach hurt, which I later learned was anxiety. But what I didn't tell my mom and dad was that I was being molested by a distant relative when my mom would leave us at a relative's house to go shopping. So there was more in play than just the shyness. But God's grace covered me because there was a sixth-grade teacher, Mrs. Hardman, who would take me in the teacher's lounge and sit beside me as I cried. She comforted me and assured me all would be well. In time, I was able to continue with school. This was just the first of many challenges in my life. There were automobile accidents, stresses in college that made me return home and go to the local university, which had its own extreme challenges. I remember whenever I had to make a speech, I'd get sick to my stomach. God surely looked on at me and gave the strength because I not only graduated from college but also obtained a master's degree and taught school for thirty years. As life went on, I became a little more "hardened" to difficulties and screwed up my courage and marched on through life. I know that each time God poured out just enough grace to help me make it to the next challenge. The grace was there each time, as was God's protection. I remember a Christian friend (who I later found out was involved in witchcraft earlier in life) told me that she felt there was a "cocoon" around me that God had put there that was protecting me. I believed it. There were a few times when I felt my life was threatened, but amazingly God intervened.

But over all that, looming larger than life itself, is child loss. I don't like the word *loss*, for I believe that my children are more alive than ever in heaven. When the doctor looked at the ultrasound and told me that Heather was gone, I fell completely apart. They even asked me to go out the back door. I was crying so hard. My sister Judy had gone with me to the appointment, and she was at a loss with how to help me. But God's grace surrounded me via the arms of my family and friends, and somehow, I kept breathing. When we got the knock on the door and went and I knelt beside my own beautiful twenty-three-year-old Erin, her beautiful blue eyes closed forever, my heart was crushed to powder. How I survived that, I still don't know! And there are days when the crushing still takes my breath away. But God opened my eyes to see David and Berry still needed me here, so I kept breathing. The call came from Scott's stepdaughter that he had shot himself. I couldn't believe, after all the prayers over him when he was in war zones time and again, that he would not open his eyes again. But God's grace covered us as we, once again, said goodbye to the dearest on earth to us.

Maybe all the trials of my life were leading up to the last great battle I have faced, the home-going of my baby boy, the joy of my heart. As I sat in the corner of the hospital or clinic room, several different occasions they called a code as he struggled to breathe, fighting with all his being to stay alive. I remained strangely calm, in face of the greatest fear a mom could know. Once, after the ambulance got to the clinic to transport him to the hospital, one of the many nurses in the room pulled me aside and said, "How did you stay calm in the face of all this?" I said, "It was only God's grace. I was praying in the Spirit." And it was true. I can't tell you how emboldened I was, this once very shy little girl, as I questioned the high-ranking doctors, nurses, and staff and learned how to do some nursing tasks myself, as I had to change PICC line bandages in a sterile environment, give shots, treat open wounds, learn about all kinds of medicines, clean up urinals, keep journals of hospital visits, and spend many sleepless nights worrying and watching. There was little shyness left in the face of insurmountable odds of keeping my son alive. I would go the distance. Looking back, I don't even know how I did it, driving in a big strange city, staying in motels or sleeping and bathing in a strange huge hospital, spending many sleepless nights praying and pleading with God for help. But in the end, I do believe that His help was always there, as so many angels in human flesh stepped up to hold our arms up.

Time and again, if it were not for God's grace and help, I would have dropped dead on the spot. There is no way I could have survived burying four of the most precious children in the world without God. He is my life force. He keeps me strong when I know that in myself I am weak. He gives me Hope when nothing but despair is ahead of me. He is my light in the darkest of nights, and I have quite a few of those. But His light shines on the path of life, and He shows me how to keep going. He is my life force.

· · · · · · · ● · · · · · · ·

September 1, 2019
Life Is Fragile

When we are young, we think everything is going to stay the same. Most of us felt secure in our families, and surrounded by them, we felt all was well. And so it was for me. I remember as a teen, my older sister went to camp for a week. She and I were very close, only thirteen months apart. We shared a room, shared clothes, jewelry, etc. When she was away, I missed her terribly! I thought then that if something happened to her, I didn't know what I'd do. And she was gone only a week! But it wasn't until I had begun my teaching career that my world was shattered by my first confrontation with death. My principal came and got me to tell me my mother was on the phone. She was frantic. My grandad was taken to the hospital and put in ICU, critically ill. She was there all alone with him. I left school and went up to be with her. He died shortly after. Everything changed in my life from that point on. My grandmother had to eventually be moved out of the big house I had come to know and love as a child. We spent countless hours there with big family gatherings and lots of playtime with my cousins. I had never seen my grandmother so forlorn. But she was so lonely, and eventually, a heart attack took her life shortly after our first child was born. Seeing the family clean out the big house and divide her belongings gave me my first real glimpse of how material things are so dispensable. Here today, gone tomorrow.

With her death, the family grew apart more and each member began to have family gatherings with their own children and grandchildren. The world I knew as a child had come to an end.

Little did I realize the impact of death on the family circle. Later, it would come full force when my husband and I lost all four of our own parents within a ten-year period, along with our own precious Erin. My safe and secure world came crumbling down around me.

What emerged was a different me. I want to tell people on the street to value the time they have with loving families, for it will surely come to an end someday. I wanted to tell a mom being very harsh with their child to pick them up and love on them, for no one has any guarantee of tomorrow.

The second and most important thing to emerge was my anchor in life's very troubled sea. The one thing that holds me together was not family, not things, but God Himself. He didn't change. He didn't leave and never will. He is the one true Father of us all. And He is a constant, faithful friend who never changes. How I realize now how important it is to know our anchor!

Life is fragile! Death and change of environment may come, but God is always there, omnipresent in this life and in the hereafter.

One of my favorite verses in the Bible reads, "When Christ, who is our life, shall appear, then shall ye also appear with him in glory" (Col. 3:4 KJV). As I took my morning walk today, this verse came back to mind. I thought of the trauma of wondering exactly *where* Erin is now. Where is heaven? Where are my David, Scott, and Heather? I think what prompted that was that we have faced death twice in the past two weeks. First, a dear friend passed suddenly, then Berry's brother passed without warning. I also had lunch with some dear friends, one whose husband is facing a cancer diagnosis after beating cancer twice in his life already.

The thought came to me that death has no hold on the believer. If we really believe that Jesus conquered death on the cross, we know our life doesn't end when the mortal body ceases to function. That thought brings such peace to me about my own children. To know that, even though I can't hug and kiss those mortal bodies, yet they are alive still in the presence of God, brings such peace to this troubled mom. Even Job said, "Though after my skin worms destroy this body, yet in my flesh shall I see God" (Job 19:26 KJV). How did Job know that? Job is supposed to be the oldest book in the Bible. And yet Job knew truths that would not be revealed until after Jesus came. He truly believed that what he said was true. If he can believe that long before it is revealed, what can't we? Is there something we are missing? Does the earthly, mortal body cease to exist upon ceasing to function? Will that body be resurrected at the last day that God allows the earth to stand? There are many questions that remain a mystery.

But this I know that Christ is our life. He is the life-giving force that God sent back to earth after Jesus ascended on high to sit at His right hand. And that life-giving force guarantees us life eternally.

DAY-1,296

· · · · · · · ●●●●● ● ●●●●● · · · · ·

September 29, 2019
The Secret Place

On one of my morning walks this week, I began to think on "the secret place." Psalm 91:1 (KJV) in the Bible reads, "He that dwelleth in the secret place of the Most High shall abide under the shadow of the Almighty." For years I have wondered just where that secret place is. Is it attainable? Is it for the ordinary man or just for the priesthood? When we were in Atlanta at the hospital, I was reading my morning devotional, and I read Psalm 18, verse 11 (KJV): "He made darkness his secret place; his pavilion round about him were dark waters and thick clouds of the skies." I felt then that I had found the answer I had been seeking for so long.

As I walked and thanked God for the day and for many other things, I realized how much that answer meant to me. To attain the "secret place of the most High" is such a great honor. But what does it take to get there? I saw in a momentary vision that it takes walking and dwelling for a while in the deepest, darkest valley that life can position us. It takes being in a place so dark that you see nothing else but God. You look up because all around you is darkness. I have been in that place a few times as I faced the deepest grief and sorrow known to mankind. I admit freely that when our youngest son, my heartbeat, left us for heaven, I was in the darkest place I have ever been. I cried out that same cry that Jesus cried on the cross, "My

God, my God, why have You forsaken me?" Although I can't really equate what I experienced with the suffering of Jesus, because He was totally separated from God the Father (for God can't look on sin), while His was a total separation, mine was a separation of my doing. For a few months I refused to read the Bible or to pray. And this was a foreign place for me since the spiritual world has been my life ever since I was five years old and came to know Christ as my Lord. In that dark place, I still refused to turn my back on God, so I didn't discount Him as God and even as Lord of my life. I just couldn't understand why He could bring such hurt and sorrow into my life. So I refused all the things that I felt had brought me closer to Him over the years.

The longer I dwelled in that dark place, the more I realized that there was no way out. I was surrounded by darkness. There was no peace there, no comfort, as I wallowed in the depths of grief. Searching within myself, in books, or on the internet brought no answers to the questions that hounded my soul day and night. Ultimately, I knew that there was but one comforter, one who could soothe my wounded soul and spirit, and it was God the Father, the Holy Spirit, and the Son of God, who loved me so much He gave up everything to reconcile me back to Himself. I knew that the only one who could help me was God.

As my walk continued, I began to be thankful. I remembered a verse that says we must "enter into His gates with thanksgiving and into His courts with praise" (Ps. 100:4 KJV). So I decided, when I begin my walk I will begin with thanksgiving. When I first began this, I found it hard to find things for which to be thankful. But as I began, I realized there is much to be thankful for. This morning I just said aloud, "God, I am thankful that when I come to You, You always greet me with a smile and let me climb up into Your lap and feel Your heartbeat as I lay my head on Your chest." That's when it hit me that the secret place of God is in the darkness! It is in those times in life when we are in a desperate state of hopelessness, helplessness, and feel there is no way out. It is in a state where *nothing* will satisfy the soul but God. And there is when we *only* see Him. Then we realize that He is the only answer, the only way out. It is then that we truly lift Him up to the position that is His alone, the ultimate, almighty, omniscient, all-powerful God, who is the source of our existence, our help, and our life.

As I continued with my walk, the thought occurred that what is ahead of me is greater than anything behind me. There was a time I wouldn't say that because my children were part of my past. But I realized in that moment that they are in my future too! There is a brighter future ahead for every believer than what we have experienced in this life. Even Jesus "endured the cross." "Looking unto Jesus the author and finisher of our faith; who for the joy that was set before him endured the cross, despising the shame, and is set down at the right hand of the throne of God" (Heb. 12:2 KJV). What did Jesus see that we are not seeing? Paradise! Can you imagine? Paradise awaits us. It will be a place with no time, no sorrow, or pain, no evil, and no tears. We can live each day with anticipation that paradise awaits us.

I'm so glad I was allowed to dwell in the secret place of God, even though it brought great sorrow and pain and still does. I can endure it for the joy that is ahead of me. I have a bright future, and so do you!

DAY-1,300

· · · · · · · ● · · · · · · · ·

October 3, 2019
One Day at a Time

Thank God we only must live one day at a time! When we live in the past or live in the future, it can be scary. We look back and compare the present to the past, if the past was so much better or filled with joy, and the present is a struggle. The future can be a blur of gray mist that contains unknown plans that fill our mind with doubt and even fear. But we can make it through twenty-four hours! Can't we? We can get through one day at a time and then deal with tomorrow, if it comes. Life is uncertain, at best. But eternity is certain.

As I anticipate my seventy-second birthday coming up next week, I could just stay in bed and cover my eyes since it will be once again spent without my children here beside me to celebrate me. But I "screw up my courage" once again and am planning a dinner out with dear family members. I will eat the cake and rejoice in the day. I can do this because I still know that what is ahead is glorious!

This morning, as I walked and prayed, I decided that for whatever time I have left on earth, I want to be the salt, as it says in the Bible in Matthew 5:13 (KJV), "Ye are the salt of the earth: but if the salt have lost its savor, wherewith shall it be salted? it is thenceforth good for nothing, but to be cast out and trodden under foot of men." Salt is a natural preservative. It is added for flavor also. But I have tasted salt that has lost its flavor, and it tastes like sand. Oh, that I might be that fresh salt that the earth needs. Oh, that I might be what others need.

It also states in the Bible that we are the "light of the world." Again, in the book of Matthew, chapter 5, verses 15 and 16 (KJV), it says, "Neither do men light a candle, and put it under a bushel, but on a candlestick; and it giveth light unto all that are in the house. Let your light so shine before men, that they may see your good works, and glorify your Father which is in heaven." If I am light, then my light has been hiding under a "bushel" for a while now. When Erin went to heaven, I searched and searched for a support group. Eventually, I found a great one online and formed a bond with other moms all over the world. It not only became a solace for me but also allowed me to become a solace for others. I began to let my light shine in others' dark places of grief. When Scott and then David went to heaven, I was at my rope's end. There was a group of ladies who visited me, and the proverbial "You can be used to help others through this" came out of one of their mouths. In the bitterness of my soul at that moment, I answered rather harshly for me, "Been there, done that. I did that when Erin passed. Is this my prison sentence? Did God take David and Scott so I could 'help others'?" (Sarcasm inserted.) The bitterness of my soul just spewed out to the precious lady who was only offering comfort.

As time has passed now, I have come to realize that I am needed. There are others who do need the "light" and "salt" that I can bring to their world. For me to shut myself off because I don't understand why God chose to take my children is not only snuffing out the light and cutting off the salt for them but for me as well. To give to others brings healing to one's self. I heard that early in my grief and resisted it with all that was in me. But it is true!

"It is more blessed to give than to receive," as the Bible says in Acts 20:35 (KJV). Giving out of our own deep sorrow opens the door to also receive.

I want to be the salt and the light! If you don't right now, wait for it. You may feel you have nothing left to give. There will come a time when you will be able to give. Embrace it when that opportunity comes. I promise it will help you.

DAY-1,306

. . . . . . ●●●●●● ● ●●●●●● . . . . .

October 9, 2019
Can We See into Heaven?

During my morning walk and meditation, I began to think on seeing my children, as is often the case. There have been what I call signs from each of them over the years. I grasped every single one as a connection to the unknown mystery of where they are now. What I am about to say may be controversial. But I feel to share.

All my children had made the decision, on their own, to accept the Christian life. According to what I have read in the Bible, as a Christian, the moment they took their last breath here, they were "present" with the Lord. Since we have been taught that heaven is His dwelling place, then we all assume that He is far, far away in the sky, somewhere beyond the blue. But I read that He said, "I will never leave you nor forsake you" (Heb. 13:5 KJV). Even when He ascended back to the Father, He stated, "And if I go and prepare a place for you, I will come again, and receive you unto myself; that where I am, *there* ye may be also" (John 14:3 KJV). As I read the last book in the Bible, Revelations, it clearly states that it is a "revealing" of Jesus Christ. Are we there yet? Or are we still waiting on Him to reveal Himself? Christ in you, the hope of glory, clearly means that He is in you. So if He is in you, where is He? Are we there yet? Or has He come yet? When Jesus was teaching the disciples to pray, He stated in that exemplary prayer, "Thy Kingdom come, thy will be done *in earth* as it is in Heaven" (Matt. 6:10 KJV). Later on, He said, "The Kingdom of God is within you." Luke 17:21 (KJV) states, "Neither shall they say, Lo here! or, lo there! for, behold, the kingdom of God is within you." "But if I with the finger of God cast out devils, no doubt the kingdom of God is come upon you" (Luke 11:20 KJV). So is the kingdom coming, or is it already here?

With all these thoughts swirling in my head, I began to think, *If the kingdom of God is within me, why can I not see my children where they are since they are present with the Lord?* It makes me wonder if they are hidden from view by my unbelief since I am granted this privilege as a child of God.

This is do know: my life began when I became a child of God. It will never end. My children's lives never ended. Jesus called the death of Lazarus (whom he later raised from the dead) sleeping. So for a believer, if we go by way of the grave, we simply "sleep" until the resurrection.

In conclusion (since I have probably thoroughly confused you now, but I hope I have provoked thoughtful meditation), I say that whether we go by the grave or live to see the end of all things as a new heaven and earth are revealed, Christ in us is the hope of glory!

• • • • • • • ● • • • • • • • •

October 21, 2019
Rebirth of Hope

What has happened to me recently can be described as a rebirth of hope. I wandered aimlessly for the past few years as I chased hope. It seemed to evade me. But the latest revelation that what is ahead of me is more glorious than what is behind me (including my children, not excluding them!) has changed my perspective. This rebirth must have occurred as a miraculous event.

As I have talked to many, many bereaved parents over the past twelve years since our Erin left for heaven, the one constant is that feeling of hopelessness. Death of a child is something that cannot be fixed. The child cannot be replaced. Several have told me they have no reason to keep living or to keep breathing. They say that life is a new challenge every day they arise. The response when I tell them I have buried all my children is one of astonishment. The question I get most is, "How do you keep living?" And I could say, honestly, I had not come up with a good answer.

Now I have an answer. The way I keep living is to keep my eyes fixed on what is ahead of me. No looking to the left or right. No looking back to try to find a happy place (although I do admit that I still do that to try to recapture the joy of when my children were growing up). But when we know our children await us in that heavenly realm and there will be a reuniting with no more parting ever, what joy that brings to a troubled soul.

This does not negate the days that will come when sorrow will come back into my heart as I face days of continued missing and longing for my children. But I can face an uncertain future with a new hope, a hope reborn out of the glorious hope presented to a Christian by the Word of God.

A Light That Shines More and More to a Perfect Day

Proverbs 4:18 (KJV) reads, "But the path of the just *is* as the shining light, that shineth more and more unto the perfect day." This verse was on my mind when I awakened this morning. No matter the circumstances of our existence in the past or even now, there is a perfect day on the horizon for every Christian. The trials that we may face in this life are nothing compared to the glory that is coming.

Years ago, I heard a sermon about "singling the eye." It was about focus. If we just look at the past or the present, especially if it is filled with sorrow, discouragement and depression are just waiting to surround us. But if we can reach beyond the pain and keep our eyes on that end goal, the "perfect day," then we can find the strength to survive the long, hard days.

I don't know about tomorrow. I don't see the legacy I will leave behind. But I do see the path ahead is filled with the light of God. And that path will take me to that perfect day.

DAY-1,321

• • • • • • • • ● • • • • • • •

October 24, 2019
The Sparrow

"Behold the fowls of the air: for they sow not, neither do they reap, nor gather into barns; yet your heavenly Father feedeth them. Are ye not much better than they?" (Matt. 6:26 KJV).

During my morning walk, a huge covey of birds began to be heard in the woods behind my house. Then I saw them flying upward and outward as they continued their migration journey to warmer climates. Who directs those small birds south? Who tells them when it is time to move to warmer places? Who cares if one gets sick and falls to the ground and dies? God does. Then I was reminded of the scripture above. As I pondered this thought, I began to realize, afresh, that nothing happens to us by chance. As I think I mentioned in an earlier chapter, our lives aren't determined by the flip of a coin. There is another powerful scripture that reads, "The steps of a *good* man are ordered by the LORD: and he delighteth in his way. Though he fall, he shall not be utterly cast down: for the LORD upholdeth *him with* his hand. I have been young, and *now* am old; yet have I not seen the righteous forsaken, nor his seed begging bread. *He is* ever merciful, and lendeth; and his seed *is* blessed" (Ps. 37:23–26 KJV). What a promise it is that our steps are ordered of the Lord! So often in my own life I have felt my life was upside down, inside out, mixed up, tangled, a mess! But after reading this, I know that even in the "mess," it is being ordered of the Lord. He knows the depths that each of us can get to before we go off the deep end.

I see more than ever how important it is to pray, "Thy will be done." When we pray for others, we don't know, but the trials they are facing are a part of that direction of the Lord. So how do we pray for them? Jesus gave us a good example when he told Peter that He prayed that his "faith would not fail." That is a great directive for prayer when we just don't know how to pray for others.

November 12, 2019
Crossing the River

Recently, I have been reading the story of the children of Israel and their many travels through the wilderness to the promised land of Canaan. As I thought on the crossing of that final river of Jordan, I remembered sermons and songs I have heard about Jordan representing death. But the more I thought on this and read, the more I see it in a whole new light. Before any of the people stepped into the water on that fateful day of reaching their promised destination, the priests bearing the ark of the Lord (which represents the presence of God) were the first to step into the overflowing banks of the river Jordan. Joshua, the leader, told the people to sanctify themselves because they had not passed this way before. Then he told the priests bearing the ark to step in the Jordan first, and as soon as their feet touched the water, the waters flowing in would be stopped. When we face death or see death come to ones we love, we can be assured that our high priest, Jesus Christ, has stepped into that water first, bearing the very presence of God. The waters will be stopped. Death has been stopped because of Jesus stepping in first. There should be no fear of death to the Christian. The children of Israel walked through that riverbed on dry ground. The water did not touch them. Do you see the comfort in this?

Years ago, when I was working with young children, we would have a short devotional together. I would always end with a question and answer time. The two things the children were most interested in were the devil and death. The Bible tells of how man is, all his life, subject to the bondage of fear of death. Since Adam's fall, man has been subjected to death. But Jesus changed everything when He came to take away the sting of death and to destroy the works of the devil.

Now when I think about all four of my children and what they must have felt in those last moments, I take comfort in the fact that the ark (presence) of the Lord went before them. They entered the promised land of heaven on dry ground. The waters of the Jordan didn't touch their feet. How amazing is that?

We can focus on the horrors of death, or we can focus on the life-giving Spirit of God. I'm so glad the Holy Spirit walks with us every day and right on into eternity.

• • • • • • • • ● • • • • • • • • •

December 1, 2019
No Closure

In conclusion, let me say that closure is not an option. As long as I breathe, there will be no closure to my grief for my children. Closure will come when they are in my arms again. My story will continue as long as there is breath in my body, for I will be a living testament of the grace of God to a grieving mom.

My heart hurts for you if you are just beginning a grief journey or have been walking this path for some time. Let me leave you with these ideas that have helped me in my grief. I pray daily for a long list of moms, dads, and siblings who grieve. My prayer is that you walk in peace. I leave you with this:

- There are no rules to grief. Grieve however you need and for as long as you must.
- Take care of you. Eat small meals and drink extra water to compensate for the outflow of tears.
- Keep a journal beside your bed. When those sleepless nights come, write your feelings in your journal. Write a letter to your child, to God, or to your surviving family.
- Don't fret if you feel your faith or hope has failed you. Faith is stronger than grief, and hope may just be a flicker, but it

will return. They won't be the same as when you first felt your loss. But hold out for them both.

- Cry. It's okay. Crying gets the grief out.
- When you are ready, begin to reach out to others who are grieving. You will find a measure of healing by helping others.
- Create your own rituals or remembrances of your child for their special days—i.e., angelversaries, birthdays, holidays. It can be elaborate or as simple as you wish, even if it is to sleep in all day. It helps to plan, for you don't know how you will feel that day.
- Don't ever be afraid to talk about your child. Say their name. Remind loved ones of special moments you shared. Keep their memory alive however you can. Create scholarship funds or gifts for other grieving parents or a random act of kindness for a stranger with a card attached with your child's name.
- Connect with other grieving people like yourself. There is such a great comfort in sharing with others who have walked a similar path. Join a forum or a community group if you are able. One size does not fit all. But try to find a group that best fits your need.
- Be gentle with yourself. Allow yourself to grieve. Others may tell you things that hurt, but remember, they don't walk in your shoes. To survive, you must give yourself permission to mourn however you need to in order to keep breathing.

May God be with you as you learn to keep living with deep pain. May you find that peace that passes understanding in Jesus Christ.

CPSIA information can be obtained
at www.ICGtesting.com
Printed in the USA
LVHW041453081220
673630LV00001B/22